THE LIVING LABYRINTH

Exploring Universal Themes
in
Myths, Dreams, and
the Symbolism of Waking Life

JEREMY TAYLOR

Paulist Press • New York / Mahwah, N.J.

Cover design by Calvin Chu
Illustrations and diagram by Jeremy Taylor

Copyright © 1998 by Jeremy Taylor

Library of Congress Cataloging-in-Publication Data

Taylor, Jeremy, 1943–
    The living labyrinth : exploring universal themes in myths, dreams, and the symbolism of waking life / Jeremy Taylor.
        p.   cm.
    Includes bibliographical references and index.
    ISBN 0-8091-3766-6 (alk. paper)
    1. Dreams. 2. Dream interpretation. 3. Mythology—Psychological aspects. 4. Symbolism (Psychology) 5. Psychoanalysis. I. Title.
BF175.5.D74T38 1998   97-40490
                                                                    CIP

Published by Paulist Press
997 Macarthur Boulevard
Mahwah, New Jersey 07430

Printed and bound in the
United States of America

Contents

List of Illustrations and Diagrams

TO MY MOTHER,
WHO FIRST TOLD ME THE OLD STORIES
AND HELPED ME TO UNDERSTAND

A Note on Anonymity
and Confidentiality
in Working with Dreams

Our dreams always reveal the deepest patterns of feeling, conviction, and behavior that determine the overall shape and direction of our lives. Sharing and exploring dreams with other compatible people on some sort of regular basis is the single best, most reliable, and most amusing way of reaching greater conscious understanding of these deeper layers of meaning and psychospiritual significance that are the foundation of our waking experience. (Chapter 9 contains a brief summary of the most basic practical hints and suggestions for setting up and pursuing this kind of participatory group dream work.)

A sense of safety and security is crucial in doing this intimate work successfully with other people. Dreamers must share a feeling of basic trust and confidence in one another in order to share personal secrets and to explore the partially formed feelings and growing edges of personality and creative possibility. Dreams regularly reveal our most intimate and potentially embarrassing "secrets" in symbolic form, especially those things we have been keeping secret even from our waking selves. For this reason, whenever we share a dream, we are always revealing more about ourselves than we can confidently judge beforehand. In order to proceed with this risk taking and self-revelation, a sense of relative safety and security is absolutely necessary. At a minimum, dream group participants need to feel relatively secure in the knowledge that they are not going to unexpectedly meet the intimate details they have shared about their lives and feelings around the next corner in the form of gossip.

One way to ensure this sense of safety is to agree at the outset that all work with dreams and the intimate waking-life feelings and experiences they reflect will be confidential. However, in addition to protecting tender feelings and confusing memories,

1

strict confidentiality also severely restricts the free and spontaneous flow of communication and emotional sharing outside the dream group. For this reason, I always urge the people with whom I do dream work to agree to *anonymity* in all their dream explorations, with the clear understanding that anyone may ask for confidentiality at any point, for any reason, spoken or unspoken, and that the rest of the people involved agree beforehand to honor any and all such requests without question or hesitation.

This means that, in the absence of any specific request for confidentiality, people in my dream groups are free to share and discuss their experiences and the insights they have gained in working with their own and other people's dreams as long as no individual dreamer is identifiable in any of the stories.

I am particularly grateful to all the people over the last more than twenty-five years who have agreed to anonymity instead of strict confidentiality in their dream and life work with me. Without your generosity and trust, it would be impossible for me to talk about dreams in anything but the most lifeless and abstract way. Thank you.

In the pages that follow, only my own dreams are specifically identified—all the other living dreamers remain anonymous. I would urge my friends, students, clients, and colleagues whose dreams I have used to illustrate and give life to the ideas presented here, to read the whole text before publicly identifying with any of the dreams mentioned, since there may be comments and implications that appear later in the text with which you may not wish to be associated. (In fact, it is quite possible that I may wish to return to some of these same dreams in works that are not yet written; so I would suggest maintaining your anonymity even after finishing this book.)

AN INTRODUCTORY ASIDE ON THE "GARBAGE DISPOSAL THEORY" OF DREAMING AND RELATED MATTERS

> We dream in order to forget.
>
> *Crick & Mitchison*

As a whole species, we are in deep trouble. We are inexorably destroying the ability of the planet to support complex, interdependent, mammalian life. This crisis has been precipitated by our sorcerer's apprenticeship in science and by the unfeeling manipulation of nature for our immediate, short-term gratification. The stunning short-term economic and political success of science and industrial applications of technology (with their reliance on narrowly focused, conscious, logical, abstract, rational, linear, specialized, seemingly unemotional thinking) has produced the secondary effect of alienating us from our deeper unconscious, more authentic, and spontaneous selves. It has also distracted us from two of the oldest and most reliable sources of restoring balance, sanity, and evolving self-awareness: myth and dream.

I want to make it clear at the outset that I am using the word *myth* here and throughout in its most generic sense: as a synonym for "sacred narrative." The word *myth* stems from the same Indo-European root its word that gives us "mouth," and it carries the implication of "meaningful speech." In this sense, any traditional story that gives specific shape to deeply held belief or deeply felt

3

psychospiritual experience is a myth. By the same token, any made-up story that succeeds in giving compelling symbolic shape to deeply held belief or deeply felt psychospiritual experience can also be said to be "mythic," whether it has a lengthy anonymous tradition of oral transmission or not. I am specifically *not* using the word in either of its two most common usages: either as a disparaging name for wild, unfounded fantasy masquerading as fact ("It's a myth that what you don't know can't hurt you") or as a belittling name for other peoples' religious beliefs ("The myth of the White Buffalo had a great influence on the Plains Indians before the arrival of the missionaries"). In the sense in which I am using it, it is fair to say, for example, that the books of the Old and New Testament constitute the narrative basis of the official "Christian myth."

It has been increasingly common since the seventeenth century and the so-called Enlightenment for well-educated and intelligent people to dismiss myths as merely the quaint and fanciful "nursery stories" of evolving cultures on their way toward superior rational, scientific mental processes, social organization, and "true religion." Today some researchers in neurobiology have carried "de-mythologizing" even further and have begun to raise doubts and questions about the ancient belief that dreams have intrinsic symbolic meaning. It is now fashionable in some scientific circles to assert that dreams are nothing more than "the epiphenomena of disordered metabolism," or "the random firing of neurons in sleep," and to disparage paying any attention to the specific content of dreams on the grounds that historically such attention has served only as an occasion for hysterical self-deception.

Perhaps the most coherent and concerted attack on the ancient belief that dreams are gifts of potential wisdom, insight, revelation, and creative inspiration came a few years ago when Francis Crick and Graeme Mitchison published a paper in which they claimed to have unraveled the ultimate meaning and purpose of dreaming. They suggested that the function of dreaming is simply to "clear the circuits" in the brain and to purge the conscious mind and the memory of "useless, irrelevant data"—a form of psychic excretion. In their 1986 article in the British scientific journal *Nature,* they suggested that "attempting to remember one's dreams should perhaps not be encouraged, because such remembering may help to retain patterns of thought which are better forgotten." (See Appendix II for detailed bibliographic references, as well as further discussion and commentary that would appear in footnotes in a more formal presentation.)

Their published conclusions had a distinctly chilling effect on the burgeoning dream-work movement around the English-speaking world. It was frightening and unnerving to many people newly attracted to paying attention to their dreams to hear that they might be doing themselves some harm by going against the supposed purpose of "dreaming in order to forget." Crick and Mitchison seemed to be suggesting that by making an effort to record and better understand their strange nocturnal adventures, people might actually be harming the brain's effort to purge itself of "extraneous impressions."

The research that Crick and Mitchison cite is quite convincing. Dreams tend to occur in a rhythmic cycle every ninety minutes or so. This cycle corresponds to the carefully observed and demonstrated cycle of "maximum attention span" in waking life. This ninety-minute cycle is intimately associated with the transfer of short-term memory impressions into the deeper and less immediately accessible structures of long-term memory. In the cyclic process of this transfer, many seemingly extraneous memories are (or at least appear to be) "lost" and forgotten. Crick and Mitchison conclude that dreams merely reflect this "garbage disposal" process of ridding the brain of irrelevant, "useless" memory data, and nothing more.

There are several problems with the work of Crick and Mitchison and the rest, not the least of which is their failure to address the fact that dreams are basically symbolic. True symbols always serve *multiple* purposes and convey many layers of meaning and significance simultaneously. This is what separates symbols from mere signs, which are specifically intended to be unambiguous and to convey only one clear message. Any analysis of symbolic form(s) that demonstrates only one layer of meaning is, by definition, incomplete and inadequate.

The evidence for the "garbage disposal" hypothesis of dreaming is quite persuasive, but in presenting it, Crick and

Mitchison simply fail to address the ambiguous, multilayered, "over-determined" quality of all dream imagery. They appear to believe that having demonstrated that dreams serve and reflect the regular process whereby seemingly random impressions are "forgotten"—that is, transferred from the short-term memory and prioritized into the less consciously accessible categories of unconscious long-term memory—they have somehow magically demonstrated that all other possible layers of significance are false.

Even on the face of it, their assertion that the impressions of short-term memory are random is clearly incorrect. All human beings live totally submerged in linguistic, historical, social, and psychological environments that are far from random. Our entire waking lives are significantly and deeply structured and patterned by our individual histories, by the conceptual categories of the languages we speak, by the economic and political systems of the particular societies and cultures in which we live and work, and so forth. In this important sense, none of our experiences and short-term memory impressions are actually random, no matter how chaotic they may appear to be from a subjective point of view at any given moment. To the extent that dreams do regularly reflect the dreamer's "day residue" of experience, they are at the very least meaningful as reflections of these larger patterns of social and linguistic experience.

In many ways, the argument that dreams are "meaningless" is like saying that simply because I don't speak some particular foreign language, those who do speak it are mouthing gibberish and that it is a waste of time (or even potentially "damaging") to try to understand them.

Imagine for a moment that an interstellar archaeologist arrives on earth in some distant future and exhumes the remains of a pleasant private library with a fireplace and walls lined with books. The current fashionable assumption in the world of interstellar archaeology is that the ink markings in the primitive barbarian earth "books" are meaningless. This scientist, examining the ashes in the ancient hearth, discovers the remains of burned paper which carry markings identical to those in the books on the surrounding walls (because the ancient bibliophile used newspapers to start the fires in that hearth).

The interstellar archaeologist publishes an important paper based on this discovery that says the ashes prove that the books that lined the walls of the ancient library were nothing more than fodder for the primitive open fire and were obviously stored in rows on the walls to make them easily accessible for tossing into the flames. Another archaeologist then goes on to demonstrate the argument "experimentally" by burning a few of the ancient books. Sure enough, they do burn, leaving ashes much like the original newspaper ashes.

At the next Interstellar Congress on the Archaeology of Primitive Social Life Forms, both archaeologists collaborate on a brilliant address that carefully argues that the recent discoveries and experimental research converge to prove that the old earth "books" are nothing more than fodder for their primitive open fires and that the continuing efforts of the "romantic" scholars to decipher them for clues about the lost civilizations of that planet are hopelessly deluded.

Books do indeed burn, and dreams do in fact play a role in and reflect the sorting out and prioritizing of short-term impressions into the categories and structures of long-term memory, but to assert that the full and proper understanding of either books or dreams is "nothing more" than this is a serious error.

Stanley Krippner addresses this problem in his anthology, *Dreamtime and Dreamwork*, when he says, "If dream content is devoid of meaning, why have scientific studies detected differences when [the dream content of] two or more groups have been compared?" He goes on to point out that consistent and predictable patterns of dream activity are regularly revealed by comparing the dreams of different groups.

For instance, statistical studies of dream content have repeatedly shown that children dream of animals more often than do adults. These content studies also show that women tend to report more nightmares and to remember the colors in their dreams more than men do. Women also tend to report a higher incidence of human interaction and speech in their dreams than do men. On the other hand, men manipulate machines and do physical battle with other characters in their dreams much more often than women or children do. These are only a few examples of the more obvious and often observed patterns of imagery revealed by this kind of statistical analysis of the manifest content of dreams. (See Appendix II for further comments.)

Krippner concludes that studies of this kind "indicate that dreams generally mirror waking activities and that people's dreams reflect detectable differences in age, gender, and cultural background." Obviously, if dreams were in fact meaningless, they would not demonstrate any of these regularly repeating patterns in their manifest content, let alone the startling and often profound truths they regularly reveal when examined at a deeper symbolic level.

As Dr. Milton Kramer said to me in 1995, "The primary question is whether dreams are 'signal,' or whether they are 'noise.' There has been sufficient evidence gathered in the last four decades to demonstrate beyond doubt that they are 'signal.'"

The most serious problem with the work of Crick, Mitchison, and the rest of the laboratory researchers who assert that dreams are meaningless "garbage" is that they fail to recognize that the very process of sorting and "forgetting" on which they place so much emphasis is itself a model of the process of the generation and perception of meaning in human consciousness.

In fact, no human experience is ever totally forgotten. Over and over again, controlled studies demonstrate that given the proper stimulus, motivation, and environment, virtually any experience from earliest infancy onward can be recalled consciously to mind. Everything that ever happens to us is stored somewhere in the deep recesses of long-term memory and can be called to the surface of waking awareness under the right circumstances. For this reason alone, the whole notion of "forgetting" on which Crick and the rest put so much emphasis needs to be carefully reexamined and reevaluated. Nothing is actually ever completely forgotten, so "forgetting" simply cannot be used as a proof that dreams are meaningless.

Even more importantly, the categories of long-term memory into which the short-term memory traces are sorted and prioritized—categories of physical, emotional, and symbolic similarity—are the fundamental structural categories of meaning itself. Long-term memory is the basic organizing principle for all human perception and awareness of meaning and significance. Long-term memory organizes and prioritizes *all* experiences for easy or less easy conscious recall by establishing their basic meaning. Long-term memory sorts and categorizes experiences in terms of both short- and long-term physical survival, embracing pleasure, avoiding pain, and satisfying fundamental desires for status, self-worth, individual and collective identity, and so forth.

Thus the supposed "proof" that Crick and the others offer that dreams are meaningless is in fact a demonstration that *dreaming itself is the universal model, the prototypical experience of the generation of a sense of meaning.*

Events, ideas, feelings, and experiences become meaningful only when they are sorted into these fundamental categories of long-term memory. Crick and Mitchison and the rest are absolutely right to the extent that dreaming is deeply and fundamentally involved in the process of sorting and storing short-term memory impressions. So by definition, dreaming is also deeply involved in the generation of meaning itself, whether any particular impression is momentarily "forgotten" in the process or not.

By the same token, it is equally naive and short-sighted to suggest that myths and other sacred, emotionally charged, symbolically framed narratives and enactments are merely "failed science." Myths are not merely "nursery stories" offering fanciful explanations for impressive natural phenomena that modern science has more adequately analyzed. Yes, there are myths that clearly have an element of imaginative, scientifically "incorrect" explanation of natural phenomena. But just like dreams, myths are symbolic forms, and *there is no such thing as myth with only one level of meaning.* The myths that purport to explain why the world is the way it is (offering reasons for the changing of the seasons, the cyclic growth and death of plants, the "first causes" of the differences between men and women, explanations for particular features of the local landscape, etc.) also give profound symbolic shape to the enduring truths about deep structures and repeating patterns of the human psyche that birthed the stories in the first place.

Far more important than the fact that some myths and folk tales are "unscientific" stories about the underlying causes of physical events is the fact that myths are also profound dramatic descriptions of our interior emotional and spiritual experience as human beings. To restrict the study of mythology to cataloguing the stories as mere historical curiosities and "failed attempts at natural science" is to miss the real point. The study of mythology is a potential source of individual and collective, psychological and cultural understanding of a very high order.

Serious and honest investigation simply can not dismiss the world of dreams as "meaningless," or the world of myth as simply "naive and fanciful." These two realms examined together begin to describe our deep, shared, unconscious heritage as human beings. Dreams and myths are living examples of the process by which we discover and renew the meaning in our lives in the ever-changing and evolving global cultural and ecological environment. It is in this realm of multiple meaning and collective significance that Carl Jung's notion of archetypes has some of its most important applications.

Dreams and myths reveal the inherent unconscious predispositions (archetypes) that have shaped both our development as individuals and our collective social evolution. It is this heritage of deep, shared, collective, unconscious archetypal patterns and energies that still forms the foundation of all our best efforts and our brightest individual and cooperative achievements.

This collective heritage also creates the context for our most profound sorrows and our bitterest failures. Our archetypal predispositions toward symbolic form and relationship give concrete shape to our individual and collective lives today, just as they have since the beginning of time. When we fail to understand them, these archetypal energies can manifest themselves in our lives in ironic and counterproductive unconscious behaviors, plunging both personal and collective human life into a chaos and misery.

I believe that only the light of increased self-awareness and self-understanding can illuminate and transform our increasingly dire situation. When we begin to see and understand these archetypal forces more clearly and consciously, we greatly increase the likelihood that these energies themselves will also inform and vitalize our best and most creative efforts to shape our individual and collective lives into the best we can imagine.

This book is an effort to promote and nurture our best creative individual and collective responses to the most pressing questions and demands of contemporary life. Our problems are both caused and characterized by the decay of civility and mutual individual regard, by the continuous threat of war and ecological disaster, and by the individual and collective loss of a sense of meaning, purpose, and creative joy in human life. I have been working with these archetypal dramas for more than thirty years, and I am completely convinced on the basis of my experience that deeper understanding of dreams and myths can have a direct and positive effect on these problems at both a personal and collective level. A deeper conscious encounter with dreams and myths can nurture creative imagination, creative self-realization and expression, compassion, and courage in ways that no other effort of attention can achieve; and these are, as they have always been, the qualities and energies we need to confront and transform our eternal human predicament.

Each chapter of this book begins with a retelling of some important mythic narrative, along with a discussion of some of its multiple layers of symbolism and significance, followed by discussion of contemporary dream narratives that embody the same basic archetypal energies and patterns. The discussions of the myths are intended to illuminate the dreams, just as the explorations of the dream narratives are designed to clarify and deepen our conscious understanding of, and emotional participation in, the myths. All of it is intended to liberate and stimulate the reader to develop a more conscious relationship with his or her dreams and to encourage dream workers to extend their work further into the all-important realm of collective, archetypal, mythic understanding.

Chapter 1
WHAT ARE "ARCHETYPES"? EXPLORING MYTHS AND DREAMS OF ENCHANTED FROGS, MOUNTAIN CLIMBING, AND SEX

> Myths are public dreams—dreams are private myths.
>
> *Joseph Campbell*

This book is an effort to address and overcome some of the natural suspicions and misgivings many people have about archetypal symbols and the whole idea of a "collective unconscious." I want to encourage people who already enjoy working with their dreams at a personal level to begin to explore these deeper layers of collective shared significance in their dream work. At the same time, this book is an effort to invite people who are already intrigued by world myths and ritual sacred practices to extend their interests and spiritual explorations into the realm of spontaneous nighttime dreams as well.

Archetypal symbol dramas appear most regularly and clearly in the myths of the world on the one hand, and in the dreams of individual people on the other. Myths and dreams address us all in this same basic language of symbol and metaphor.

The fundamental similarities in symbolism and structure shared by the dreams of individuals and by the official sacred narratives and other mythic stories from societies around the world offer compelling evidence of the shared *collective* unconscious unity of the human species in the very midst of our undeniable individual uniqueness and cultural diversity.

Lately, more and more people are discovering that paying attention to their dreams can be a most interesting, illuminating, growth-promoting, and enjoyable activity. Many of these people have also found that getting together and sharing their dreams with one another greatly enhances their ability to appreciate and understand their confusing nocturnal adventures. (For a succinct presentation of the most useful basic hints for individual and group dream work, see chapter 9.) In the course of these discoveries, many have come upon the work of Carl Jung and the idea of "archetypes of the collective unconscious"—that is, fundamental structures of the psyche that appear to be among the deepest sources of our own individual dreams, as well as of folk tales, myths, legends, and sacred narratives from all periods of history.

Sometimes people get this far and falter, thinking that now they have to "go back to school" and/or poke through vast, dusty, untidy piles of obscure mythological, religious, and occult materials in order to begin to grasp and better understand these fascinating collective symbols in their own and their friends' dreams. Often this appears, even at best, as a hopelessly daunting prospect.

This book is an effort to cut through that sense of paralysis and provide a comfortable and easily accessible introduction to some of the more salient of these collective symbolic patterns and energies. I also hope the book will demonstrate that even a rudimentary awareness of different sacred narratives and mythological traditions can illuminate our individual dreams and psychospiritual problems and offer practical insights into the deeper sources of our most pressing collective, social, political, economic, and cultural dilemmas as well.

The "Aha!" of Insight

When we dream an image born out of our childhood experience, we already "know" in some unconscious way what that memory means. Even if we can't quite articulate it in the moment, the unconscious knowledge is there, just below the surface of waking awareness. When someone else speaks and suggests an interpretation of such an image, the dreamer is very likely to experience an "aha!" of recognition. This "aha" is a demonstration of previously unconscious memory and is the *only* reliable touchstone in this work of dream exploration and symbolic analysis.

Just as with these personal memories and associations, we already possess an unconscious awareness of the sonorous meaning(s) and significance of archetypal symbols, even though we have no conscious knowledge of any of the obscure myths that use the same imagery. When archetypal images and energies appear in our dreams—and they always do, even when they wear the disguise of mundane and "trivial" images—at some level we *already know* what they mean, and our "aha's" demonstrate this collective unconscious awareness.

With regard to archetypal symbols, our task is, as always, to access this preconscious knowledge and bring it up to the surface of waking consciousness—to make it "speech-ripe." These deeper, collective, archetypal levels of understanding can be drawn to the surface of waking awareness in exactly the same way as are the more personal levels of comprehension. As with the personal layers of symbolism and meaning, the "aha" of recognition is the most reliable indicator of subtle, deep-seated truth.

In short, although conscious familiarity with the world's mythology and religious scriptures is interesting and valuable in the process of understanding dreams more fully, it is not necessary. The fundamental symbolic truths of archetypal images can also be recognized and made more conscious out of the dreamer's own intuitions and associations in the same way his or her more personal symbols can be drawn to the surface of waking awareness—primarily through introspection and dialogue with others.

Around the World with the Enchanted Frog

The classic folk story of the enchanted prince or princess who has been turned into a frog may serve as a specific extended example of a collective, archetypal symbol drama. The story demonstrates how such stories carry multiple levels of meaning, creative energy, and possibilities of relationship. Mythic narratives such as this persist in large measure because of the ways in which they embody and transmit deep symbolic truths about human development on the one hand, and about the nature of the particular society in which we live on the other.

"The Frog Prince(ess)" is a story that appears in many different versions around the world; and each version implies a fundamentally similar psychospiritual message in each of its manifestations, despite seemingly endless variations in detail from culture to culture. The basic story is familiar to almost all people from childhood, regardless of the society in which they were raised.

At the same time, contemporary men and women in widely diverse cultures also dream with some regularity about magical amphibians with many of the same symbolic characteristics and implied qualities as the enchanted frogs in these myths and folk tales. When a person dreams an image that appears to be some version of an "enchanted frog," the whole complex of resonant associations and symbolic implications of the collective myth are introduced into the dream. The appearance of such an image in a dream suggests that the dreamer is dealing with the same range of individual and collective social issues and dilemmas in his or her waking life that have always been associated with the image of the frog in these traditional stories.

For most native English speakers, the versions of "The Frog Prince" that have been traditionally told in the British Isles are usually accepted as "canonical." Most English speakers are not even aware that this famous story has so many other versions in other lands. The universal appearance of repeating symbolic story motifs such as the enchanted frog in the mythological traditions of the world is one of the most compelling evidences for the existence of a deep shared stratum of the human psyche.

In the traditional British versions of the story familiar to most Americans, a beautiful but haughty princess loses some precious object—a ring or a jeweled hoop or ball—down a well or in a deep pool. A talking frog appears and offers to dive down into the watery depths and fetch the carelessly lost treasure back for her. Before he will perform his task, however, the frog demands that the princess promise to give him a kiss as payment for his trouble. The princess is disgusted by this prospect, but her desire to retrieve her lost treasure is greater than her revulsion at the idea of kissing the frog, so she agrees. The frog dives down and recovers the lost treasure; and the princess, sometimes after trying to persuade the frog to accept several seemingly more valuable and attractive substitute rewards, eventually kisses the frog. When she kisses him, he transforms into a handsome prince. He then reveals that he had been placed under an enchantment to stay trapped in the shape of a frog until he could persuade a woman of royal birth to kiss him. The former-frog-now-turned-prince and the somewhat chastened and less haughty princess marry and "live happily ever after" (Fig.1).

Figure 1. (British Isles) The Enchanted Frog offers to retrieve the Princess's lost treasure.

The basic outline or archetypal pattern of the story remains essentially the same all over the world, even though many of the details appear to change radically from one language and culture to another. For instance, the German language versions of this tale are essentially the same, except for the fact that the frog's transformation back into human form is accomplished in quite a different fashion from the British "kiss." In the German versions of the story, the careless and haughty princess is enraged and disgusted by the frog's importunate demand for a kiss as payment. In some versions, the frog demands "three wishes," each an escalation of intimate contact with the princess. She agrees to his terms, but secretly plans to break her promise when the time comes for payment. The frog fulfills his part of the bargain; and when he demands his reward, the princess picks him up as though to kiss him, but instead she dashes him against a wall with all her strength in an effort to kill him. In the Germanic versions of this archetypal story, it is this sudden impact with the wall that accomplishes the frog's transformation back into human form, not a kiss. Despite this betrayal, the frog prince and the haughty princess are married (although in most versions, their subsequent happiness or lack of it is not mentioned).

There are several inferences that may be drawn from just this one variation in the tale, not the least of which is a difference in the basic cultural attitudes toward romantic love that tend to prevail in English and German cultures respectively. In the Anglo-Saxon cultural tradition, the unspoken assumptions of romantic encounter require that lovers at least make an effort to keep even their most extravagant promises to one another. In Germanic culture, inconstancy among romantic lovers is expected, particularly from women, who tend to be viewed as inherently fickle. In the Germanic culture pool, it is generally understood that romantic attraction is a form of madness, and that therefore wild promises made in the heat of passion are not to be taken as seriously as promises made under more conscious and sober circumstances. This basic cultural attitude is one of the ongoing justifications for arranged marriages and for the collective disparagement of romantic love as a source of committed relationship. At the same time, arranged marriage is also a crucially important tradition in the perpetuation of class distinction and accumulated family wealth.

Looming behind this first level of inference are also strong intimations of even deeper and more fundamental differences in collective cultural attitudes toward the archetypal feminine. The behavior of the princess in both versions reflects (and plays a part in perpetuating) collective cultural opinions about the significance and worth of "feminine" emotional experience itself. Each version of the tale suggests the generally accepted social expectations and limitations regarding the acceptable expression of "feminine" emotional and interior life by both men and women. In the English language versions of the tale, the subjective world of emotional experience is understood to be basically trustworthy; whereas in the German tradition, subjective emotional experience is viewed with cynical suspicion. In both versions, there is an implied assumption that the princess (simultaneously symbolic of the feminine aspects of the psyche on the one hand, and the "basic nature of women" on the other) is "careless" and "haughty" *by nature.*

Both versions also suggest the generally dependent economic and emotional status of women in actual British and German society. In neither version of the story is there any question of the princess stripping down and recovering the lost bauble herself.

In general, the status of women relative to men in any given society is a clear predictor of the value generally placed on psychologically feminine (interior, relational, creative, sensual, intuitive, cyclic, repeating, emotional) experience (of *both* men and women) in that particular culture. In societies where women own property and have a great degree of autonomy, there tends also to be a general acceptance of the reality and reliability of feminine forms of experience and behavior. Conversely, where women are considered to be property, and have relatively little autonomy, there is also a collective tendency to ritualize the expression of strong emotion and to deny the relevance and importance of spontaneous feminine feelings and intuitions.

Just this one variation in the symbolic structure of the story also points to collective cultural differences in the underlying, unspoken assumptions about relationships among the various social classes in the Anglo-Saxon and Germanic cultural traditions. In all the different English versions, there is never any real question about whether or not the princess will actually keep her word and kiss the frog once she has promised to do so. As long as the frog is not diverted from his purpose by her offers of substitute rewards, we know she will kiss him in the end. In the various Germanic versions, however, quite another social contract is revealed. It is understood that the princess, by virtue of her "superior" class standing, has no real obligation to keep her word to the frog. In the German versions of the tale, the princess's subsequent attempt to kill her animal benefactor is presented as acceptable; this is conveyed symbolically by the restored prince and princess marrying in the end. It is acceptable for the princess to betray the frog because he is a mere animal. His animal being, at this level, is a symbolic statement of his status as a member of a lower order of society. The enchanted frog prince himself understands these social arrangements perfectly. He expects her to break her word—in fact, he is counting on it, because it is being dashed against the wall that will free him from his cursed frog form. Nor does he expect a woman of his own class to keep her word to a mere lower-class talking frog.

The duplicity of the princess in the Germanic versions of the story not only reflects a collective masculinist cultural assumption about the emotional untrustworthiness of women in general and the corresponding untrustworthiness of the internal realms of feminine psychospiritual experience in particular, but it also reveals a common assumption of class warfare that has generally been much more overt and intense in the Germanic cultural tradition than it appears to be in the more "polite" (and covert) English language culture pool.

These multiple layers of symbolic meaning and implicit social order resonate from and cling to the archetypal figure of the enchanted frog wherever it appears, in both the collective world of folk narrative and the interior world of waking fantasy and sleeping dream.

Moving eastward, following the archetypal theme or *mythologem* of the royal adolescent who is forced by circumstances to kiss and/or marry the enchanted frog who is then transformed back into (royal) human form, we discover that in Russia, the standard versions of the tale reverse the roles of the prince and princess. In the Russian and other Slavic language versions of the story, it is the prince who is forced to marry the enchanted frog princess.

In most of the Slavic versions of this traditional tale, the young prince and his older brothers are all ordered by their father to seek wives by following a rolling ball or a shot arrow. Each must marry the person to whom his "magical seeking object" leads him.

This magical object is symbolically analogous to the princess's precious lost toy in the British and German traditions. At one level, the Russian prince's arrow and the British and German princess's ring or ball are both Freudian, gender specific, symbolic images of awakening sexual desire accompanying physical maturity. At another related level of archetypal symbolic significance, these images also embody the internal wholeness and harmony that is both the birthright and the desired outcome of the increasing emotional and spiritual maturity that accompanies natural physical growth and social development.

In the Russian stories, the prince's older brothers all have their "seeking objects" retrieved by beautiful princesses, but the youngest is led by his to a talking frog (Fig. 2). In spite of his initial revulsion, he fulfills his pledge to his father and marries the frog. She does not change back into human form until quite a while after their marriage, and then only after she has helped her husband succeed in a series of seemingly impossible tests and competitions devised by his father and his arrogant and increasingly envious brothers. In many versions, she is also pitted against her human sisters-in-law in contests of refined domestic skill.

One of the implications of these trans-Caucasian variations in the story is that in the Slavic, in contrast to the Germanic and Anglo-Saxon culture pools, husband and wife are not generally expected to reveal their true emotional feeling and sexual warmth to one another (i.e., revert to authentic human form) until after they have both clearly demonstrated

Figure 2. (Russia) The Enchanted Frog retrieves the Prince's arrow.

their respective socially defined abilities as (male) providers and protectors, and (female) helpers and nurturers. Of necessity, such demonstrations of "earned" affection and intimacy can not take place until some time after the formal marriage has taken place.

At the level of the story that depicts social class relations, the Russian versions of the tale also suggest that the apparently low social standing of the frog princess is the main reason for the harshness and brutality of the tests that she and the prince are subjected to.

These Slavic versions of the basic archetypal story reflect the same levels of social and psychological organization. In all its national and ethnic versions, the tale serves as a tool for preparing each successive generation to accept and perpetuate the basic social class and gender role arrangements of that particular society.

The Enchanted Frog as Spiritual Guide

At the same time, the story in all its versions and variations from culture to culture also suggests at a deeper level that the individual must resist and avoid simple, unthinking adoption of conventional attitudes if he or she is to discover and express his or her own unique personality. Every young person must discover his or her own unique and authentic self while at the same time assuming appropriate traditionally and socially defined gender-specific roles and tasks.

Regardless of the particular society a person lives in, he or she must be trained to accept the traditional social arrangements and gender roles of that culture with a minimum of struggle and resistance in order for that society to perpetuate itself. At the same time, the individual must also discover and express his or her unique personality, gifts, and energies, and with these energies, discover his or her true and unique relationship with the transpersonal intuitions of the divine. If large numbers of individuals fail either to adopt appropriate social roles and values or to discover their authentic identities and gifts, then the societies in which they find themselves will inevitably fall apart and fail. Myths, sacred narratives, folk tales—and most of all, *dreams*—all serve to "coach" or "shepherd" the individual though this simultaneous acquisition of deeper self-knowledge and awareness on the one hand, and adoption and assumption of acceptable social role and status on the other.

The various versions of this one traditional tale type reflect and influence the universal, transcultural process of personal/psychological self-discovery and increasing spiritual awareness that must always take place within the confines of a specific society—the universal process of psychospiritual development that Carl Jung called "individuation."

In all its multiple versions throughout the world, the enchanted frog prince/princess story makes the same kind of multilevel symbolic reference both to personal, interior, emotional, psychological, and spiritual issues and to social-cultural gender and class arrangements at the same time. These two orders of psyche and society forever reflect and shape one another. The myths and dreams of members of that society regularly reflect both social and psychological realities, always in the context of the individual's efforts to find meaning by harmonizing and integrating these levels of experience into a single individuated whole.

The multiple versions of the archetypal enchanted frog prince/princess story all point simultaneously to the universal human instinct for discovery and expression of increasing individual self-awareness on the one hand, and to the particular social and cultural circumstances and expectations that limit and define the range of human expressive and relational possibility on the other. The same thing may also be said of dreams in which these archetypal motifs appear. The appearance of an archetypal image like an enchanted frog in a dream is a clear indication that the dream relates the dreamer to society, as well as to the development of unique personality and character.

The Enchanted Frog in Southeast Asia

Following the motif of the enchanted frog prince/princess redeemed by royal marriage even further east, we find multiple versions of the same essential story in Mongolia, China, the Himalayan region, Southeast Asia, and the Indian subcontinent. In these societies, it is once again the princess who usually marries the enchanted prince in frog form. (See Appendix II for full bibliographic information on quotes and sources for the text, as well as discussion of related issues and ideas that would appear as footnotes in a more formal academic presentation.)

In Thailand, for example, the princess marries the enchanted prince who has been transformed into a "Negrito," who is as small as a frog, lives by fishing, and is constantly compared to a frog because of his wide mouth, short stature, muscular legs, and close association with the water.

The prince, the true first-born son of the king, is enchanted into the form of a tiny, frog-sized Negrito born inside a conch shell. This spell is cast by an evil magician hired by of one of the king's other wives who wishes her own son to inherit the throne. This bizarre birth of the conch shell with the tiny, frog-sized, enchanted prince hidden inside it (hidden even from his mother) disgraces the king's favorite wife. Mother and enchanted son hidden in the conch shell are forced into shameful exile in a foreign land.

Once out of the country, the enchanted frog prince emerges from his natal shell and reveals himself to his mother. They are both treated as total outcasts even in their newly adopted home. The Negrito frog prince grows up in solitude, in nature, supporting his mother by his uncanny abilities as a fisherman.

In the middle of the story, the enchanted frog prince hears about a haughty princess who has refused all of her royal suitors. He goes to visit her and "causes her to see his true form when no one else can see it." She marries him and accepts the outcast fate

Figure 3. (Thailand) The Enchanted Prince reveals his true form to the Princess, while the God Shiva watches from the clouds.

that goes with it, for she too is driven into shameful exile for marrying such an inappropriate husband. In time, the princess grows to love her mother-in-law and learns about the life of the lowliest people of the land firsthand. In this process, self-knowledge and compassion are awakened in her heart (Fig. 3).

This is the same archetypal task of "overcoming haughtiness" that the British and German princesses and the Russian prince must also accomplish. The shaming and exile of the Thai princess can be seen as an extended elaboration, exploring the implications of the more compressed moment of "kissing and marrying the frog" in the Northern European and Russian versions.

By "going into exile" and "discovering the lives of the peasants," the princess becomes increasingly aware of her own true identity and of the common humanity she shares with all the people as a separate question from her socially defined role as princess. This act of fundamental human self-recognition, separate from socially defined role and status, is what each human partner of the enchanted frog must always discover. Once it is discovered, the "enlightened" person must publicly acknowledge the relationship to the enchanted frog by "marriage," and be willing to suffer the opprobrium of the majority of others who have not achieved this same level of self-realization.

It was ever so.

Eventually, the exiled princess discovers her authentic feelings and thoughts and learns to express them clearly. She proves her love for the enchanted Negrito frog prince and prevails on him to throw off his "disguise" and save her father's kingdom from invaders, which (of course) he does, redeeming the "lost treasure" of his own true identity and the endangered kingdom simultaneously.

This story has been a staple of the traditional dance theater of Thailand for centuries. One of the most popular versions is the traditional dance and chant presentation *Sang Thong*. The race and class tensions inherent in the story in all its versions around the world are highlighted in Thai society, as demonstrated by the events surrounding a production of the play in the modern era, under the royal sponsorship of King Rama V.

In 1956, King Rama V determined that the version of the

ancient story written by his ancestor, King Rama II, should be revived and produced once again in free public performances for a new generation of Thais. He further determined that the role of the enchanted prince should be performed by an actual ethnic Negrito actor/dancer from his own household, a man named Kenang. The majority of native Thais are deeply and traditionally prejudiced against their Negrito neighbors, viewing them as less than human. These ancient Thai prejudices were still so strong and deep at the time of King Rama V's production of *Sang Thong* that even though the story was totally familiar to all who saw it, and even though the production was under the most prestigious royal sponsorship, the presence of an actual Negrito actor/dancer on the stage caused riots among both the aristocratic and peasant audiences wherever it was performed.

The disturbances occasioned by the king's "liberal" royal theater performances ironically echo the archetypal significance of the story itself. The audience's collective rejection of an actual ethnic Negrito in the role of the enchanted prince is exactly the same archetypal action as the rejection of the princess by her family and her society in the traditional story when she marries the enchanted frog prince.

The ancient archetypal enchanted frog prince/princess story in all its global variations suggests that if true happiness and spiritual fulfillment are to be found, individually and collectively, the authentic energies of the deep self must be brought into creative expression, *even though these energies often appear initially in the form of the most lowly and despised "nonhuman" elements in both the psyche and the society.* Habitual, unthinking, socially determined rejection of "the despised" (both within and without) must be overcome, for it is only with the conscious acknowledgment and integration of the traditionally despised element (the archetype Jung called the Shadow), that personality and society can achieve healthy balance and responsive, creative wholeness.

These "enchanted frog" stories, whether dreamed or told as traditional entertainments, help prepare each person to succeed in the universal task of maturing to social, emotional, intellectual, and spiritual adulthood. Despite the multitude of cultural variations, the basic archetypal direction and "point" of the story in all its versions is always the same: *In order to be healthy and whole, each person must recognize the superior, hidden worth of the most lowly and despised elements of both psyche and society.* All the versions of the story point symbolically to the necessity of an individual act of courage and wholehearted acceptance of that which has been rejected by collective convention. The archetypal story also promises in all its many versions that if such an act of courage and embrace is genuinely accomplished, the "lost treasure" will be restored, and miraculous happiness and productivity will result.

As an archetypal pattern, the story exists in all its various forms to remind its global audience that no matter what the particulars of their social arrangements may be at any given moment, the energies they repress and deny are always and inevitably the same energies that are required for authentic health and wholeness. Psychologically and spiritually speaking, every person must "kiss the frog" of his or her own worst, most repressed, and most neglected aspects of personality in order to recover the lost treasure of integrated personality and experience a meaningful life.

At this important level of archetypal symbolism, the enchanted frog always represents this despised element that has been separated, repressed, and rejected, whatever it may be in any particular person or society. It is this universal applicability across wide differences of specific personality and culture that marks the tale(s) as truly archetypal.

The Universal "Lost Treasure"

At this same level, the "lost treasure" (or "magical seeking object") always represents, at one level, the experience of harmonious balance and wholeness that has been "lost" because the person has simply accepted conventional attitudes without any accompanying authentic self-exploration and discovery. The enchanted frog story always depicts the struggle for self-awareness and self-expression in a relationship that is genuine and not merely a reflection of the conventional wisdom of the society.

The persistence of this enchanted frog story in so many

widely different societies also suggests clearly that these psycho-spiritual acts of self-awareness and integration can, in fact, be achieved within the social and cultural context(s) of each community. The world's cultures provide widely varying contexts for this universal task of individuation; however, the task itself remains essentially the same *and is as necessary for the preservation and continued health of society as a whole as it is for the "salvation" of the individual.*

Put in more overtly spiritual terms, the story in all its global variations points to the presence of the divine in everything, most particularly and importantly in the creatures, situations, and internal energies that are most ignored, despised, and repressed. *There is no place where God is not.* Even the most devout and pious believer is always in danger of failing to perceive and embrace the divine element in the lowly and despised figures in his or her dreams. Even if pious good works are dutifully offered to the lowly and despised in society on a regular basis, if these acts of charity are offered "without love" (that is, without a realization that there is a fundamental human similarity shared by the giver and the receiver), then (to quote Saint Paul) these acts "are meaningless noise and amount to nothing."

In all the different versions, the enchanted frog story affirms the necessity of recognizing and reaching out and embracing the despised element *within* if the lost treasure of expanding psychospiritual awareness, deeper self-acceptance, and awareness of the presence of the divine, as well as of finding one's right livelihood and place in society, are to be "recovered" (that is, experienced consciously again) in each new generation.

Put in more psychological terms, no one can invent a partial, "fake" personality (with all the nasty, messy, problematic, and frog-like Shadow elements edited out) and then expect that inauthentic, partial, essentially fictional character to have any deep sense of meaning, wholeness, or awareness of the excitement, purpose, mystery, or creative possibility of life. Short of a miracle, the construction of an inauthentically "good" and self-deceptive personality simply guarantees a slow loss of a sense of meaning and excitement and an absence of a reliable sense of meaning and purpose in that person's life. In such a situation, the most distressingly "dark and scary" dreams are likely to arise to criticize the inauthenticity of the dreamer's *persona* (or conscious, social "mask") in order to open a path back to a deeper awareness of meaning and creative vitality.

This is not to say that such secretly frightened, repressed, anguished, and sometimes embittered people are not occasionally opened up by the mysterious experience of what most Christians call "grace" (analogous to *baraka* in the Islamic tradition). But short of the unpredictable operations of grace, the inevitable consequence of the failure to embrace the revolting, enchanted-frog parts of myself is to live with the aching absence of a felt sense of the presence of the divine, the lost treasure, and with a sense of hopelessness and meaninglessness, no matter how repressed or secret that anguished sense may be.

Countless other versions and variations of the archetypal enchanted frog prince/princess story can be found in all parts of the world, including African, Pacific Island, and Native American traditions. Each version reflects the particular, unique social, gender, and class arrangements that obtain in that particular society, while at the same time pointing to the same universal, cross-cultural truth: Only through increasing self-awareness and acceptance of those previously denied aspects of the psyche can an awareness of harmony with the authentic self and the divine be achieved. The tale symbolically depicts a truly universal process of psychospiritual development that Carl Jung would call an "archetypal drama."

The enchanted frog tale is only one manageably small and specific example of the multitude of folk expressions, myths, and sacred narratives of the world that present essentially the same set of psychological and spiritual truths, always dressed in the outer garments of the particular cultures in which they appear, but also always telling the same essential, archetypal inner collective human story.

The myriad of endlessly repeating archetypal stories that appear in various forms in virtually every culture testify to the fact that there are basic similarities in the minds and hearts of people in all these diverse cultures. The fact that these same images and themes appear in the dreams of contemporary people also suggests that although specific and particular differences of personality and society abound, there is a deep layer of universal humanity that makes these particular images and motifs universally appealing across even the most dramatic boundaries of language, culture, tradition, religion, and gender.

The Enchanted Frog in Dreams

Recently, a man whom I will call "Bob" was working in a dream group I was facilitating. His dream may serve as a counterpoise example of the enchanted frog story appearing in a uniquely personal form.

> In his dream, after going through a series of vaguely sinister, embarrassing, and potentially compromising situations involving uncompleted sexual encounters with both women and men, Bob escapes and meets a frog on a mountain path. The meeting with the frog suddenly changes the tone of the dream from anxiety and menace to increasing relaxation and cheerful confidence. Bob follows the frog up the mountain path with a sense of release, freedom, and even joy. "The frog keeps looking at me over its shoulder, and urging me on with its almost human eyes..."

Bob confirmed with his own "aha's" of recognition that this dream was focused on a recent decision he had made to abandon a very lucrative and socially prestigious, but emotionally and spiritually barren, profession as a corporate lawyer. At the time of the dream, Bob had given up his previous career and was searching for something more satisfying, as yet undefined. His "aha's" were generated out of the group's work of asking questions and projecting their feelings and ideas onto his dream as though they had each dreamed it themselves.

The archetypal symbolism of the frog in Bob's dream, as well as in the various enchanted frog stories from around the world, grows directly out of observation of the life cycle of real frogs in nature. The frog achieves its adult form through dramatic physical metamorphosis and transformation. As such, the frog is a natural metaphor for archetypal human intuitions regarding profound, life-changing psychospiritual growth and transformation. Initially, the frog is born beneath the water in a fish-like form, without arms or legs. Later it undergoes a dramatic transformation, acquiring limbs and digits and losing its fishy tail. It then climbs up out of the watery depths onto dry land and into the sunshine. The frog is a natural archetypal metaphoric figure of transformation. The fairy-tale transformation of the frog into a prince is a symbolic extension and humanization of the natural transformation of the tadpole into the adult frog.

This same quality of natural archetypal symbolic analogy links water, the direction "down," and cool, fecund dimness into a constellation of symbols for unconsciousness and the experience of being relatively un-self-aware. By the same quality of natural symbolic analogy, the polar opposite of this constellation—brightness, warmth, dryness, and the direction "up"—is a complex of archetypal metaphors associated with consciousness and increasing self-awareness. Thus the natural life cycle of the frog, as it moves from water to dry land, and from fish to land animal, without ever losing its connection to the waters from which it came, becomes an extraordinarily apt natural archetypal metaphor of all forms of human psychospiritual development from relative unconsciousness and immaturity toward increasingly conscious and self-aware participation in life. It is as though we all start in the watery unconscious, like tadpoles, and then transform ourselves with increasing self-awareness; so that as we become more mature, we "climb up out of the water into the sunlight" of increasingly conscious self-awareness.

Another layer of archetypal resonance in the image of the frog is its deep connection with water and rain. In nontechnological societies (and in the deep unconscious minds of even the most sophisticated city dwellers) the frog is connected with the transformation of the natural world by rain. Throughout our evolution as Homo sapiens, we have heard the frogs "calling the rain" and seen the rain appear. As a species, we have come to associate the transformation of the land we live in—from dry to wet, from barren to fertile, from tan to green—that regularly accompanies the arrival of the rains with the frogs that "call the rain." This ancient natural association again puts the image of the archetypal frog at the center of a cosmic drama of profound transformation and change that affects not only the individual, but also the structure of society and the natural world as a whole.

Frog deities, particularly in tropical cultures, are inevitably associated with rain and the fertility of the land at an exoteric level, and with the transformation of spiritual life and awareness at an esoteric level. Frog gods and goddesses are worshipped and propitiated both to ensure rain and the fertility of the crops and as guardians and patrons of spiritual development and advancement, since the waters they inhabit and control are both the actual waters necessary for continuing physical existence and also the symbolic unconscious, emotional, and spiritual fructifying and vitalizing "waters of life."

The frog in Bob's dream reveals itself to be an archetypal image closely associated with all these levels of meaning. Its "almost human eyes" make the specific connection to the enchanted frog motif even clearer. Further confirmation comes in the frog's ability to totally transform the emotional impact and tone of the dream experience. Because it is still in its frog form, there is reason to suppose that Bob's transition to his new life and the internalization of the new values that accompany it are far from complete, but it is also a clear indication that the process of metamorphosis is well under way.

The transformative archetype of the enchanted frog always has spiritual as well as psychological implications. This brings us back to Bob's dream again from another direction. The "mountain path" is in itself an archetypal metaphor of spiritual striving. "Going to the mountain top" has always been a way for many spiritual seekers, particularly male-oriented seekers, to achieve communion with the divine "above." The fact that the frog leads the dreamer "up the mountain path" is further indication of the archetypal forces at work in Bob's life, reflected in his dream. Bob has come to recognize the real value in many of the previously despised and suppressed elements of his financially successful but emotionally barren and ethically ambiguous "fast lane" life. These awkward, unfashionable, previously ignored emotional and spiritual intuitions are now guiding him "up" to greater self-awareness and transpersonal experience "on the mountain top."

From an archetypal point of view, the enchanted frog is a most appropriate guide on this journey. Without a dawning recognition of the true value of the previously ignored and repressed emotional and spiritual elements of his old life that the frog embodies, he would not be able to reach the mountain top of greater self-acceptance and spiritual awareness.

The path to the mountain top can be successfully traversed only by someone who is relatively *whole,* one who has consciously explored and accepted even the more problematic and negative aspects of his or her personality. No one can be whole without this kind of conscious self-knowledge and self-acceptance. Metaphorically speaking, each one of us must learn to trust, and eventually "kiss and marry," the part of ourselves that is most "enchanted" (i.e., unconscious) and seemingly most repulsive, underdeveloped, and frog-like.

The cumulative implications of both the personal and the archetypal associations to the "frog with human eyes" in Bob's dream point to the spiritual as well as the emotional and psychological significance of the dream. The vaguely sinister erotic images that precede the appearance of the enchanted frog also have similar archetypal implications.

Overt Sexual Encounters in Dreams

The menacing and ambiguous sexual encounters that precede the meeting with the frog on the mountain path in Bob's dream are, at one level at least, simply reflective of the multiple, relatively shallow, and unsatisfying sexual encounters that routinely went with his old "fast lane" life. At another level, they are metaphoric examples of the somber, threatening absence of real joy and meaning in his apparently successful life as a whole.

Explicit erotic encounters in myths and dreams are always highly significant from an archetypal point of view, particularly as they tend to reflect and depict the dreamer's (and, at another level, the society's) overall state of integration and wholeness. When sexuality and erotic encounter appear in an unmasked overt form, there is almost always a level of reference to the life of the spirit. This layer of archetypal significance in overtly erotic symbolism appears to be constellated by the basic nature of human sexual experience itself.

All sexual encounter is energetically stimulating and arouses deep emotions. Even nasty, oppressive, unsatisfactory sexual encounters will still activate and energize all of a person's limbic systems, even if that total arousal is disappointing or even traumatic; whereas happy, satisfying, orgasmic sexual union is one of the most intense, pleasurable, and transformative experiences of which human beings are capable. For this reason, overt erotic activities in dreams (and myths) tend to be symbolic of the next "octave" of human experience: intuitive, transformative spiritual encounter.

Authentic spiritual experience has the same quality of being naturally and totally energizing and involving. This level of natural symbolism makes spiritual encounter like sex. The analogy is "natural," in the same way that the archetypal analogy of the frog's and butterfly's physical transformations are naturally symbolic of human psychological and spiritual intuitions and transformations.

In myths and dreams, a second, "masked," symbolic variety of sexual energy regularly appears. There is the kind of sexuality that Freud spent so much time exploring and naming, where virtually every image and action has a symbolic reference to genital sexual encounter. In a myth, a folk tale, or a dream, going through a door has sexual implications; *not* going through a door has sexual implications. Every element of the symbolic experience has a level related to the dreamer's genital/sexual/emotional/relational life or lack of it.

Freud's insights into the essentially sexual/erotic nature of all myth and dream symbolism are regularly confirmed by work with contemporary peoples' dreams. The relative freedom of sexuality and sexual expression in our era, as compared with Freud's, has not changed the basic dream pattern.

Freud's blunder was to reduce *all* dream experience to repressed, symbolic sexual desire, ignoring the other multiple layers of meaning and significance that are also always woven into every dream. But he wasn't wrong about the sex. We are essentially sexual beings; and all our actions, awake and asleep, do always have unconscious symbolic sexual motivations and overtones.

In Freud's view, all human activity is ultimately motivated by sexual desire. Over the course of his life and work, he came to use the term *libido* to cover the spectrum of sexual/"life energy" desires. The all-inclusiveness of the term *libido* eventually elevates it to a philosophical/religious/spiritual term (although Freud himself would undoubtedly be appalled at the suggestion). Any term that comes to stand for the deepest felt sense of meaning and motivation in a person's life is by definition a religious, spiritual, or at least an all-encompassing philosophical term.

Freud also suggested that the primary function of dreaming was to "protect sleep." He saw the dream as a tissue of masks, distortions, and displacements, turning the natural, "raw," uninhibited, and consciously unacceptable sexual "wishes" that float to the surface of awareness in sleep into more or less acceptable images, so that the dreamer was not regularly awakened with horror at the recognition of his or her rapacious desires. If Freud were correct, however, we could reasonably expect that no one would ever dream of overt, unmasked sexual imagery, or that if one did, it would immediately precipitate one into agitated awakening. This is simply not the case, as Bob's dream and countless others regularly show. People often dream about overtly erotic, seemingly nonsymbolic sexual encounters, and only rarely do they awaken from them in horror.

At this level, the nasty, ambiguous sexual encounters at the beginning of Bob's dream represent his increasing unhappiness at the spiritual barrenness of that life. The sinister and unfulfilling sexual encounters in Bob's dream reflect his deep, frustrated desire for a good deal more than satisfying sex. The frustrated quality of these overtly erotic images also reflect his sense of frustration at having "made a mistake" by involving himself in a life that initially offered promise of emotional or spiritual fulfillment, but that required the suppression of large portions his authentic personality, thereby making the satisfaction of such spiritual longings virtually impossible. In just the same way, the sexual encounters in the dream (and in his previous fast-lane life) offered only the illusion of real love and emotional/relational satisfaction.

In Bob's dream, one of the implications of the shadowy, unfulfilling, and ultimately unsatisfying sexual encounters at the beginning of his dream is that there was, at least initially, some way in which his previous professional life did seem to offer a promise of deeper emotional and spiritual fulfillment. But it had failed to deliver on that promise. The encounters suggest that Bob may have tried to force his idealism and spiritual longing into the mold of his professional activities, rather like a person who continues going to church in the hopes of "feeling closer to God," even when the actual experience no longer produces that effect.

Given the idealistic public image of many of the traditional skilled professions (medicine, law, architecture, ministry, and the like), in contrast to the nasty, trivial, competitive, and shortsighted way they are all too often actually experienced and practiced, the image of the ambiguous, failed sexual encounters is archetypally resonant with many professionals' contemporary experience. The situation in which Bob found himself at the time of his dream is all too common for many professionals; the drama of failed idealism and spiritual longing is an archetypal experience of the modern world for many people.

Sex and Spirit–the Longing to Be One

The hunger for totally fulfilling emotional/spiritual experience—for experience that is not only immediately gratifying to the waking ego, but also embodies an authentic sense of participating in a broader drama of meaning and significance that extends beyond the details of personal circumstances, even beyond the seeming beginning and end of individual life—is an instinctive/archetypal human need. Even more than language and tool use (both of which have recently been demonstrated to be shared with a growing number of "lesser" species), this instinct and desire for all-encompassing, transcendent meaning appears to be the quintessential human instinct. The desire for it is so deep that many people in contemporary Western society are even afraid to admit to themselves that they have it, because they fear their lives would become insupportable if they admitted it to themselves consciously and then failed to find it.

This archetypal drive for a sense of transcendent meaning is deeply ingrained in human beings and has a myriad of specific expressions as wildly varied as the range of expressions of our sexual/relational urges. The natural symbolism of human sexual experience is an archetypal metaphor for this next octave of human instinct. The sexual/erotic situations and circumstances in our dreams regularly give symbolic shape to the specific state of development of this universal drama in our own particular lives.

The association between overt sexuality and spiritual search is deep and ingrained in the collective unconscious. It expresses itself both in the familiar prohibitions against sexual expression in many of the world's conventional religious traditions on the one hand, and in the emphasis on sexual expression in the "left-handed" spiritual traditions like Tantrism, Gnosticism, and Tibetan Buddhism on the other. Below the surface of contradictory appearance in both these attitudes toward sexual expression and spiritual striving is a single archetypal assumption: *Sexual energy and desire is deeply connected with the psychological and emotional energy used in striving for a more consciously felt sense of the presence of the divine.* Whether sexual expression is specifically forbidden or consciously cultivated in this endeavor, it is recognized as deeply and metaphorically associated with the energies of spiritual search.

All over the planet, mystics from all traditions resort to sexual/sensual/erotic metaphors in the attempt to make their mystical encounters with the divine comprehensible and communicable to people who have not shared the experience. This is precisely because the ecstasies of sexual love are the closest natural analogy to the ecstasies of spiritual communion. In ancient Egypt, Mesopotamia, Greece, Rome, and the Celtic world; in the Americas, Asia, and Africa; in all periods of history, the mystic testifies, "I met the divine, and it was like meeting the lover. I prepared myself, as I prepare for my beloved. The joy of our union was like the joy of wildly abandoned and satisfying sexual love, and the separation was like the misery of separation from the loved one."

In prehistoric, matrifocal religious traditions, overt sexual expression and erotic encounter were recognized and accepted as ritual pathways to communion with the Goddess. The temple prostitutes against whom Jeremiah and so many of the other Old Testament prophets inveighed so shrilly were clearly priestesses devoted to sexual expression as a meditation on, and a means of direct communion with, the divine in feminine form. The connection is deeply ingrained in the collective unconscious; and in matrifocal religious practice, the spontaneous appearance of overtly erotic sexual imagery in dreams and meditative visions was understood to be "a gift of the Goddess," a confirmation that the individual's spiritual efforts were being rewarded.

Ironically enough, this archetypal connection between sexuality and spiritual "success" casts the testimony of the desert hermits of the early Christian church into a new and different light. The Desert Fathers, like Simon of the Pillar, Anthony, Jerome, and the rest, all fled from town life because the constant bustle of human interaction and commerce tended to distract them from their spiritual labors. Even the quieter countryside turned out to be too filled with plants growing and flowering, and animals living their unashamedly animal lives; so the spiritual seekers fled even further from the distractions of squishy, wet, messy biological life, into the dry, leafless solitude of the desert. But even in the stark and barren desert, they were plagued with dreams and visions of the most overtly and explicitly erotic and sexual nature. They have left fairly lurid accounts of their visions and struggles (a favorite subject for proto-pornographic medieval Christian painting) and of their passionate desire to create a "new man" in whom these spontaneous sexual desires and visions would finally be rooted out.

However, from the point of view of the collective unconscious and the more harmonious balance between the psychospiritual energies of the masculine and the feminine that accompanies successful psychospiritual development, their visions can be recognized as the same kind of encouraging confirmations of the sincerity and depth of their spiritual striving that were given to seekers in the earlier matrifocal religious tradition under similar conditions of asceticism and sacrificial self-discipline. The ironic difference is that the earlier tradition embraced and accepted such visions as objective, divine confirmations of spiritual progress, whereas the Desert Fathers interpreted their experiences as indications of unregenerate "sinfulness" and spiritual failure.

The stated desire of Christianity to create a "new man" [*sic*] must be reevaluated, I believe, in the light of this constellation of spontaneous archetypal patterns of symbolism. The deep natural association between sexuality and spiritual striving, for example, suggests a truth very close to the truth of the enchanted frog story. Once again, the thing that is despised—in this instance, sexuality and the physical world in general, and the feminine in particular—is the very thing that has been left out, the beautiful thing that has been enchanted into the repulsive frog form, without which full, authentic, satisfying, meaningful communion with the divine can not be achieved.

For Bob, his previous life finally became insupportable; and the elements of sincerity, authentic emotion, vulnerability, spiritual search, and service to others that had been missing and despised as "naive" and "weak" were the frog that had to be kissed in order to retrieve the lost treasure of a satisfying, meaningful life. For Christianity in general, and the Desert Fathers in particular, it is the physical world, nature, the body, sexual expression, and particularly the archetypal feminine that have been rejected and despised as "fallen" and "sinful"; and it is precisely these "disgusting" (archetypically frog-like and inherently transformative) elements that must be embraced in order to achieve a truly felt sense of the presence of the divine. The particulars of the drama may vary, but the essential elements remain archetypally consistent.

Is the "new man" of Christianity actually in greater harmony with the depths of his or her authentic being and with the divine, both within and without, than the supposedly less conscious and more self-indulgent "pagan" he is supposed to replace? I think the evidence of disrupted ecology and both institutional and interpersonal inhumanity speaks for itself. The health and wholeness of individual people and of global society as a whole is not served by the denial of the body, sexuality, the divinity of the feminine, and the sacredness of physical matter itself. Our current crisis of global ecology and culture can be seen as the direct result of the effort to cut ourselves off from these deep wellsprings of the collective unconscious, as manifested particularly in our dreams, and in the traditions of sacred, archetypal stories of myth and folk tale from around the world.

Archetypal encounters with the frog and with the host of other animals that speak always tend to represent the authentic, harmonized, instinctive spiritual life. Like the similar articulate animals and monsters in "Beauty and the Beast," "Snow White and Rose Red," "Swan Lake," and so forth, the enchanted frog has many levels of meaning. But one of the most important and consistent is this layer where the magical animal embodies and symbolizes the deep, unconscious, inner, instinctive, natural, "animal" promptings of feeling and conscience that it is time to live a more emotionally authentic and genuinely expressive and creative life. Just as in the many versions of the frog prince/princess story, the result of beginning to live this kind of life is often ostracism and ridicule from one's former friends and associates; but the benefits far outweigh the seemingly inevitable loss of status.

In Bob's dream, "following the frog up the mountain" stands clearly as a metaphor for following the unfashionable inner promptings of feeling and conscience that it is time to change and leave his old life behind, despite the consequent loss of income, social status, and ultimately even the dissolution of his marriage and the loss of all his old fast-lane friends. One of the most painful and internally disorienting losses occasioned by the abandonment of his career in law was the loss of his "manliness" in the eyes of his old friends and colleagues. However, by the time he had the frog dream, Bob was already beginning to experience the joys and energies of his new, less certain, but more authentic and expressive way of life and to understand that there are indeed many more ways of "being a real man" than engaging in gladiatorial combat in the arena of the law.

The archetypal promise of the enchanted frog story, in both myth and folklore, and even more particularly in the dreams of individual people, is that if the risk is taken and the unfashionable transforming "frog" is embraced and loved as a life's companion, then the lost treasure of self-worth and spiritual meaning will be recovered, and ultimate success beyond the wildest imaginings of the previous worldview are assured.

SUMMARY

*The striking similarities in theme, motif, and specific imagery
shared among the world's myths and folk tales on the one hand, and
among the dreams of individual people on the other, offer compelling
evidence that there is a corresponding stratum of shared unconscious
similarity in all human beings. Carl Jung called these repeating similarities "archetypes of the collective unconscious."*

*The story of the enchanted frog prince/princess is one good exam-
ple of this class of archetypal narratives that appear in multiple versions in virtually all cultures around the world.*

*Several versions of the story from different parts of the world are
presented and discussed with regard to what the variations in the narrative from culture to culture may have to suggest about the differences
among those various cultures on the one hand, and the fundamental
human similarities they share on the other. All the versions of this
worldwide tale suggest the particular traditions of relationship to the
archetypal feminine and gender-role behavior that obtain in each culture. At the same time, the story in all its versions also suggests a single
psychospiritual truth: that the divine is in all, especially in the most
repugnant and despised elements of society and of the psyche. The archetypal story goes on to suggest that if the "lost treasure" of happiness and
a fulfilling sense of spiritual meaning on the one hand, and satisfactory
and just social arrangements and relationships on the other, are to be
discovered or recovered, then the "frog" of rejected energy must be "kissed
and married"; that is, embraced and accepted.*

*When the same enchanted human/frog image appears in the
dreams of specific individuals, there is equal likelihood that it has essentially the same archetypal message to convey. A dream from "Bob," a
man who had voluntarily retired from his fast-lane profession to seek
more emotionally satisfying and spiritually rewarding work, is discussed in detail.*

*Overtly sexual/sensual imagery is related to mythology on the one
hand, and to the psychological and emotional issues embodied in Bob's
and other dreams on the other. The appearance of overt sexual, erotic
imagery in dreams (and myths) is also archetypically associated with
spiritual concerns. There is an inherent tendency in the shared human
psyche to symbolize spiritual experiences as erotic encounters, in part*

because sexuality is one of the most totally involving experiences human beings are capable of, and as such, sexual encounters are a natural analogy to spiritual experiences. The more satisfying the symbolic sexual/sensual encounters, the more they tend to reflect satisfactory spiritual developments in the dreamer's life.

The metaphor of "climbing the mountain" that appears in Bob's dream has long been associated with upward spiritual striving. The appearance of the mountain climbing image in Bob's dream further implies the depth and breadth of the spiritual journey the dreamer has undertaken.

Whenever archetypal images such as enchanted frogs, sexual encounters, and climbing mountains appear in the dreams of an individual, there is every reason to look for levels of symbolic meaning in the dreamer's personal life that echo and reflect the symbolic meanings and weight these images have always carried in world mythic narrative.

Chapter 2
MORE METAPHORS OF THE COLLECTIVE UNCONSCIOUS: BUTTERFLIES, ALIEN ABDUCTIONS, AND LOST CIVILIZATIONS

> Today there is a wide measure of agreement, which on the physical side of science approaches almost to unanimity, that the stream of knowledge is heading toward a non-mechanical reality; the universe begins to look more like a great thought than like a great machine....We discover that the universe shows evidence of a designing and controlling power that has something in common with our own individual minds.
>
> *Sir James Jeans*

The most natural analogy for constantly self-replicating archetypes of the collective unconscious lies in the basic anatomical structure of the physical body. All human beings (indeed, all vertebrates) share a common archetypal pattern of physical form. Each person and creature is a unique physical organism, while at the same time, each body re-creates exactly the same basic pattern of tissues and organs in the same relationship that is present in all other vertebrate bodies. In this sense, we may speak about basic archetypes of the brain, heart, and liver—the blood, the kidneys, the skeleton, the muscles, the nerves—as well as basic archetypal patterns of relationship among these organs and tissues. These fundamental, unchanging archetypal forms are reproduced in endless specific examples and variations.

At the level of physical anatomy, we have no difficulty understanding that all human beings are both unique and separate, and yet at the same time totally similar to one another. Whether we choose to emphasize the unique aspects of our physical bodies or to concentrate on our universal anatomical similarities is solely a question of our observer's bias and point of view at any given moment.

As it is with physical anatomy, so it is with the psyche. All human beings reproduce the entire spectrum of archetypal forms and energies shared by all other human beings, while at the same time giving them unique expression in our individual lives and experience. These spontaneous archetypal images and dramas are universally resonant and recognizable from China to Chicago and from Terra del Fuego to Vladivostok. As the ancient Chinese philosopher Kuo Hsiang observed in the second century, "If we differentiate things according to their differences, everything is different from the other. If we consider things similar according to their points of similarity, there is nothing which is not the same."

In working with dreams, the appearance of multiple versions of the same images and themes in the dreams of different individuals (or in a series of dreams from same individual) often marks an archetypal theme or pattern and is a reliable indication that there is a universal issue or situation being addressed in the life of the dreamer(s). The same is true in the world of myth and folklore. When a similar motif (like an enchanted frog or an arduous upward climb) appears in many different versions of the same story (or at a structurally similar juncture in different stories), even when these stories are scattered across different cultures in different periods of history, we can be quite sure that at some important level similar archetypal social, psychological, and spiritual issues are being symbolized and addressed.

In all cultures, folk tales have always served as vehicles for the appearance of archetypal motifs. Children's stories and fairy tales always play a crucial role in shaping the basic social and psychological attitudes of children in their most unconsciously formative years.

It may be that today in the industrialized world, film and television have usurped this heuristic function of traditional spoken folk narratives; but since the basic (archetypal) fairy-tale plots and emotional tensions between and among the characters in television cartoons and cinematic dramas still remain very much the same and still reflect much the same sorts of gender roles and class arrangements portrayed in the traditional fairy tales, the seemingly great changes in the technological form of the psychosocial modeling may not actually make as much difference as many critics of contemporary culture suppose. Despite the dazzling diversity of seemingly different plots and stories, recognizable patterns of basic relationship repeat endlessly, beyond and below the surface of appearance.

Just as the heart always pumps the blood, and the stomach and intestines digest the food, it is always that same despised element, the "Shadow" (regardless of the specific shape it may assume in each individual's life and collectively in each different culture), that invariably holds the very energy and experience necessary for real health and wholeness.

These archetypal symbolic dramas usually appear most clearly in close association with common experiences shared by all human beings, such as the universal tension between authentic, individual self-knowledge and self-acceptance, and the pressure to conform thoughtlessly to the stereotyped norms and mores of one's social milieu. One way of thinking about the archetypes of the collective unconscious is to see them as natural, instinctive, symbolic statements of common, universal human needs and experiences. On several occasions, Jung equated the archetypes with "instinctive tendencies" akin to those involved with language, reproduction, finding nourishment, and so forth.

Dreaming as Archetypal Symbol

The universal experience of dreaming itself, together with the recurrent ways in which it is viewed in widely dispersed cultures at different periods of history, may serve as another example of how archetypal energies are given particular, diverse forms while still reflecting the same essential patterns.

One level of archetypal symbolism inherent in the dreaming experience itself is our instinctive predisposition to imagine that our dreams hold clues to the deeper meaning and significance of our lives. *All* peoples, at *all* periods of history—and, we may safely assume, in prehistoric times as well—have exhibited this instinctive archetypal tendency to search for and find symbolic meanings in their dreams that resonate, one way or another, with their most important waking desires and frustrations.

At an even deeper level of archetypal symbolism and intuition, people all over the planet at all periods of history have also tended to see in their dreams some reflection or anticipation of after-death experience. On numerous occasions, Shakespeare makes use of this archetypal association between sleep and death and between dreams and the afterlife: "Our little life is rounded with a sleep..." When Hamlet is contemplating suicide, the metaphor is enough to give him pause: "To sleep—perchance to dream. Aye, there's the rub!" In their chants for the recently dead, the Tibetan Buddhists say, "You are dead, but you dream on ..." In West Africa, the word for "to dream" *(drokuku)* means "to be half dead." Native Americans of the Great Plains have a traditional saying: "To die is to walk the path of the dream without returning." Examples of this particular archetypal analogy are legion. Whenever we find individuals and cultural groups as diverse as Shakespeare, Tibetan Buddhists, West African shamans, and Plains Indians all using the same basic metaphor, we can be sure we have come upon an archetypal idea or symbolic form.

Although the specific expressions differ, the basic metaphor itself—sleep = death, dream = after-death experience—is completely cross-cultural and conveys the same basic instinctive human notion, the same basic archetypal speculation about the profound relationship between dream experience and the idea of an afterlife. It is worth noting that our Western technological society is the only culture in the entire history of the planet that has systematically attempted to collectively ignore and suppress these instinctive, archetypal intuitions of the similarity between sleep, dream, and death.

An even deeper level of archetypal symbolism associated with sleep and dreaming is revealed in the astonishing unanimity of the world's myths and sacred narratives in their assertion that human beings communicate with the divine more often and more reliably in dreams than in any other regular state of consciousness. This is perhaps the most dramatic example of the archetypal predisposition to view the dreaming experience as related to the deepest questions of meaning and significance in our lives. The Hebrew Talmud; the Christian Bible; the Moslem Koran; the Buddhist Dhamapada; the Hindu Upanishads; the Australian Aboriginal songs of the Dreamtime; the Pacific, African, and Native American stories of creation and world shaping—the list is virtually endless. *All* the sacred narratives testify that God and the gods, goddesses, spirits, and ancestors communicate with human beings directly in their dreams. The same archetypal idea can be put into more abstract and psychological language: We are inherently predisposed to find in our dreams intimations of and clues to our potential relationship with the most profound energies and ideas that we are capable of formulating and experiencing consciously at this point in our personal and collective evolutionary development.

This startling unanimity among all the world's religions is a symbolic statement of the inherent health-and-wholeness-promoting quality of dreams. Dreams do not come in the service of the ego or in support of repression and denial. They come to connect us more consciously to the deepest and most profound energies of our lives. The psychospiritual wholeness that dreams reflect and promote is much more complete and authentic than the sense of "conscious self" that is defined (and limited) by the waking ego.

Jung saw this archetypal quality of dreams as the source of the dream's "compensation" for the limitations and premature closures of the waking mind. Over and over again, he says that the dream experience "compensates" for over- and under-estimations and valuations made by and in the dreamer's conscious attitude. Although this is certainly the case, over the years it has become increasingly clear to me that "compensation" is more accurately viewed as an inevitable consequence of the basic health-and-wholeness-promoting quality of dreams and dreaming. *Wholeness* is not a compensation for incompleteness and premature closure; it is a positive force and value in its own right. This consistent promotion of psychospiritual wholeness will always compensate for whatever errors of judgment and prejudices the dreamer may have adopted and perpetuated; but the purpose is not some sort of static balance, but rather a continuously developing and evolving experience of, and interaction with, life in ever larger and more resonant metaphors of relationship and meaning.

Our dreams always place the waking ego in a symbolic landscape that reflects the collective, conventional attitudes and opinions of our given society or culture, while at the same time pointing to the larger, more universal human needs that may or may not be met by that particular society. Thus, dreams always tend to subvert prematurely closed attitudes and ideologies. Even if a religious intuition was first born from the same collective unconscious source as our dreams, as soon as authentic spiritual inspiration becomes frozen in creed and dogma, the dreams themselves will begin to criticize and subvert it in the interest of the next evolution of psychospiritual wholeness that the dogmatic formulation closes off prematurely.

For this reason, it is easy to see why dream work is so strongly disparaged in the daily practice of most mainstream religions, despite the unambiguous affirmations of sacred scripture that dreams are a primary means of personal communion with the divine. Indeed, these affirmations are so frequent and unambiguous that if dream work were not specifically discouraged, then it would be virtually impossible for any merely local, human ecclesiastical authority to maintain order in any congregation. The biblical precedents (to say nothing of the scriptural statements of other religious traditions) are so clear that without the practical "administrative" prohibition against dream work, it would be possible for anyone (the scruffier and more malcontent the better) to stand up and proclaim: "Last night I had a dream, and God told me to tell you..."

The tradition of marginal, socially outcast "prophets" proclaiming "God's will" through their dreams is in itself another octave of the same basic archetypal theme. Like the theme of the enchanted frog prince, it points symbolically to the absolute spiritual necessity of finding the divine in all, and most particularly in the despised and collectively denied elements of both psyche and society. For it is precisely in those despised elements that the energy for the next transformation of self and society into a state of more complete wholeness and harmony with the divine lies waiting.

"Nightmares" as Urgent Messages

The "nightmare" reveals another specific layer of this archetypal symbolic drama of dreaming and waking. Our survival, both individual and collective, has always depended to a very great degree on our ability to pay immediate and focused attention to threatening stimuli. For millennia, we have had to mobilize all our wits and energies the moment we are menaced or attacked. Animals who can pull off this "trick of consciousness" tend to survive, and those who can't quite get it together tend not to. For millennia, the forces of natural selection have been at work, shaping the species; and for this reason, we are *instinctively predisposed* to pay close attention to any startling, surprising, menacing, or seemingly negative stimulus.

When the unconscious, the deep source within, has particularly important information to convey to the waking mind (particularly when we are not in the habit of remembering dreams), our dreams are very likely to assume nasty, negative, "nightmarish" forms *simply to grab and hold our attention.* In this vitally important sense, the nightmare itself is another example of a primary archetypal form. Nightmares, like all other dreams, come in the service of the dreamer's health and wholeness. Their scary and compelling form simply grows out of and reflects our inherent (archetypal) predisposition to pay attention to the threat of the negative.

In this important sense, the generic message of all nightmares in all cultures in all periods of history is essentially the same: Wake up! Pay attention! Here is a survival issue! Sometimes the "survival issue" has to do with the dreamer's physical health; but even when physical health is not an issue, there are always psychological, emotional, and spiritual survival issues depicted and given symbolic shape and form in nightmares.

One of the best ways to grasp the nature and significance of all the archetypes and archetypal forms is to understand that they are categories of instinctive, evolutionary predisposition toward particular kinds of emotional symbolism, built up over the entire history of our evolution as human beings. Our instinctive predisposition to give immediate and focused attention to threatening stimuli, and therefore to symbolize particularly important unconscious information in a seemingly negative form, is just one example of how an archetype manifests in multiple forms and appearances, all of which carry the same essential meaning.

Sleeping and dreaming is only one example of a universal human experience that has global, archetypal symbolic resonances and associations. All truly universal human experiences have a tendency to evoke strikingly similar symbolic images and similar emotionally charged relational dramas. These deep similarities in symbolic image and emotional charge persist no matter what specific personalities, societies, or periods of history give them their unique shape and style in any particular instance. Australian Aborigine artists, Siberian hunters, South African miners, and San Francisco urban sophisticates—all are instinctively predisposed to pay immediate and focused attention to nasty, threatening stimuli in waking life and to their "nightmares," as are all other human beings in all parts of the world at all periods of history. It is a pan-human patterned response that takes specific form in individual people, shaped and colored by our unique individual personalities and diverse cultural backgrounds; but it is essentially and demonstrably similar symbolic behavior, regardless of the individual and cultural variations we bring to this archetypal theme.

Cataloguing Archetypes as "Folk-Tale Motifs"

By the middle of the twentieth century, the basic field work and scholarship of collecting and cataloguing the archetypal stories with repeating universal symbolic motifs, like those revealed in the enchanted frog tales, had been more or less completed. The two great scholars in this area of ethnographic research and compilation, Anti Aarne of Finland and Stith Thompson of the United States, collaborated in creating an elaborate and still definitive system for categorizing and cataloguing these recurring myth and folk-tale motifs. The basic frog prince/princess story, for instance, is labeled "Tale Type #440" and includes many subcategories, such as "B211.7.2—frog capable of speech," "B655—marriage to frog in human form," and "D395—transformation, frog to person," and so forth.

Once these basic archetypal motifs had been collected and catalogued, it was increasingly difficult for the academic world to ignore the fundamental similarities of plot and symbol shared throughout the world's myth and folklore. These global similarities in folk and sacred lore constitute one of the most powerful arguments for the reality of the collective unconscious. We are now in a position to add the testimony of dreams to this growing list of evidence for the fundamental unity of the human psyche, both individual and collective.

Carl Jung concluded that the cumulative evidence of both individual psychology and folklore was indisputable—all human beings share a deep layer of psychologically similar "instinctive" intuitions, and these "archetypes" of shared human mind and heart are the primary source of the dramatic similarities in world myth. He even suggested on a number of occasions that if all artifacts of language and culture were simultaneously obliterated and only preverbal human children survived, those children would reinvent all the same essential stories, beliefs, and ritual social structures all over again in the space of one generation as they acted out the archetypal intuitions welling up out of their shared objective psyche.

Other scholars and psychologists have argued that these similarities are not the products of fundamentally similar minds, but rather the result of "diffusion" of a single set of spiritual ideas and rituals from a single source. They argue that these repeating themes all result from the rise of a primary *"UrKultur"* that spread its influence—particularly its religious visions and mythic narratives—around the globe in prehistoric times.

Many people find the evidence quite persuasive for such global diffusion of culture from the fertile basin of the Tigris and Euphrates Rivers in what is now Iraq. However, even if it is the case, it only postpones the question of the reality of the collective unconscious by one step. Even if the striking similarities among all the world's myths and folklore do reflect the diffusion of culture from a single primary source, the question still remains: Where did these particular ideas and images come from originally, at the source? Even more important from a contemporary point of view, why do these particular stories and ideas *still* continue to exercise such a fascinating and persuasive effect on *all* the people who encounter them now, long after the original *UrKultur* has crumbled into dust and become virtually forgotten?

The compelling fascination and vitality of these archetypal stories and themes has persisted for millennia. Even if the diffusion hypothesis is historically correct in one instance or another, the inevitable implication still remains that there is something inherent in the panhuman psyche that finds these particular stories, these particular symbols and dramatic images, so eternally and compellingly appealing.

So even if we accept the evidence for cultural diffusion, we are still talking about basic human affinities for particular kinds of symbolism and dramatic narrative shared by all human beings around the globe that cause these stories to retain their fascination long after the social and cultural situations that gave them birth initially have disappeared. In other words, we are still looking at persuasive evidence of the reality of a "collective unconscious" or "objective psyche" of some sort. The evidence for cultural diffusion points clearly to the reality of a *collective,* shared level of unconscious functioning in the human species, analogous to our shared physical anatomy.

Archetypes as "Chariots of the Gods"

The tendency of many renegade scholars and occultists to attribute these similarities of world symbolism not to the legacy of ancient Near Eastern civilizations, but to "space travelers" who visited the planet in prehistoric times, or to the lasting effects of even earlier "lost civilizations" like Atlantis and Lemuria, is in itself a persistent modern myth. These ideas of "fantastically advanced lost civilizations" are, among other things, archetypal symbolic representations of the collective unconscious itself. The stories and theories of Atlantis and the "ancient astronauts" are, at one level at least, archetypal symbol dramas expressing (as myths have always done) collective psychospiritual intuitions about our deepest selves.

The influence of the collective layer of the psyche is felt and can be seen everywhere. It is a natural part of our being, yet at the same time, it feels strange when we experience it and encounter evidence of it directly. The conscious encounter with the collective unconscious invariably feels "weird" and "fascinating" and "alien" and "compelling," all at the same time. Symbolically, the influence of the collective unconscious does indeed come "from another world" than the world of the waking ego. The persistent myths of the "travelers from other worlds" and the "great, lost, advanced races" that are ultimately responsible for the spooky similarities in the symbolism of world culture are themselves emotionally evocative, symbolically accurate, archetypal representations of what it feels like to encounter the deeper layers of the collective "objective psyche." This aspect of intrapsychic life feels so much older and wiser, and so very distant. Yet at the same time it is almost all-powerful, pressing against our limited sense of waking self, but still hidden.

As Emerson says, addressing the same archetypal intuition that gives birth to the myths of Atlantis and the visitors from other worlds: "'Within' is so great as to be 'Beyond.'" The stories of "chariots of the gods" and "lost master races" give concrete narrative form to these intuitions of the deep, unconscious, archetypal "within" that is simultaneously "beyond." The adherents of these nonconformist theories tend to argue most passionately for the truth and accuracy of their views, in large measure because these ideas give concrete conscious shape to what they experience unconsciously and emotionally as true.

As Carl Jung points out: "Practical experience shows us again and again that any prolonged preoccupation with an

unknown object acts as an almost irresistible bait for the unconscious to project itself onto the unknown nature of the object
and to accept the resultant projection, and the interpretation
deduced from it, as objective." This is as true of the inchoate perception of the collective unconscious itself as it is of particular
archetypal forms arising from the collective levels of the psyche.

In this sense, the contemporary fascination with UFO's and
alien abductions is another example of the same archetypal pattern. The direct experience of the archetypal energies of the collective unconscious always *feels* overwhelming and purposeful,
even though that purpose is fundamentally unknown and
unknowable, in exactly the same fashion as are the actions of the
"aliens," who are also perceived as having some grand and mysterious plan and purpose.

The repeating elements in the stories of alien abduction
have led many, including the brilliant and courageous Harvard
psychiatrist John Mack, to conclude that the "abductees" are
reporting real experiences in the waking physical world.
Whether these encounters are physically real or not, they reveal
an archetypal symbolic pattern associated with direct encounter
with collective unconscious itself.

The experiments in cross-breeding that the aliens are supposedly conducting are associated in the abductees minds with
the transformation of the human species in the face of our
increasing pollution and destruction of the natural environment. These stories give concrete (symbolic) shape to our deepest fears of our own potential for evil. We human beings know we
are capable of destroying the planet's ability to support life; and,
as always, we long to be "saved" from ourselves.

Instinctively, we realize that we must evolve if we are to overcome our propensity for (self) destruction. The stories of alien
abduction, even if they are journalistically accurate, remain as primary examples of the archetypal mythological impulse taking contemporary, postmodern shape. The stories give compelling
symbolic narrative form to the deepest intuitions of the urgency
and reality of impending collective change in the face of the escalating disasters of contemporary life at the turn of the millennium. Dr. Mack himself draws conclusions that point clearly to this

archetypal symbolic resonance in the stories told by abductees: "With the opening of consciousness to new domains of being, abductees encounter patterns and a design of life that brings them a profound sense of interconnectedness in the universe."

We human beings are inherently predisposed to seek such experiences of deep and profound connection with larger patterns of meaning, and to generate experiences and create compelling symbolic narratives that convey those feelings of communion and direct participation in those larger patterns. Indeed, any story that succeeds in evoking that felt sense of participating in larger and more meaningful patterns of truth than our own individual comfort or discomfort is, by definition, a "sacred narrative," and will have a tendency to attract adherents who take it literally. In that sense, the alien abduction stories are only the latest in a noble line of sacred narratives where "God" and/or "the gods" intervene directly and "save" humanity by transforming our awareness of our special relationship to these larger divine (archetypal) energies.

The increasingly conscious encounter with these deep archetypal energies in the shared human psyche is metaphorically "creating a new hybrid species," just as it has always done at moments of collective social, cultural, economic, and religious change. Each individual who encounters these archetypal energies in the details of his or her life will feel "manipulated" by forces beyond his or her comprehension or control, forces that will be experienced as simultaneously "alien" and "intimately personal," as symbolized in the stories of the examinations, experiments, and coerced cross-breeding that the abductees report.

The contemporary literature about UFO's and abductions is filled with commentary and debate about how many of these reports may have originated in dream experiences that were mistaken for waking events. When a person remembers a dream that includes images and metaphors of this sort, it is always worth exploring the imagery for its possible symbolic relevance to the dreamer's evolving relationship with the collective unconscious itself.

In his *Flying Saucers: A Modern Myth of Things Seen in the Sky*, Carl Jung reports the following excerpt from the dream of one of his female patients in her early forties (I have modified the text to read in the first person, present tense):

> In my dream, I am standing in a garden, when suddenly the humming of an engine becomes audible overhead. I sit down on a garden wall to see what's going on. A black metallic object appears and circles over me; it is a huge flying spider made of metal, with great dark eyes. It is round in shape and is a new and unique airplane ["aeroplane" in the original]. From the body of the spider there issues a solemn voice, loud and distinct; it utters a prayer that is intended as an admonition and a warning to everybody, for those on earth as well as the occupants of the spider. The gist of the prayer is: "Lead us downwards and keep us (safe) below... Carry us up to the height!" Adjoining the garden is a large administrative building where international decisions are being taken. Flying incredibly low, the spider passes along the windows of the building, for the obvious purpose of letting the voice influence the people inside and point out the way to peace, which is the way to the inner, secret world. There are several other spectators in the garden. I feel somewhat embarrassed because I am not fully clothed...

I will not attempt to reproduce Jung's (brilliant) commentary on this dream and the others in the series. I offer it here because the dream is a clear example of the intrusion of collective/archetypal energy into the waking consciousness of the dreamer, making use of the archetypal UFO image to carry the collective energy in the dream and render it into a symbolic form that is fully visible on the one hand, and also capable of carrying all the potentials of the unconscious that are not yet sufficiently differentiated to be visible on the other. Dreams in which the archetypal energies of the collective unconscious make themselves known often use imagery of this sort, as well as imagery evocative of the "fathomless ocean," the "infinite sky," "angels" (and/or "demons"), "ancient lost continents and civilizations," and so forth.

This particular dream invites the dreamer to overcome her fears, to go beyond her limited conscious awareness of her creative potential, and to begin to take increasing responsibility for manifesting her deeper life purpose in the world. There is always a danger of "inflation" when such tremendous collective ener-gies surge to the surface of waking awareness; hence the healthy compensatory awareness of being "not fully clothed." As Jung says in commenting on this dream, "Increased knowledge of the unconscious brings deeper experience of life and greater con-sciousness, and therefore confronts us with apparently new situa-tions that require ethical decision."

The Promise of the Butterfly

Whenever an archetypal image (like a "flying saucer" or "the ocean") appears in a dream, a symbolic narrative, or even a waking life situation, it always carries with it the weight and energy of its collective resonances and evocations of archetypal meaning, whether those layers of significance are immediately conscious and obvious or not. For example, as discussed in the first chapter, a fundamental natural (archetypal) analogy exists between the life cycle of the frog (involving as it does the physi-cal metamorphosis of tadpole into adult amphibian) and the symbolically "transformative" human experience of emotional and psychological development. A similar natural archetypal analogy exists in the life cycle of the caterpillar/butterfly.

This quality of natural symbolism that characterizes all archetypal forms can be understood more clearly in a comparison of the two. In nature, butterflies undergo a radical metamorpho-sis similar to that of the frog, and for this reason butterflies—along with moths, cicadas, dragon flies, and the rest—also have an arche-typal resonance with symbolically analogous human interior psy-chospiritual transformations. The appearance of caterpillars and butterflies in dreams, myths, and folk tales is, like the appearance of frogs, often associated with radical changes of belief, way of life, and worldview.

However, because butterflies undergo their metamorpho-sis with a central death-like stage, lying apparently lifeless in the "tomb" or "coffin" of the cocoon or chrysalis, the butterfly tends to be even more closely associated with spiritual intuitions about the transformation of life energy into a discarnate "soul" after physical death. In many nontechnological societies, moths and butterflies are believed to be the actual spirits of the dead returning for visits to the land of the living.

Moths, primarily because of their generally nocturnal habits, have a slightly different and more somber archetypal symbolic resonance. In many nontechnological cultures, moths are believed to be "damned souls," wandering in the night, irresistibly drawn to light and flame in a desperate attempt to escape the darkness to which they have been condemned. Conversely, butterflies, because of their generally brighter and more cheerful coloration and their appearance in bright sunshine, are much more often associated with "saved" or "liberated" souls.

The other day, I saw a cartoon depicting a caterpillar crawling along and looking suspiciously up at a butterfly flying by. The caterpillar mutters to itself, "You'll never catch me going up in one of those things!" This cartoon captures much of the archetypal human suspicion and ambivalence about the intuitive promise of continuing life after death. The fearful and resistant attitude that causes some people to avoid airplanes and say things like, "You'll never catch me going up in one of those things!" echoes and symbolically resonates with the same "conservative," rationalist suspicions about life after death. The cartoon caterpillar strikes us as funny because we recognize an internal, archetypal drama in the image it presents us. We are as unaware of the actual circumstances beyond the grave as the caterpillar is of the continuity of life it shares with the transformed butterfly. And so we laugh (and secretly wonder...).

At a related level of symbolic resonance, the drama of insect metamorphosis points to the possibility of total spiritual transformation in this life—a transformation so radical and complete that the previous way of being and living is perceived to be "totally dead." The image of death, when it appears in dreams, is the single most common and frequent archetypal metaphor of real growth and change in the dreamer's psyche.

There is a famous story of the second century B.C.E. Taoist sage, Chuang Tzu, who dreamed that he was a butterfly, happily flitting from flower to flower. "Suddenly, I awoke, and there I was, undeniably Chuang. But I can not be sure whether I am

Chuang who just dreamed he was a butterfly, or a butterfly now dreaming that I am Chuang."

Master Chuang's playful conundrum predates Descartes' parallel realization about his dream by several centuries. It also echoes with the archetypal resonances of the symbol of the butterfly, symbolism much closer to the surface of conscious awareness in his contemporary Chinese audience than it tends to be in our own. One of the "hidden" symbolic layers of this story is the same joke as the grumbling cartoon caterpillar. Chuang Tzu gently reminds his readers that they do not *know* what happens after death, and a little good humor and suspended judgment are in order. The life of the butterfly is notoriously short and ephemeral. Chuang Tzu calls his audience to recognize the symbolic parallel, to see that our own lives may be as fleeting as the butterfly's, and to seek joy and give joy, as the butterfly does, in the limited time available.

Unlike the butterfly, the frog undergoes its transformation without retreat into the "tomb" of the cocoon. A dramatically fleshy creature that changes without any period of unconscious dormancy, the frog has tended to be an image more associated with the psychological and emotional transformations of the living than with intuitions of transformations after death. Neither does the frog leave behind a husk that reminds us of the shriveled corpse as the butterfly and the other metamorphic insects do. The frog in its fat (by human standards) corporeality does not change into a light, shimmering, brightly colored, winged flying form. But it does change radically, so it becomes the "natural symbol" for radical developments in thought, feeling, and intuition among humans that symbolically parallel the natural life cycle of the amphibians.

Here we can see one of the subtle distinctions between the symbolic metamorphosis of the frog and that of the butterfly. The frog's transformation tends to turn human attention to the connection to society and the body. The enchanted frog prince/princess is always concerned at some important level with his or her role in society and how it does, or does not, adequately reflect and serve his or her authentic emotional and psychological character. The butterfly's transformation, on the other hand, tends to evoke questions and issues of a more directly and dramatically spiritual nature.

Archetypes, Addiction, and Transformation

When a person dreams of these images, the images always bring with them into the dream(s) the whole web of collective associations and resonances that have become deeply associated and attached to them over the evolutionary history of humankind. The greater the need for deep change in the dreamer's life, the more likely it is that the dreams will reveal archetypally resonant images of this sort.

A woman dreams:

> I pick up a book and open it. As I open it, the book assumes the shape of a butterfly, and I think to myself in the dream, "Oh, yes—the words in this book are in the shape of a butterfly...!"

The dreamer, a writer herself, is finding that in waking life her writing is acquiring a more and more spiritual quality—something that comes as rather a surprise to her, given her lifelong avoidance of organized religion. Among other things, the dream celebrates the dreamer's increasingly relaxed acceptance of the legitimacy of her own spiritual desires and intuitions, along with the realization that the meditative exploration of consciousness that writing is for her opens quite naturally and normally into increasingly spiritual dimensions.

Desire for transformation and increased conscious connection to the deepest sources of meaning is an archetypal drama that is at the center of many lives plagued with alcoholism and other addictions. The longing for connection to the divine is frustrated, and at a deep unconscious level, the addicted person feels "justified" in his or her addictive behavior because it expresses the utter revulsion at a life that has failed to reveal a greater meaning than personal ego gratification. As the contemporary theologian Matthew Fox says, "Alcoholism is failed cosmology." Carl Jung had a similar understanding almost fifty years earlier. It was his comments to an American alcoholic about alcoholism being a symptom of failed spiritual search that eventually led Bill W. and Dr. Bob to focus their efforts to overcome their own addictions on efforts to evoke a generic "higher power." It is this emphasis on the spiritual aspects of addiction that makes the "12-Step" programs like Alcoholics Anonymous such an effective force in contemporary Western society.

When faced with the interior knowledge that the deepest needs and desires for a fully alive and meaningful life have been frustrated, individuals often turn to various sorts of addiction to distract themselves from the full impact of the realization. In fact, any repetitive activity that functions to distract a person from the full conscious awareness of the depth and strength of his or her feelings and experience deserves the name *addiction.* In the world I travel in, I know many people who are addicted to prayer and good works. They are as terrified by the full range of their emotions as any alcohol, drug, or sex addict. These people, when they notice the scary, unacceptable thoughts and feelings pressing toward the surface of awareness, immediately look for "someone to help."

Sadly, such addictions to good work almost invariably have the ironic effect of poisoning and rendering ineffective their efforts to help and serve. Unfortunately, a large proportion of our efforts to "do good" in the world come to naught; and in fact, they succeed only in creating larger and larger metaphors of the very problems they are trying to solve, because the "do gooders" are using their efforts unconsciously like addictions—as excuses for avoiding and suppressing their own authentic interior lives.

In my work with recovering alcoholics and other addicts over the years, I have been impressed again and again with the importance of the metaphor of "suicide" when it appears in their dreams. Suicide, particularly in the dreams of men and women in recovery, tends to have very positive implications. "Death" is the most common archetypal symbolic image of psychospiritual growth and change; and when that death is self-inflicted in a dream, it implies that this time, it's going to work. This time, the dreamer's conscious effort to reshape his or her psyche and personality to overcome the habits of addictive behavior is likely to succeed. Suicide becomes an exquisite metaphor of the personality that is still addicted choosing to transform itself so radically and fundamentally that the only appropriate metaphor is self-inflicted death.

In situations other than the recovery from addiction, the metaphor of suicide in the dream tends to have the same arche-typal symbolic resonance. Even in cases where a person is afflicted while awake with compulsive thoughts and fantasies of self-destruction, it is still true, in my experience, that the primary energy for those "obsessive" thoughts is the tendency of the psy-che to reflect its deepest desires *symbolically*. The potential wak-ing-life suicide is also struggling with the desire to change his or her life so radically that the only adequate metaphor is the com-plete destruction and death of the old personality. The famous Jungian analyst Robert Johnson has been overheard on more than one occasion to say to people who appeal to him for help with their compulsively suicidal thoughts, "OK—commit suicide—but do not injure your body!" In the dream world, suicide accom-plishes this all-important psychospiritual task.

Whenever any character or figure in a dream appears to die, it is inevitably connected with the growth and transforma-tion of the dreamer's personality and the evolution of his or her authentic character. In my experience, it doesn't make a tremen-dous difference who dies; if *anyone* or *anything* is experienced as dying, then some aspect of the dreamer's total psyche is trans-forming—having the life energy withdrawn from it—so that pre-sumably it can be reborn in some more whole and complete, fully vital form.

When the dream ego dies, it is always symbolically a form of suicide, since everything and everyone in the dream is, at some level or another, a metaphor of some aspect of the dreamer's own psyche. The "death" in a dream of the dream ego always suggests that the processes of growth symbolically depicted in the dream have reached a level where there will be noticeable changes and differences in the dreamer's waking sense of self.

Most often, this process of ego dissolution and reconstruc-tion can be observed taking place over a series of dreams, with the "death" happening one night and the "rebirth" revealing itself in later dreams, remembered days, weeks, or even months later. From time to time, however, the whole process can be seen clearly in the course of a single dream. In my experience, this "compression" of the archetypal "death/rebirth" process into a single dream experience is often associated with particularly focused and wholehearted efforts to facilitate psychospiritual growth with conscious intention and practice on the part of the dreamer.

A perimenopausal woman in her early fifties dreams:

> I am lying in a dark room. The door opens, the light shining in the hallway silhouetting my child. The child raises a knife and runs toward me, then plunges the knife into my chest, killing me instantly. The scene shifts and I'm pushing a shopping cart across a construction site, maneuvering it around chunks of concrete, gravel, discarded 2x4s, etc. I know the child who has killed me is now dead. I have a bridal gown in my shopping cart, and I am taking it to the "new child," who seems to be some sort of reincarnation of the dead child.

Here all the archetypal themes are clearly visible. The menopause itself is a collective/archetypal experience, as well as being absolutely personal and experiential. The sense of self as a fertile woman must "die" in order for there to be "space" for the new sense of self as creative and life-giving in other ways to take its necessary place. There is a collective biological inevitability about it all; and at the same time, there is conscious construction work that is required to make it all happen as well.

In this way, the collective/archetypal dimensions of dreams and the unconscious symbolic resonances of waking-life experiences constantly influence the flow of mood, feeling, thought, and physical sensation. We live, awake and asleep, totally immersed in a sea of unconsciously meaningful symbolic events and reactions. Greater conscious awareness of the nature and structure of these archetypes of the collective unconscious tends to enhance our ability to grow and change and to lead responsible, loving, creative, expressive lives.

The poet Rilke is reported to have ended his experiment in psychoanalysis after only a couple of meetings, expressing the fear that it might not only "dispel his demons, but drive away his angels as well." He gives voice to the very common fear (bolstered by Freud's theory of artistic creativity and inventive inspiration as "sublimation" of more primary, less "civilized" instincts) that neurosis is the main energy source for creative expression. All I can say is that the evidence of thirty years of working with the dreams of artists and other creative people suggests a very different conclusion: As personal neuroses become more clearly understood, and waking life becomes more choiceful and less "driven," the dreams open into wider and even more satisfying and resonant realms of possibility and manifestation. There may be a period of seeming "death" in the "tomb" of depression, but it reveals itself to be the necessary time in the chrysalis before the new form(s) of thought, feeling, expression, and relationship finds its transformed wings.

SUMMARY

The best analogy for the archetypes of the collective unconscious is the anatomical structure of the human body; the same organs, performing the same functions in the same relationship to one another, are endlessly reproduced each time a new human being is conceived and born. Each human being (other than an identical twin) is a unique physical being, while at the same time embodying exactly the same archetypal pattern of anatomical structure as all other people. In the same fashion, the entire spectrum of archetypal energies and relationships is reproduced in the human psyche, endless repeated, yet producing unique new combinations in each repetition.

Dreaming itself is a universal human experience that carries universal, cross-cultural, archetypal symbolic significance. All over the world at all periods of history, dreaming has been seen as carrying clues to (1) the deeper meanings of the dreamer's personal life and future, (2) his or her relationship with the divine, and (3) the nature of the experience of the discarnate soul after death. Sleep = death; dream = after-death experience is a universal symbolic analogy.

The collective unconscious itself is often depicted in dreams and myths as "coming from another world," being "unbelievably powerful" and yet simultaneously "distant and mysterious." Images such as UFO's, the ocean, and lost ancient civilizations often appear in dreams as symbolic reflections of the individual dreamer's encounter with the collective unconscious itself.

Creatures that undergo metamorphosis in the natural course of their development, like frogs and butterflies, share a collective symbolic association. When they appear in dreams, they bring with them the entire collective tendency to symbolize the possibilities of transformative growth and change in the lives of individuals. Specific individual and collective examples are presented and discussed.

Chapter 3
STORIES OF LOVE AND FEAR: ARCHETYPES AND AUTHENTIC GENDER

Heavenly King was intelligent,
Spat a lot of spittle into his hand,
Clapped his hands with a noise,
Produced Heaven and Earth.
Tall grass made insects,
Stories made men and demons,
Made male and female.
    How is it you don't know?

Miao Creation Myth

In the Japanese myth and folklore tradition, the First Parents, the semidivine primordial beings from whom all human beings descend, are named "Izanami" and "Izanagi." In most of the versions of their story, they are referred to as "sister and brother," either because they appear together without mention of their origin or because the Supreme Creator drew them forth at the same time, out of the same divine substance.

The traditional stories go on say that once the supreme god(dess) had made Izanami and Izanagi, the other gods and goddesses who already occupied the cosmos became concerned and fearful. They foresaw a seemingly inevitable outcome; if Izanagi and Izanami were allowed to marry and procreate, as the Great Demiurge desired, then their voracious children would grow so numerous and uncontrollable that they would devour the entire earth. (Today, anyone who is paying any attention can hardly fail to sympathize with their concerns.)

However, it was the will of the Divine Creator that Izanagi and Izanami should marry and have children, so the nuptial ceremonies were planned and preparations began. Since the fearful and jealous gods and goddesses could do nothing to prevent the wedding, they conspired together to prevent the marriage from being consummated. They separated themselves into two delegations; the male gods went to help Izanagi prepare, and the goddesses paid a similar visit to Izanami.

When the gods came to Izanagi, ostensibly to help him prepare for the marriage ceremony and to advise him regarding his first night of love with his new bride, they put on long faces and warned him that he should be very careful and avoid thrusting his erect penis into Izanami's belly, no matter how aroused he became, because, they told him, her vagina was like a second mouth, full of terrible sharp teeth, and when he thrust himself into her, she would not be able to control herself, and she would bite off his penis and he would die a horrible and painful death.

Putting on masks of false solicitude, the goddesses went in a group to Izanami and her told a similar tale. They told her she must not open her belly to Izanagi under any circumstances, because once inside her, there was no limit to the size his penis would grow. If she allowed him to enter her, he would swell and enlarge and tear her apart, even if it was not his desire to hurt her.

In this way, the gods and goddesses hoped to prevent Izanagi and Izanami from copulating and procreating, even after they had followed the command of the Creator to marry (Fig. 4).

After the wedding ceremony, Izanagi and Izanami approached one another in the darkened marriage chamber with great caution and trepidation. Izanami was so afraid that she held her hands down defensively in front of her vagina to better gauge the size of Izanagi's penis and, if necessary, fend it off as he approached her. Izanagi for his part was so apprehensive about Izanami's supposed *vagina dentata* that he decided to probe her genital area with his knee before attempting to follow his desire to enter her with his more vulnerable and sensitive penis. In the dark, he encountered Izanami's long and elaborately manicured fingernails with his knee and mistook them for the teeth for which he was so fearfully prepared. For her part, Izanami felt the size and muscular hardness of Izanagi's flexed knee, "as big and hard as a watermelon," and knew that she could never take such a huge thing inside herself and survive.

Figure 4. (Ancient Japan) Izanagi and Izanami, having been given false advice by the gods and goddesses, prepare to marry.

In this way the plans of the jealous gods and goddesses were fulfilled, and for a long while Izanami and Izanagi were afraid to have intercourse even though they had married as the Creator had commanded them to.

Some versions of the traditional story go on to say that the Divine Creator saw all this and smiled. The divine androgynous he/she simply waited and watched until the time was ripe. Izanami and Izanagi learned how to make dwellings, use fire, and till the land. One day the Creator saw them working together in the rice fields. They had their clothing rolled up and tucked into their sashes to keep it out of the water, and their legs and thighs glistened and flashed as they stooped and rose in unison in the rhythmic ritual dance of planting the rice seedlings. It was then that the Creator touched them secretly and inspired passion and desire in their hearts. Izanagi and Izanami were moved to make love with one another right there on the spot, with their eyes open, in broad daylight.

And what came of that, as the teller of traditional tales is so fond of saying, "is another story"—one that is still unfolding.

Animus and Anima

In these accounts of the early lives and exploits of Izanagi and Izanami, the "high" mythological world of gods, first beings, and first causes blends and merges with the "low," folkloric world of sexually explicit humor and ribaldry; and in doing so, it reveals the ultimate unity of these two archetypal realms (despite the concerted efforts of academic class warriors to keep them separate).

Even though this story has its origins in the prehistoric culture of the Japanese archipelago, it speaks the universal, symbolic, archetypal language of myth and dream. It gives concrete, dramatic narrative shape to much of the complexity and ambiguity of sexual differences and gender identities that simultaneously divide and unite the human species. Virtually anyone who meets this story is moved to smile at the clever interlocking deceptions of the gods and goddesses, and subsequent anxious blunderings of Izanami and Izanagi. The smile is born, in part at least, from a wry recognition of resonantly similar preconscious energies and anxieties deep within our own interior lives.

The story symbolically names some of our own fears and metaphorically describes some of the defensive/protective strategies that are born out of our uncertainty in the face of the radically unknown and seemingly unknowable experience of the other gender. In Izanami's fear of Izanagi's infinitely expanding phallus, we can see, at one level, an archetypal image of the physical agonies of pregnancy and childbirth. At another level, it is also a metaphor of the seemingly "infinite and limitless" energy for "growth and expansion" in the archetypal masculine. This is the energy that has led to building and expanding political and economic empires and to the creation of imposing architectural structures that dominate and blot out the natural skyline. Both men and women have this archetypal masculine energy in their psyches. It is what drives Western men and women in particular to strive in each generation to outstrip the one that preceded it.

In similar fashion, Izanagi's fear of *vagina dentata* can be viewed as an archetypal symbol of the feminine quality of the physical world in general, and the earth herself in particular, inexorably and inevitably "devouring" all her children in death, no matter what love and success she may bestow on them while they are alive. The image echoes the "devouring" and "cutting off" of seemingly infinite possibilities by the particularity of actual choices and events. At an emotional level, the archetypal *vagina dentata* is an image for the sense of limitation that particular, monogamous, committed relationship brings to the animus's seemingly insatiable hunger for new and exotic emotional, erotic, relational experience. (For a more complete discussion of the "castration fear" embodied in this myth and its connection to the archetype of the "Great Mother," see chapter 4.)

Even though this gender-identified "other" is always experienced in external encounters with other people of the opposite sex, it is primarily a projection of an interior reality. Our perceptions are shaped by the versions of the archetypal energies within which we project forth in illusory opinions and emotional responses to the men and women who actually are different from us. The differences are real, but our reactions to those authentic differences are always shaped, colored, and distorted to some extent by our own interior experience of the masculine and feminine energies in our own psyches.

In the dreams of each individual and in the myths of the world, certain figures regularly appear that embody and give specific symbolic shape to our deepest knowledge and intuition about what it's like to be "the other." Izanami and Izanagi are specific examples of figures of this kind. The actions of these archetypal figures give specific symbolic/narrative shape to our deepest intuitions, hopes, fears, and fantasies about the experience, secret desires, and unexpressed feelings of the other. Jung named this archetypal figure of the man within a woman and the woman within a man *animus* and *anima* respectively.

Anima and *animus* are gender-specific Latin words for

"spirit" (i.e., "female spirit" and "male spirit" respectively). The Latin root *anim-* denotes vitality and internal motivating energy, and appears in other English words like *animal* and *animate.* The feminine form, *anima,* is sometimes translated as "soul," in contrast to the masculine *animus* or "spirit."

Gender and Shadow

To the extent that the archetypal gender fantasies about "the other" that are promoted by the ancient Japanese gods and goddesses are immediately negative and designed to engender fear and lack of spontaneity in Izanagi and Izanami respectively, they can also be understood to embody the archetypal energy that Jung called the *Shadow.*

The archetype of the Shadow tends to manifest in dreams and myths as a seemingly negative figure who, in fact, holds as a hidden possibility the greatest thing or possibility in the dreamer's (or the culture's) life. In this story, for instance, it can be seen that in the seemingly negative and "shadowy" ideas of the vagina with teeth and the infinitely expanding phallus, there lies hidden the joys of love, sexual union, and the propagation and evolutionary development of the individual and the species as a whole. At another level, the creative possibilities of personal and social innovation also lie hidden in the image of the ever-expanding penis. At an even deeper level, the implication that the fears of Izanami and Izanagi are illusory and ultimately groundless suggests the possibility of reconciliation even with the fear and knowledge of our own inevitable deaths.

Unless Izanagi and Izanami are able to overcome their fear and bring the metaphoric light of expanding consciousness to their relationship ("making love in broad daylight") their/our story must remain mired in ritual repetition (often called "perseveration" in the psychological literature) and offers no possibility of growth and transformation. However, when they/we "see each other clearly" (another metaphor of increasing conscious self-awareness and the withdrawal of projections), then the entire drama of human life is released and freed to flow forward into evolving forms and new expressions.

In fact, this is the great ironic secret of the archetype of the Shadow. The distinctly frightening quality and seemingly negative appearance of the shadow figure is always a reliable measure of the value of the positive energy and gift for transformation that lies hidden within it, held hostage by the negative way in which we view it. The more distressing the image, the greater the gift it hides below the ugly surface of its appearance.

Jung was adamant about the specific gender link in the definition of animus/anima and Shadow. He said on many occasions that a man does not have an animus, and woman does not have an anima. In classical Jungian theory, the anima is always the "feminine soul" within a man, and the animus is always the "masculine spirit" within a woman. He was equally adamant about the gender image of the Shadow in dreams *always* being the same as that of the dreamer.

However, the fundamental nature of all archetypal figures and the collective energies they embody is multifaceted and ambiguous. True archetypes and archetypal figures ultimately defy containment in any rigid intellectual definitions or categories. All archetypal images have a distressing tendency (distressing at least to the rational mind) to expand beyond the limits of their formal definitions, to become increasingly multivalent, and ultimately to transform into one another. Jung observed this universal pattern of behavior in archetypal forms and borrowed the term *enantiodromia* from Heraclitus to describe this predictable tendency of seemingly polar opposites to flip over and turn into one another at precisely the moment when they seem to be most in opposition.

On many occasions, Jung made reference to the fact that all archetypes are "bi-polar" and carry within themselves dual aspects of "positive and negative, light and dark, good and evil, male and female, etc." He went on to say that the tendency to "split" our perceptions of archetypal forms into "opposing, dichotomous images" was a symptom of lack of psychological (and spiritual) development and sophistication. One specific example he used regularly to clarify his point was the tendency in patriarchal societies and cultures to "split" and divide the archetype of the deep feminine into the seemingly irreconcilable images of the Immaculate Virgin Mother and the Terrible Seductive but Sterile Whore, and to force living, complex, multifaceted women into one or the other of these two-dimensional, stereotypic models. Experience suggests that he was right and that this very real and oppressive tendency is a direct consequence of the collective failure of patriarchal culture to acknowledge and creatively express its own regularly repressed, irrational, emotional, relational, intuitive, physical, "feminine" side.

It seems obvious to me that Jung's own tendency to divide animus, anima, and Shadow images into rigid gender-exclusive categories is an example of precisely the same neurotic "splitting" phenomenon. Jung's continuous assertions that "men have no animus" and "women have no anima," to say nothing of his oft repeated assertion that the archetype of the Shadow always appears in the dreams and fantasies of particular individuals as the same sex as the dreamer, is yet another specific example of this archetypal tendency for unresolved anxiety in the face of ambiguous archetypal energies to result in an arbitrary and distorted "twinning" of the images generated by that archetype into dichotomous and apparently mutually exclusive opposites. The more exciting truth of the matter is that we can't have one without the other, because they are literally different faces of the same energy. The universal tendency of human beings when operating out of fear to "split" and "twin" images of multivalent archetypal power is one of the reasons why Jungians generally tend to ascribe "unconsciousness" to the number two.

Both Izanami and Izanagi, as well as the gender-specific goddesses and gods, can be viewed as anima and animus figures respectively. They embody, in concrete symbolic form, universal confusions and intuitions about the interior, subjective experience of the opposite sex. At the same time, they can also be viewed from just slightly different angles as examples of the Shadow and the Trickster archetypes as well; for they embody the dark, irrational fears and suspicions that gather around the gifts of relationship and sexual encounter on the one hand, and playful, unexpected, and surprisingly effective resistance to seemingly superior and overwhelming power and dogmatic authority on the other.

Archetypes and Stereotypes

Jung's formulation of animus, anima, and Shadow is essentially (and to a great extent, I believe, unconsciously) conventional and masculinist. It begins to describe the psychospiritual reality of traditional heterosexual men and women, but it does not adequately describe the reality experienced by all others—lesbians, male homosexuals, bi- and transsexuals, and so forth. Jung was himself a victim of unconscious gender stereotypes; and although the majority of his most talented and sensitive students and protégés were women, in the details of his personal life he also appears to have participated in the generally unexamined masculinist sexism of his era, while at the same time playing an important role in formulating the theoretical psychological insights that paved the way for the revaluation and restitution of the feminine in modern life.

Even more importantly, the complex gender imagery of dreams and myths simply does not conform to or sustain his rigid formulations. For these reasons, we must begin to reformulate these descriptions and definitions of the archetypes of authentic gender to more adequately reflect the reality of normal, multivalent, complex, human sexual/relational experience.

Even in the dream worlds of heterosexual men, Jung's dogmatic assertion that "men don't have an animus" is simply not borne out. The fundamental nature of mature archetypal male experience is as ultimately mysterious to the heterosexual man as it is to everyone else. Men regularly encounter mysterious male figures in their dreams who embody their own deepest, as yet unrealized feelings and intuitions about "what it *really* means to be a man." It seems to me that these figures deserve the name "animus" as much as the corresponding male figures in the dreams of heterosexual women.

The same is also true of the ultimate mysteries of the archetypal feminine. Contemporary women regularly dream female figures that embody their evolving relationship to the archetypal

feminine and "the Goddess." These figures also fit the definition and deserve the name of "anima" as much as the corresponding female figures in the dreams of men. (For a fuller
discussion of the complexities of the archetype of the Great
Mother, see chapter 4.)

The whole issue of definitions of *animus* and *anima* might
simply be dismissed as a relatively trivial and narrow academic
argument over technical terminology, were it not for the fact that
these classical Jungian formulations of archetypal patterns are
increasingly being employed as diagnostic tools in psychother-
apy, in the legal determinations of sanity, culpability, and competence, as well as in the formulation of public policy. When
these noninclusive and socially oppressive notions of rigid gender links with anima/animus and Shadow begin to acquire the
weight and status of unquestionable authority, law, and expert
testimony, the impact on the lives of individuals and society as a
whole is increasingly negative.

Traditional heterosexual desire and behavior is simply not
the benchmark of "normality" and "sanity" any more than is a
particular height, hair color, or body weight. There is a wide *range*
of authentic gender and sexual orientation that is just as broad as
the normal range of body type, intelligence, musical ability, dex-
terity, and so forth. Human experience is much more authentically diverse than any average or stereotype can encompass. The
phenomenology of the dreams and the repeating shapes of world
myth and sacred narrative also demonstrate this diversity, while
at the same time revealing the repeating archetypal patterns that
point to and affirm our deep common humanity.

Longing for the Lost "Other"

The mythology of the world abounds with stories about the
sense of incompleteness and longing that comes with separation
of the species into multiple gender experiences and expressions.
Plato retells an ancient Greek myth from the Orphic tradition
that says that originally human beings were "whole." The wholeness of these first beings took the form of round bodies with
multiple arms and legs. These androgynous first beings were so

powerful in their completeness that the gods became jealous and fearful and split them in half. As a result, all human beings now live their lives in a state of desperate incompleteness and longing, forever searching for their split-off "other halves."

In this myth, whether the lost and longed for other half is a figure of the same sex or the opposite sex, or even an amorphous figure of the longed for lost wholeness (of union with the divine), the deep archetypal feelings of incompleteness and desire for union are fundamentally the same; and in myth and dream, sexual and spiritual longing often stand symbolically for one another. The archetypal tendency of overt, unmasked sexual and erotic imagery in dreams and myths to make reference to spiritual desires for more conscious "union" with the divine is born again and again from this universal metaphor analogizing the one passionate longing with the other.

Even the spiritual traditions that promote celibacy and the idea that sexual union, masturbation, and all forms of sexual fantasy and expression should be avoided altogether are still saying quite clearly that it is the same physical psychospiritual energies that would otherwise be "wasted" in sexual expression and the pursuit of intimate physical and emotional human relationship that should instead be rechanneled and devoted exclusively to achieving more conscious union with the divine. Thus even the celibate traditions that suppress and disparage sexuality still reflect the same essential archetypal symbolic truth that undeveloped individual human consciousness is incomplete, and that the energies for the development of that higher awareness are essentially erotic. As suggested in chapter 1 in the discussion of the overtly erotic elements in Bob's dream of the frog with human eyes, there is a deep archetypal association between specifically erotic imagery in myth and dream and the stage of evolutionary development of individual and collective spiritual awareness.

The Myth of the Bogadjimbri Boys

The Aboriginal inhabitants of Northern Australia tell sacred stories about the divine twins, the Bogadjimbri Boys, "huge, like giant trees, stretching up to the sky." These two

Figure 5. (Australia) The Bogadjimbri Boys create the differences between men and women (after the visual style of the "outcast" Wadjari People of the Murchison River area of Western Australia).

primordial demiurges are born of Earth Mother Dilga without masculine intervention or assistance. They then go forth and create everything in the physical world, including the first human beings. These newly created people are sexless and infertile, and they "meander aimlessly" through the world. Seeing this state of affairs, the Bogadjimbri fashion male and female genitals from two species of fungus (which still exist in the North Australian ecosystem, and do indeed look most evocatively phallic and vaginal), and attach them to the aimless people, giving them excitement and purpose, but also unsatisfiable longings. In most versions, this activity of dividing the human beings into two groups by gender also leads to the first experience of death (Fig. 5).

The Bogadjimbri laugh when they see the people they have created suddenly dashing and sneaking and scurrying around, driven by the energy and longings of sex. The wild cat Ngariman is offended by their laughter and slashes them with its claws, killing them. The Earth Mother, Dilga, is so angered and saddened by the slaughter of her two sons that she causes the earth to be flooded with her milk in an archetypal deluge that drowns all the cat people. She then resurrects her two sons, making one into a giant water snake, and the other into a particular cloud of stars visible in the sky of the Southern Hemisphere at certain seasons of the year.

The Archetypal Marriage of Love and Death

This connection between sexual love and death is very deep. At one level it is obvious, in that every complex living thing that is born must come into being out of a sexual union of some sort. It is equally obvious that every living thing conceived and born in this way is doomed to die. In this sense, sexuality and erotic expression "invite" death while at the same time "defying" it. Viewed from another angle, this connection between the arousal of erotic impulses and the specter of death is simply ecological, since any species must procreate more prolifically in the face of increased death rates in order to survive. (There are important clues to the erotic motivations for warfare and for certain kinds of ugly, violent, "morbid" pornography in this ancient archetypal connection.)

The Nupe people of what is now Nigeria tell their version of this universal intuition about the intimate relationship between erotic activity and death in this way:

> In the beginning, say the Nupe, the Great God created tortoises, people, and stones. He made male and female of each kind—tortoises, people, and stones. He gave life to all of them, but none of them could have children. Instead, when they got old, they would not die; they would just go to sleep and wake up young again.
>
> The tortoises, however, longed to have children. They went to the Great God and said, "We want to have children. Please make it so that we can have children."
>
> But the Great God said, "I have created you. I have given you life, but I have not given you permission to be like me and make life. You may not have children."
>
> The tortoises were chastened and sad and went away without speaking any more, but the longing to have children would not die in their hearts. So, after a while, they came back and asked again if they might be allowed to have children,

and again the Great God refused, but still the desire for children did not diminish in their hearts, and after a while, they came back and asked a third time, and this time the Great God said:

"You always come and ask me to let you have children! Don't you understand that if you have children, after a while, you will have to *die?!*"

"Even so," said the tortoises, "let us have children so that we can see them grow, and then we will die." When they said this, the Great God granted their wish (Fig. 6).

Later, when the people saw the tortoises having children, they came in a group to the Great God and asked to be allowed to have children too.

"Don't you understand?!" the Great God said again, "If you have children, after a while you will have to die. That's the only way!"

But the people insisted. "Let us see our children grow, and then we will die!" And so, the Great God granted their wish.

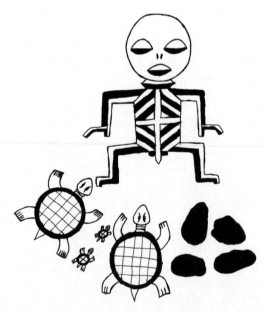

Figure 6. (Central Africa) The tortoises ask the Great God to be allowed to have children, even if it means they must die, and the stones choose otherwise (after the visual style of the Yoruba People of Nigeria).

This is how death and children came into the world together. Only the stones decided that they didn't want to have children, and so they never die.

Without ever having talked with either the Australians or the Africans, the Maidu people of the Northern Sierra Nevada in California tell their own version of the sacred archetypal tale of how sexuality and death come into the world together in a similar way.

In the Maidu cosmology, Earthmaker and his troublesome compatriot Coyote are the primordial pair. Earthmaker travels around, shaping the landscape and peopling it with creatures and plants and spirit beings of all sorts; but Coyote tries to imitate him, continually spoiling Earthmaker's "perfect" work with the twin gift/curses of love and death.

First, Earthmaker says that people will make children when they are lonely by laying reeds and sticks on the ground between them when they sleep and commanding them to become children. But Coyote doesn't think much of this way of doing things:

> Then, in a little while, Coyote spoke up and answered him
> "That which you say is bad!
> Why will we not make it so that men and women hug and kiss,
> and tickle one another and laugh and feel good?
> When people get married, they should make love
> and then, a little later,
> they should lie down together and feel good!
> And then, when they have finished lovemaking,
> they should laugh a lot and talk with each other.
> But if they never hug and kiss each other
> but just go to sleep and get angry with each other—
> if that's the way they do, then that's bad.
> It's just not going to be that way!"

Earthmaker argues that his original plan is better because "the woman will not suffer/ but will go about having children," but Coyote is adamant; his way is best, even though it means "women weeping, straining, will give birth,/ and later, after a while, they will have children./ And some of them will die, and some of them will live" (Fig. 7).

The two of them go on arguing, and Coyote becomes more

Figure 7. (North America) Coyote and Earthmaker debate how the world should be, while the renewing snakes look on.

and more eloquent and adamant. Earthmaker argues for monogamy, and Coyote argues for multiple sexual encounters and sex outside of, as well as within, marriage. Coyote argues for the vitality and rejuvenating feelings of sexual encounter:

> "Now a leader should really say what is good!
> But you, Earthmaker,
> are not speaking for human contentment and joy!
> But I speak for a world where men can laugh
> and feel good and come to take delight in themselves
> and in the women they care for.
> So then, an old man,
> flirting and playing with a young woman,
> should feel like a lad again.
> And a woman should feel that way too.
> I too am a great man
> and what I say is very good!"
> Thus spoke Coyote.
>
> Then Earthmaker said nothing,
> but he thought to himself:
> "You, Coyote, have overcome me in everything;
> so then, without my saying so,
> let there be death in the world."

Earthmaker departs in silence leaving "two scouring rushes on either side of a rivulet," and Coyote goes about enjoying the world he has made. Eventually Coyote sends his son to fetch water, but the rushes Earthmaker placed beside the stream turn into rattlesnakes and kill the boy.

> Then Coyote cried out.
> "May I never say such things again!
> Come back! Let there be no death in the world!
> You must make my son come back to life!
> Come back! I will never say such things again!
> From now on, I will always do what you say!"
>
> He ran after the Great One,
> who paid him no mind but kept on hitherwards.
>
> Coyote pursued him, but could not overtake him,
> and he turned back.
>
> "I am full of grief!" he said.
> "In spite of the very many times I have won out over him,
> he has done this to me! He has killed my child!"
>
> The Coyote stopped in his tracks.
> "I will chase him no longer," he said.
> "I will never catch up with him."

Stories of this sort abound in world myth and folk tale. The darker side of love is fear, grief, and death. Human beings appear to be inherently predisposed to respond with increased erotic desire in the face of death and the threat of death.

Pairs of Opposites and Human Consciousness

All of these narratives also suggest an archetypal quality to the number *two*, alluded to briefly earlier. In many of these origin and creation stories, love and death are created together; and the creation is accomplished by two figures or demiurges who are in continuing tension with one another. At one level, this is a symbolic representation of the potentially creative tension that exists between the "twin" heterosexual energies of male and female; but at another level, there are implications here of the archetypal symbolism of numbers themselves.

At another level, the appearance of "two's" and "twins" is an example of the tendency of freshly surfacing, previously totally unconscious archetypal contents to emerge into the first tentative formulations of conscious awareness in the form of perceived opposites. Jungians are fond of saying that "two is the number of unconsciousness," but it could equally well be said that two is the number symbolizing the emergence of previously unconscious material into consciousness.

As noted above, there is a tendency for archetypal material to be perceived, initially at least, as embodying antagonistic or even mutually exclusive oppositions (good/bad, dark/light, up/down, hot/cold, wet/dry, divine/demonic, etc.). In fact, the archetypal energies themselves form the field of perception where the seeming dichotomies exist, and thus true archetypal energies can never be adequately divided and separated into "opposites." The great Romantic poet of the archetypes, William Blake, said it quite clearly and bluntly: "Opposites are never True Contraries."

The classic Yin/Yang image of Taoism ☯ is a graphic example of this archetypal wisdom. The black "tadpole" always has a white "eye," and the white tadpole always has a black eye; so even if one were to succeed in wrenching them apart and throwing one away (in some sort of millenarian fantasy of the ultimate conquest of good over evil), the remaining form always has the seed of its seeming opposite sprouting from within it.

Spiritual Geometry

Two is the number symbolizing this initial separation of the unconscious primordial unity (symbolized by the predominantly feminine *zero* and the predominantly masculine *one* respectively) into two, the perceived tension of supposed opposites. To the extent that this perception of irreconcilable opposition is in error, two is indeed the number of unconsciousness; but to the extent that the unconscious material that first emerges is the perception of the tension of apparent opposition, then two is also the number of emerging self-awareness in process.

One consequence of this archetypal quality of two is that political, economic, social, and cultural arguments in waking life that depend on terms and definitions of irreconcilability are always inevitably fraught with unconsciousness and self-deception; and they regularly turn out to have devastatingly counterproductive results, even (and particularly) when they are pursued with monomaniacal zeal and sincerity. Economic and political (to say nothing of psychospiritual) wisdom requires other solutions to problems than the "triumph of virtue." Here, I believe, is a very important clue to the deeper meaning of the seemingly anomalous New Testament admonition, "Resist not evil."

At the same time, two is also the number of linearity in general, and the experience of linear time in particular. Two points imply and generate a straight line. The "line" is the symbol of linear events, moving steadily from the "frozen past" into the "inevitable future." The appearance of *two's* in myth and dream is often a reliable clue to the concern for the passage of time and its impact in the form of aging and the inexorable approach of death.

It is from the interplay of perceived opposites that all the phenomena of experience and history are created. For the Taoists, Hindus, and Buddhists, the symbolic shorthand of this play of opposites is "the ten thousand things," standing for all possible and actual phenomena. In this sense, the equation of the emergence of conscious into the world is $0 = 1 = 2 = 10,000$. Many forms of Eastern and Western meditation practice and striving for "enlightenment" consist of reversing the formula so that it reads and is experienced as $10,000 = 2 = 1 = 0$.

For traditional, nontechnological peoples whose sacred creation narratives involve the generation of the world and love and death from the interplay of two seemingly opposed forces or divine characters, these narratives and divine energies are almost invariably believed to be "ever-present," just behind or beyond the surface of appearance. In this way, these stories always hold forth the promise of reversing the experience of the diversity and complexity of phenomenal awareness into the experience of eternal oneness. In Coyote's conscious acceptance of his grief and pain at the loss of his child and his understanding that he cannot "catch up" to Earthmaker, there is a spiritual awareness of the simultaneous distance and closeness with the divine that incomplete and evolving human consciousness provides.

It is also worth noting that when the reeds Earthmaker left by the water come to life and turn into rattlesnakes and kill Coyote's son, the snakes are created in exactly the way Earthmaker proposed that new creatures come into being in the first place. In that sense, none of Coyote's "cleverness" changes Earthmaker's original plans, despite the appearance that Coyote has triumphed.

There is in this irony also an implication that Earthmaker's original promise of immortality is fulfilled, but in a way that Coyote had not anticipated. Just as Earthmaker had originally commanded, the reeds turn into living things, the snakes that kill Coyote's son. But they are resonant with the "reeds and sticks" that Earthmaker had originally said would "become children," so the implied promise of immortality and rebirth resides at the center of the same tragic drama that causes Coyote's (and our) fear and grief at the reality and prospect of death.

As a wise friend of mine is fond of saying: "Who we think we are dies, but we aren't who we think we are."

"Two-ness" is an archetypal metaphor embodying and implying this entire, endlessly repeating drama.

The Waters of Life

These myth narratives also demonstrate an archetypal resonance between the life-giving waters of nature—particularly the fresh water of rain and the rivers and streams—and the life-giving bodily fluids of human beings—particularly milk, saliva, blood, and semen, but also including tears, sweat, and urine. There is a strong archetypal tendency to analogize rain and tears, and many fertility rituals in nontechnological agrarian societies attempt to arouse "the gods and goddesses" to make rain by moving them to violent sexual arousal and tears.

In ancient China, for example, there was a rain-making ceremony that consisted of two teams, one of naked men and another of naked women, engaging in a ceremonial battle and striking one another in order to provoke the gods "to tears." The ancient Chinese oracle book, the *I Ching,* says, "Male and female mix their essential forces (the Chinese word is *jing,* literally "seminal fluids"), and the ten thousand things come into existence." As noted above, "the ten thousand things" refer to the entire physical/phenomenal world—all the seemingly separate but intertwining and interpenetrating processes in which opposites interact to produce the objects and experiences of life.

All human beings exhibit an archetypal predisposition to symbolize the struggles and tensions of *all* opposing, polarized forces as both forceful and sexual. Psychospiritual intuitions of wholeness and the hunger for their fulfillment are all seen as deeply analogous to sexual longing. The quality of that longing is essentially the same for all gendered beings, and one of the most common archetypal metaphors for the fulfillment of those desires is vigorous, languorous, orgasmic sexual union.

These fundamental, endlessly repeating metaphors influence every aspect of human activity that is either tinged with spiritual longing on the one hand, or charged with sexual desire or repulsion on the other. Every time a person enters into an increasingly intimate emotional and sexual relationship with another person, the (in many cases unconscious) desires for spiritual fulfillment are activated and energized as well.

Romantic love in particular invites the projection of these desires into the experience of physical and emotional relationship. One of the main reasons why so many romantic liaisons end in tragic disappointment is that this element of spiritual longing remains unconscious and can not actually find satisfaction in the daily details of personal relating. The romantic lovers separate in stormy disappointment, many times without ever realizing that the true cause of their disappointment and "falling out of love" is not the inevitable inadequacies of the other person, but rather the fact that the desire for increasing relationship with the divine can not be adequately fulfilled within the limitations of a purely personal, psychological, emotional, physical relationship with another person.

The matrix of personal relationship is (or at least can be) a supporting container for the individual's search for more conscious awareness of the divine. The primary problem with celibacy as a spiritual discipline is that is tends to force the issue of love into more and more arbitrary, inauthentic, and "generalized" forms. Most of the truly spiritual celibates that I have met (and I grant that this is a biased sample) have achieved their genuine spiritual awareness *despite* their celibacy, not because of it. By far the greater number of what seem to me to be authentically spiritually aware people achieved their awareness through an increasingly deep, complex, and intense experience of emotional and sexual relationship with specific partners. The process of discovering and creatively expressing authentic gender is in itself an invitation to increased awareness of the divine.

There is a basic truth here: A modicum of sexual self-awareness and conscious self-control of sexual urges is absolutely necessary for any kind of authentic psychospiritual development, but to exaggerate this simple truth into the assertion that celibacy is a necessary or superior state for spiritual development is a subordination and distortion of that basic idea in order to make it serve the purposes of oppressive collective male dominance. There is, in my experience, no more legitimate reason to believe that celibacy is a superior spiritual path than there is to believe that women or gender minorities ought not to be ordained to priesthood and ministry. Both notions are inherently oppressive and unfortunately continue to distort countless people's sincere efforts to achieve greater conscious awareness of themselves and the divine.

Gender in Dreams

Dream figures of the opposite sex regularly symbolize evolving energies in the psyche that are absolutely necessary for further growth and development of character and personality.

A successful professional man in his early fifties reports a dream:

To his surprise, one of his daughter's college friends, a diminutive young Chinese-American woman, is driving a big tour bus. The dreamer gets out of the vehicle he is driving, a jeep, and boards the bus. He seats himself in the front seat, just across the aisle and to the right of the young driver.

The route is mostly along cliffs overlooking the ocean. On the straightaways, the young woman smiles and turns to chat with him, but on the curves she has to concentrate on steering the bus. The young woman pilots the bus through Greece (a favorite holiday destination), Northern California (his current residence), and the rural New York State community where his grandparents lived during his early childhood, all in quick succession. In the dream, he is struck by the young woman's wry good humor about being physically so small and having to work so hard to steer the bus around the tight alternating curves. Her efforts are so strenuous that her long, straight, black hair keeps falling in her face as she drives, and she is forced to resort to puffing out her cheeks and blowing the strands of hair away from her eyes, because she can't take her hands off the big black steering wheel to brush the hair away and still be sure of her control of the bus.

A number of archetypal energies echo in this short dream, but one of the most significant is the image of the young woman herself. In waking life, she is not well known to the dreamer. This in itself makes her a very likely figure upon whom to project newly emerging aspects of his psyche. In general, people in waking life who are not very well known often appear in dreams as figures representing unintegrated energies of the dreamer's psyche precisely because there is so little actual information to get in the way of or to cloud the projection. In this case, the young woman appears to be a classic image of the evolving anima.

Now that he has reached middle age and his children are grown, the dreamer is faced with emotional energies and possibilities of action that he "put on hold" at the end of college when he got married and embarked on his career. He is also reexperiencing his own developmental stages as his young adult daughter passes through these same stages herself. Parents always reexperience the drama of their own growth and development from childhood to maturity as their children grow and achieve the same developmental milestones. At each point of development, parents face again their own conscious and unconscious memories of their struggles and choices, triumphs and disappointments.

In the dream, the young woman conducts a quick "tour" of several important scenes in the dreamer's life, from childhood to the present, connecting them all together into a single "journey." The tour specifically includes "Greece," a place still filled with romance for him, where he has found he can experience himself more fully and put his thoughts and feelings into a broader and more coherent context than in the more habitual and familiar surroundings of the United States. This tour becomes a symbolic statement of the dreamer's emerging emphasis on emotional as opposed to intellectual awareness, as he consciously examines his history and begins to consider what different road he may take in the second half of his life.

In waking life, the dreamer is not entirely confident of his ability to manage this sort of change in his career and his way of being in the world. At that level, the dream comes to answer in the affirmative his unspoken question about his own competence and emotional capability. Diminutive though the young anima/woman is, she is both strong and determined, and in the dream she is fully equal to the demanding task of "steering the bus."

Vehicles in dreams are often metaphoric of relationships and relationship issues in the dreamer's life. In this instance, the "jeep" that the dreamer parks beside the road and "abandons" in order to ride on the "bus" suggests, at one level, a decreased expression of and exclusive reliance on "rugged independence" and a voluntary acceptance of more "collective" interactions. Vehicles for personal transportation are often metaphoric of personal relationships, whereas vehicles for collective, multipassenger transportation are often symbolic of corporate or institutional activities and relationships.

Hair in dreams and myths is often a metaphor of the other things that come spontaneously out of our heads, namely, our thoughts and opinions. Breath, wind, and smoke (which makes the otherwise invisible breath and breeze visible to the eye) are also often symbolically associated with spirit. The young woman's persistent good humor in the dream and her curious

and poignant gesture of "blowing the hair out of her eyes" suggest strongly that the dreamer's waking-life attitudes of serious-
ness and intellectuality may well need to be modified through
increased playful, yet determined, attention to his emotional and
spiritual life. He must not let "his long dark (thoughts) get in the
way of his 'vision.'"

Water in myth and dream, particularly the ocean, most often
carries archetypal connections to the world of feeling and emotion. The implied danger of driving the bus off the cliffs and
plunging into the ocean that forms the background of most of the
dream also suggests that the dreamer's renewed attention to emotion in middle life must be carried out with some care lest these
feelings become overwhelming. The fact that is the "ocean," and
not some lesser body of water, also suggests that although this
development of emotion and spiritual vision is personal, it is also
archetypal. Developing deeper spiritual awareness and understanding in midlife is a task for *all* people, even though it can only
be accomplished in the specific experience of each person.

The fact that the young woman is Asian is a further clue to
the emerging unconscious energy of the dreamer's anima. For
inhabitants of the Western Hemisphere, the Orient is the part of
the world that is sunlit and awake and active while the Western
Hemisphere is covered in darkness and Westerners are asleep.
This also symbolically describes dreams and the energies of the
unconscious. Much of the "enigmatic" quality ascribed in popular
Western opinion to the "Eastern mind" is a symbolic projection of
the "inscrutable" and "baffling" experience of encountering the
unconscious in our dreams and in its many other spontaneous
moods and surprising intrusions into waking life.

The dream described above suggests a relatively cheerful
and amicable encounter with the developing and evolving energies of the woman within, but this is not always the case.

A Navy chaplain returning to seminary for a year of sabbatical study dreams:

> He is in the big new library of the Graduate Theological
> Union (GTU) at the University of California at Berkeley. In
> his dream, he sees a female seminary student sitting at a
> table, apparently lost in her studies. In waking life, he con-

fesses to being secretly attracted to this woman, both as a potential sexual partner and as an emotional confidant. In the dream, he struggles with the tension between his desire to go over and speak to her and his fear that she will reject him. As he gathers his courage to approach her, he glances up and sees windows set high up above the bookshelves near the ceiling. He realizes with surprise that this large reading room must be underground, because he sees people standing around on the grass outside these high windows looking down into the room and watching him. He sees that they are "mocking him and spying on him," and he awakens in distress and agitation.

In this dream, the woman seminarian is another unique and specific image of the archetypal anima. Here she appears tantalizingly close, but seemingly unapproachable, in contrast to her good-humored relational presence in the previous dream. When the chaplain worked with the dream in his dream group, he discovered that the people "looking down on him" (all puns unconsciously intended) in his initial encounter with the woman were both his "old Navy buddies" and the "arch-feminists" of the GTU community.

In waking life, he confessed to feeling disparaged and threatened in classes and in less formal settings by the "feminists." He also acknowledged his fear that his compatriots in the Navy would not understand or respect his new-found awareness and appreciation of women, and particularly the feminine aspects of the divine, both of which his GTU studies were fostering within him. In waking life, he was also becoming increasingly aware of his tendency to project his own internalized critical and judgmental energies outward onto others, feeling himself judged and found wanting in the eyes of others, and also engaging in (unspoken) harsh judgments of the very people he perceived to be appraising him negatively. (It is ever so with projection.)

Over the months of his sabbatical studies, as his interior emotional experience became more conscious and vivid, his desire for deeper and more intimate relationships with women became more real and urgent. Among other things, the dream reflects these interior developments and their increasing impact on the dreamer's external reality. The internal critical voices in his psyche take the shape of masculine and feminine stereotypes that, while seemingly at war with each other, still unite in their condemnation of him and his newly emerging emotional life. The seemingly opposite figures of macho career Navy officers and feminist theologians and seminarians are both extreme gender and social stereotypes.

Stereotypic, cliché images, both in dreams and in waking life, are almost always associated with repression and projection. Like the jealous gods in the story of Izanami and Izanagi, the "Navy buddies" and the "GTU feminists" represent conservative, gender-stereotyped elements of the psyche opposed to change. Their hostility and their ability to evoke fear and self-doubt in the dreamer mark them as Shadow figures as well. In that sense, the chaplain's emotional dilemma can be seen as an example of the archetypal dilemma embodied in the Japanese myth; and his dream reveals striking parallels to the Izanagi/Izanami story. In his dream, he approaches the seminary student with essentially the same poignant mixture of desire and fear with which Izanami approaches Izanagi in the darkened bridal chamber. The setting and the characters are completely contemporary and specific, but the *story* is universal. The outer drama of emerging possibilities of relationship mirrors the inner drama of self-exploration. As the myth suggests, the scene (both in the dream and in the waking-life situation it mirrors and elucidates) is probably much less threatening than the dreamer's erroneous assumptions about his own and the woman's feelings cause him to imagine.

A contemporary woman, I will call her "June," dreams:

In the Front Row with Gorilla-Man
I am sitting in a black dress in the front row—right up to the stage almost. I think Stan (her current intimate man friend) is with me. I see Kent (Stan's son by a previous marriage) a bit to the left and perhaps Alex (her own son by a previous marriage) is close by too. The curtain goes up and there's a macabre scene—big men dressed as drag queens—lots of black and white. It's fascinating and frightening at the same time. I recall one man in white satin with black polka dots with a ruffled neckline, similar to a clown's. My black dress becomes covered with green English ivy, sending tendrils and leaves outward toward the audience.

The next scene: there is the star "villain" of the show—a big man in a gorilla costume. He comes down into the first row. I am somewhat afraid and regretting our first row location, glancing to the left to see if Kent is afraid. I am scrunched down and am facing the audience to keep an eye on the Gorilla-Man. Now he comes right to me and lifts me up easily. I am apprehensive, but not in terror. He carries me up to the stage. He is really a *big Man!* I can see his real face amidst the costume, and his eyes are kind and loving. His face is attractive to me (black stubble-beard). He kisses me tenderly on the forehead or cheek very quickly. I'm sure he didn't intend to be seen—it goes against the role he's playing.

I suddenly feel very safe and am not afraid at all. I feel cared for. I look forward to the next scene.

Awoke with a feeling of peace and well-being that lasted all morning long.

Note: the men are big enough to be considered giants—the size of NBA basketball players easily—6'8" or 7' tall.

Here we see essentially the same archetypal drama experienced from a heterosexual feminine point of view. Just as every man, to be fully mature, must come to a creative, accepting accommodation with the feminine/emotional/irrational/relational/anima aspects of his psyche, so must each woman come to grips with, accept, and integrate her own masculine/strong/linear/decisive/animus side.

The first scene of the dream places the dreamer directly "in the front row." The phrase "front row" suggests several things simultaneously. On the one hand, it implies "the main struggle" (suggested in part by the punning double meaning of "row"). At the same time, it also suggests "right next to the stage" (of development). There is also an implication of June's personal struggles with class mobility; "front row seats" are the most expensive and the best, always reserved for those who can afford them.

When "Gorilla-Man" takes her from the front row up onto "the stage," it implies the dreamer's unconscious readiness to move to this new phase of greater conscious understanding and public expression of her animus energies, despite her more conscious fears and apprehensions.

At a more collective level, the initial setting suggests that the personal details of the dreamer's struggles with her own interior masculine energies are also deeply resonant with the larger archetypal forces at work in the "battle of the sexes" in society as a whole. At both the personal and the collective level, the "drama on the stage" seems "macabre—both fascinating and frightening at the same time." The "black and white costumes" worn by the huge men appear, at one level at least, as metaphors of rigid, black-and-white (conventional) thinking about the issues of gender and social class that restrict and define the possibilities of relationship between and among men and women. There are also implications of this same sort of conventionality with regard to creative expression and its ambiguous relationship to earning a living (the setting is a "theatrical production").

The "polka-dot clown collar" costume stands out in particular in the narrative, like a modern rendition of the black and white costumes of the sad clown Pantaloon, Silvio, and the lovesick Harlequin. These archetypal androgynous rejected male lovers of Renaissance theater regularly lose their loved ones to more aggressive and typically macho male figures, in part because of the dictates of social convention, and in part because, despite their grand passions and delicate sensitivities, they lack the grit and toughness necessary for fully achieved and mature heterosexual masculinity. These "costume dramas," like all true myths, are not simply theatrical stories; they depict archetypal forces and situations present in both psyche and society in every moment.

The feminine longing for male energy that is both emotionally sensitive and wisely strong, both cooperative and decisive, both gentle and ruggedly determined is ancient and deep in both women and men. Sensitivity without clarity and strength is ultimately as incomplete and unsatisfying as strength and unswerving decisiveness without emotional self-awareness or expressiveness.

June's dream is specific. The issue involves her and all the males in her immediate life about whom she has the deepest feelings: her son, her lover, and her lover's son. The other nameless, faceless, and masked men also suggest that it is not just a personal issue; it has larger, more generalized, abstract, and collective levels. In this sense, there is a strong parallel between these figures and the vaguely seen "window watchers" in the chaplain's dream, who suggest the same kind of collective layers of significance.

Her own black dress suggests a one-sided, conscious, waking ego, persona participation in the games of sex- and class-role stereotypes. Jung appropriated the term *persona* to refer to the archetypal form of the "mask" that each person wears in social interactions. The clothing we wear and the hairstyles we adopt reflect interior ideas, ideals, and self-definitions, both in dreams and in waking life. These details of physical appearance always have symbolic significance and "fill in the blank" of our own versions and expressions of the archetype of persona.

In waking life, the dreamer is quite elegant and fashion conscious. She moves freely in several different social circles where the fashion standards vary widely. She is careful to be "dressed right" for each setting and to keep these "worlds" relatively separate in her life by not moving from one to another without changing her whole "look."

At this level, there is a another personal implication of being "abducted and taken up on stage." In waking life, June's lover, Stan, is, among other things, a talented musician and songwriter. For some time, he has been trying to persuade her to join him on stage and sing the songs he writes. Her ambivalence about this prospect is multileveled. Her conscious desire to transcend her class-conscious upbringing leaves her with deep fears about loss of status on the one hand, and performance anxiety on the other. Her dream suggests that the strong, self-motivated masculine energy in her psyche (energy which she does not yet totally trust) is ready to "go on stage" and "join the show." This suggests at least one of the specific consequences likely as a result of accepting the "gorilla"/animus in her that has "primitive" desires for public acknowledgment and success.

The large size of all the men, and the Gorilla-Man in particular, at one level reflects the "oversized" pressures of male dominance in our society. Woven into this image is also a suggestion at another related level of the disproportionate size and influence of adults in the lives of children. "Giants" in dreams often hint at and point to the influence of parents and other adults in the lives of children. The "abduction" of the dreamer by the huge Gorilla-Man implies not only the size of her own masculine animus energies, which she is just beginning to accept in herself, but also the actual proportionately "huge" physical size of her father when she was a little girl.

It is always the father (or a father substitute) who first puts a particular shape and stamp on the archetypal energies of the animus as they well up naturally in the psyches of little girls. Conversely, it is always the mother (or some other older female substituting for the absent mother) who provides the first concrete image for the upwelling anima/feminine energies in little boys. Relationships with parents in childhood always create the background and determine the particular sexual/relational issues that must be addressed in adult life.

If there is not a certain felt sense of acceptance and sexual attraction between the developing child and his or her opposite-sex parent figure, then the development of these crucial potentials for emotional and sexual relationship in adulthood will be skewed and damaged. Too much attraction, inappropriately expressed, can be equally damaging. Like so many other tasks of adult life, parenting requires a balanced, appropriate, and proportionate expression of emotional and physical affection and support.

One specific implication of the Gorilla-Man in June's dream is that no matter what other problems there were with her father when she was growing up, there was at least a fairly healthy and happy emotional connection with him, despite whatever collective "macho" persona/"gorilla" mask he may have worn.

In fact, the dream implies fairly clearly that this relationship with her stubble-bearded father beneath the "mask" is one of the reasons she now prefers the company of men who appear macho and stereotypically masculine, but who have "good hearts under the disguise," to the "new age men" who have the public/persona "costumes" of acceptance of the feminine, but whose secret emotional lives may still be quite unregenerately and oppressively sexist.

The Archetypal Abduction

The quality of "abduction" in the Gorilla-Man's action of picking the dreamer up bodily and carrying her up on stage, together with the interesting detail of her dress suddenly sprouting out in "ivy vines," suggests another deep archetypal mythological resonance to this drama of hunger for balance of masculine and feminine, mutual love, and interior wholeness.

In ancient Greece, one of the stories about the cyclic alternation of the seasons involves Demeter, the Great Mother of All Living, and her perpetually youthful and beautiful daughter, Persephone. Zeus, the King of the Olympian gods, is said to be Persephone's father, although in earlier matrifocal myths, she is her mother's daughter, born into the world without male assistance of any sort.

In the patriarchal versions of the story that Hesiod and the others handed down to us in writing, Father Zeus is approached by his shadowy brother Hades, King of the Underworld, who has no wife. On the basis of past debts and obligations (primarily his having sided with Zeus and fought at his side in the earlier war against the Titans), Hades demands Persephone as his wife. Zeus agrees although he knows that Persephone's mother, Zeus' sister (and in some versions, his mother) Demeter, will never agree to the marriage of her daughter to Hades, or to anyone else for that matter. So Zeus tells his brother Hades to watch for an appropriate moment and simply abduct Persephone and make her his queen by brute force.

One day while Persephone is playing happily with her handmaidens, dancing in the fields and gathering flowers, Hades causes the ground to split open at Persephone's feet. He leaps up from the depths, seizes her, and carries her back with him down into the underworld. Demeter discovers that her daughter has been abducted and learns of Zeus' collusion in the crime. She rages at her husband/brother/son Zeus for his cruelty and callousness in forcibly separating mother and daughter (Fig. 8).

In her sorrow and fury, Demeter leaves Olympus, takes on the disguise of an old woman, and wanders on earth incognito, refusing to allow any births, animal or human, to take place, and causing all the vegetation on earth to wither and die. This means not only that humankind is faced with misery and starvation, but also that there are no offerings or sacrifices to lay on the altars of the other gods and goddesses. The lives of Olympians themselves are threatened by Demeter's "strike." They all join together and call on Zeus to change his mind and bring Persephone back so that Demeter will relent and allow the earth once again to be fertile, green, and joyful, and so that the gods and goddesses can once again receive their sacrificial nourishment.

Figure 8. (Ancient Greece) Persephone is abducted by Hades (in the style of Attic vase paintings).

Demeter is adamant: Life and birth will be restored only when her abducted daughter is restored to her. Hermes, the archetypal messenger/diplomat, is dispatched to the underworld to bring Persephone back to the surface. He negotiates with tenacity and skill and eventually strikes the compromise that sets the seasons in motion. Because she ate six pomegranate seeds while in the house of Hades, Persephone will spend six months of the year in the underworld as his queen and the other six months in the world of air and sunlight with her mother. True to her threat, Demeter withdraws the energies of life in fall and winter when her daughter is in the underworld, and releases them again in spring and summer when Persephone returns.

On the surface, this is a story about abduction and coercion. It serves in part as a piece of patriarchal propaganda, replacing an older, matriarchal sacred narrative, in which the powerful decisive characters are all women, with a story about the lives and fates of women being determined by the superior strength of men.

Most likely, the now-lost Pelasgian Greek narrative(s) describing the cyclic death and rebirth of the vegetable world with the turning seasons ran parallel to the Middle Eastern myth of the goddess Innana's descent into the underworld to recover her lost lover from her sister Erishkigal, the Queen of the Dead. The similar narrative preserved in later Roman sources, of Psyche's descent into the underworld to recover her lost lover, Eros/Cupid, is, in all likelihood, another direct descendant of this lost matriarchal sacred tale. (It is not accidental that it is from this latter myth that the word *psychology*, "knowledge and study of the interior life of the mind and soul," is derived.)

At another level, however, both the patriarchal versions of Persephone's abduction by Hades and the matriarchal versions of the same descent into the underworld, undertaken more voluntarily as an act of rescue, are all symbolic stories of the necessary integration of male/animus energy into the psyches of the maturing adult women. In this vitally important sense, Persephone, the archetypal maiden/child, can never achieve full womanhood and become the adult emotional and social equal of her own mother without a difficult and uncomfortable descent into her own psychospiritual depths, and the subsequent "redemption" and "release" of her own interior masculine/animus energies.

In June's dream, the "vines" that sprout from her dress mark her as a woman embodying the archetypal energies of Demeter and Persephone in her waking-life struggles. The issue in her life is psychospiritual "fertility" and productivity, and it is this ability to produce new, fresh, creative life even after her primary role as mother has been fulfilled that can not be released without the embrace of the animus.

The dilemma of how to relate to this wild, coercive, brutal, deceitful, but ultimately strong, generative, and decisive masculine aspect of the psyche is embodied in these ancient myths and in June's dream of Gorilla-Man. The same emotional and intellectual paradoxes resonate in essentially the same symbolic forms in both the dream and the myths.

Without the archetypal animus energies of Zeus/Hades (the energies of formally logical, linear, decisive, relatively unemotional analysis and discernment), the ambiguities of deep emotional connection, commitment, and mutual dependence would prevent Persephone from separating from her mother and establishing her own life. The "abduction" at this level depicts the emotional difficulties of separation and establishment of autonomous adult life for the woman. It is painful, and the energies seem to "pop up out of the ground." But they are undeniable, and they lead to the establishment of the perpetually young princess as a truly adult queen in her own right.

At this level, June's Gorilla-Man is a modern example of the ancient figure of Hades the Abductor, dragging the young woman away from her relatively comfortable and passive "audience" role in her own life and launching her onto a new and more autonomous "stage" of her personhood. Like Beauty in "Beauty and the Beast," another archetypally similar tale, her task is to recognize the terrifying, potentially destructive power of the male/beast within and to transform both it and herself with acceptance and integration of that energy into her life. This is a deeply heroic and important act. At all periods of history, in all parts of the world, this act of accepting the darkest and most frightening aspects of the self has been recognized as the necessary precursor of authentic *love*.

For a woman, it is symbolically the act of loving the abductor/beast of the animus. For men, it is portrayed as the task of accepting the committed relationship with the dangerous, imprisoning, emotionally coercive and judgmental, transforming Hag/anima.

The failure to accomplish this act of acceptance and transformation results in a number of psychospiritual problems and dilemmas for both men and women. For men, the failure to integrate the anima in maturity often creates versions of the "Don Juan" scenario. Psychospiritual injury to the archetypal feminine results in an endless series of emotional/sexual connections that never culminate in satisfactory committed relationships. Sometimes it results in the seemingly opposite scenario of an outwardly conventional, monogamous marriage, but one without any real "juice" or emotional growth, which is perpetuated out of convenience or simply out of fear of "being alone." In either case, the failure to find deep active satisfaction in an ongoing committed relationship often stems from the same source: The feminine energies necessary for continuous conscious awareness of deep feeling and emotion (and thus for deep emotional commitment) have not been accepted and integrated. For the man or woman that has failed to integrate these anima energies, deepening emotional relationship is experienced primarily as a threat to independence, a trap, and a limitation, rather than as a means of authentic, satisfying self-expression. For men and women with injured anima, emotions themselves are experienced only as passing, trivial, and unreliable "moods," rather than as deep, consistent feelings.

For both women and men, the corresponding failure to integrate the animus often results in the tortures of endless emotional vacillation and indecision about the most important aspects of their lives.

Gender Roles in Patriarchy

In a patriarchal society such as our own, young men and women inevitably receive the message in childhood that their life possibilities are severely and arbitrarily limited by their gender. This message is usually first delivered by parents, both mothers and fathers. Even in those rare instances where enlightened parents attempt to protect their children from the depredations of sex-role stereotypes, the children are often ironically even more vulnerable to the pressures of peer group, school, and societal expectations to conform to relatively narrow class and gender formulas because of their intensified sense of isolation and separation from their peers and age-mates because of their "different" upbringing.

For many intelligent and sensitive women and men, the pains and disappointments of these betrayals by the masculine domination of family and society lead to a profound distrust, not only of men in general and in particular, but also of the decisive masculine energies within their own psyches. This appears at the level of feeling and behavior as a terribly ironic relationship to decision making, discovery of "right livelihood," and the ability to find satisfaction in long-term relationships. Women (and men) with this form of animus injury are often superb administrators, able to make all sorts of complex decisions within a given external context of job or family; but they are also seemingly unable to define or alter those overall contexts for themselves, or to make the larger decisions necessary to direct their own lives and careers and to serve their own ultimate best interests.

This curious combination of demonstrated administrative ability and deep indecisiveness is most often a direct consequence of mistrusting the archetypal masculine, both externally and internally. Healthy decisiveness requires the ability to discern clearly and cleanly when the information gathering phase of decision making is complete and when it is appropriate to take determined action, despite whatever "loose ends" of emotional consequence and relational nuance may still be unclear. This is an essentially "masculine" ability, in both men and women.

The balance between these developing energies is crucial. Increases in self-awareness must be accompanied by concomitant increases in freedom, autonomy, and self-direction. Without this balance, increasing self-awareness without accompanying growth in the power to act freely and expressively leads only to deep and debilitating depression; while increasing freedom and the power to act without deepening reflectiveness and self-awareness leads only to aggressive triviality.

Dreams and Gender Liberation

It is sadly clear that this animus ability to come to decisive closure and take action without vacillation or immobilizing concern about future consequences has gone berserk in contemporary patriarchal/industrial society. The vast majority of today's collective political, economic, cultural, and ecological problems are the direct result of animus energies operating in grotesquely exaggerated fashion without the balance and correction of their opposite and corresponding archetypal anima energies of open-ended awareness of relationship, subtle connection, and long-term consequence. This obvious and demonstrated "untrustworthiness" of collective animus energy, unbalanced and unchecked in the world, is so clear that for many people (both women and men), their own internal masculine is viewed and experienced as equally untrustworthy.

Mary, a mature woman returning to college after raising her children into adulthood and then separating from her husband, dreams:

> She is alone in the college building where most of her classes meet. It is night. She is standing in a well-lit classroom when suddenly a man dressed in sweatpants and a hooded sweatshirt and wearing boxing gloves comes dancing and shadow boxing into the room. His hood is pulled forward obscuring his face. He dances across the front of the room sparring and punching at the air. The dreamer is filled with fear, but she gathers her anger at being made to feel afraid simply because she is a woman alone and shouts at the intruder: "Who are you?! What do you think you're doing in here?!"
>
> With that, that man whirls to face her. He raises his boxing gloves to his face, and using the protruding thumbs, flips the hood back to reveal his face—the huge face of a mosquito, as large as a man's head.

The shock of this unexpected revelation is so great that it propels her into full, tingling wakefulness.

When she worked with the dream in one of my ongoing university classes, we came to the understanding that the figure of the boxer with the giant mosquito head was an archetypal animus figure with a very curious and particular lineage.

Mary is an ardent and strongly committed feminist whose anger at the depredations and oppressions of masculinist sexism is deep and abiding. However, at the time of the dream, she was still frustrated with her inability to make use of her deep anger to accomplish her most cherished goals and desires. For the most part, her surges of rage and righteous indignation simply irritated and frightened her and "sucked her dry" (one layer of the "mosquito" imagery).

As she worked with the dream, she realized that much of her feminist rhetoric and organizational activities amounted to "shadow boxing." This was a distressing realization, but it was also accompanied by a certain amount of awe and wonderment at just how "buffed up and strong" this shadow-boxing animus was. This realization was followed immediately by a recognition that shadow boxing is also an excellent form of training for actual fighting, and that she was nearing the point where her training was likely to start paying off in actual matches and victories.

In this act of recognizing the potential for positive, creative action suggested and embodied in this initially frightening figure, Mary began to accomplish the archetypal heroine's task of "Beauty" to recognize and love and thus transform "the Beast" in the specific feelings and decisions of her own life and psyche.

In the group, we tried to place the dream in successively larger and larger "amplified" archetypal/mythological contexts. One layer of larger context is related to the mosquito as "a blood sucker" and therefore a kind of natural "vampire."

Vampires and Projection

"Vampires" exist in the folk traditions of virtually all societies and exhibit a curiously similar set of attributes. Regardless of their period in history or the cultures in which they appear, they are "deathless" (the "living dead"). They must preserve their immortality by feeding regularly off the lifeblood of other non-vampires. They are wary of sunlight, and they either cannot see or cannot abide looking at their reflections in mirrors or other reflective surfaces.

Symbolically speaking, these attributes describe the experience of repression and projection. The person locked into the internal denial of repression "cannot die"—that is, cannot grow and change and mature. Once again, the metaphor of death is the symbol of psychospiritual transformation and change. The "immortality" and "eternal youth" that is achieved is the self-deceptive feeling of internal completeness and consequent immunity from change. It is the "living death" that is stagnation viewed from outside, but that feels like "safety" and "superiority" from within. The person trapped in the self-deception of repression and projection is cut off from the psychospiritual energies of growth and change that are regularly symbolized as death and rebirth in the archetypal symbolism of myth and dream.

Since the vital energies of authentic feeling and emotion are repressed, the "vampire" must live vicariously off the perceived (projected) emotions of others, gaining nourishment only from the "lifeblood" of other people's lives. In order to accomplish this preservation of the illusion of life without change, "sunlight" (the classic image of consciousness) and "reflection" (the act of honest self-observation) must be avoided at all costs.

The "giant (vampire) mosquito head" on the body of the "shadow boxer" was an archetypal image of the extent to which the dreamer's theater of feminist rage was a cover-up for fear and a projection of unacceptable *internal* "masculine" energies onto men in general as well as onto particular men with whom she struggled.

Another interesting and important archetypal association is with one of the oldest traditional stories of the "battle of the sexes." In the sacred narratives of many cultures, First Man and First Woman by definition have no one to marry but each other. Even though they are not fond of one another, they come together to live and produce children. They make efforts to get along, but their mutual irritation with one another only grows. Finally, in many stories, in a fit of rage and frustration, First Man overcomes First Woman with his superior physical strength and kills her.

Fearful that his crime, the "First Murder" (the symbolic equivalent of the first murder of Abel by his brother Cain in the Old Testament), may be discovered either by God or the gods or by his children, First Man decides to destroy the evidence by burning the body of First Woman, and to explain her disappearance with the story that she became so angry with him that she deserted him to live alone. As he consigns her corpse to the consuming flames, the sparks that fly up are filled with all the unexpressed anger and rage of First Woman. Animated by this fury, the sparks transform into the first mosquitoes that plague "man" for the rest of eternity in vengeance for the unjust murder of First Woman.

Even though the dreamer had never encountered any of the traditional narratives that include this story of the origin of mosquitoes in the heat of gender injustice and feminist rage, the archetypal quality of the image makes it perfect for the symbolic representation of her personal, contemporary, internal reality. In the service of health and wholeness, the dream comes to name the energies that are being squandered and wasted in the drama of "shadow boxing" with repressions and projections. These energies are essentially creative energies that are lost without an evolution of increased consciousness and self-awareness—an evolution that was in large measure accomplished by the dream and the dreamer's subsequent *aha's* of understanding that grew out of the group's work with dream, and particularly the exploration of the archetypal/mythological themes and images embodied in it.

Archetypal Imagery in the Dreams of Individuals: Implications for Dream Work

It is important to notice that although the dreamer had no conscious knowledge either of the archetypal connection between "vampires" and the repression/projection phenomenon, or of the worldwide tales of First Man's murder of First Woman and the consequent creation of mosquitoes, her dreaming self still made use of these archetypal symbols because they so aptly expressed her emotions and the complexities of her evolving self-awareness. It is equally important to note that the dream work that unpacked the levels of meaning around the frustrated expression of masculine energies in "shadow boxing" got very close to the heart of the matter without recourse to any archetypal amplification. The archetypal associations, or "amplifications," of the images deepened and extended the meaning and pointed more directly to the collective, transpersonal layers of the dream, but the essential message of the dream was already clear.

As suggested earlier, excellent dream work can be done whether or not one knows these myths and folk stories. When the dreams call up archetypal images, the unconscious dreamer already knows what the basic story is, whether or not the interesting parallels to sacred narratives in other distant and obscure cultures are immediately available to consciousness. The universal themes can be discovered and revealed by "ordinary" exploration of the images for their personal associations and basic symbolic implications. The archetypal amplifications drawn from knowledge of the religious and folk traditions of other cultures enrich the work; but they are not necessary, since the same essential symbolic dramas and relationships can be revealed by the dream images themselves, even without their specific archetypal associations.

The ironic, archetypal truth of all these dreams is that without the responsible, mature internal embrace and creative integration of those very same out-of-control, "inhuman" (gorilla/giant mosquito) masculine energies, the solutions to our individual and collective dilemmas will elude us. Unless the person who has been injured by an out-of-control "masculine" tendency toward premature closure and blindness to long-term consequences and connections can find those same energies in his or her psyche and make creative use of them, the frustrating and self-destructive dramas of both personal and collective life will grind on to their seemingly inevitable conclusions.

Unless the woman who does not trust the masculine predisposition to bring things to a conclusion and move on to the next linear agenda item learns to make use of that very ability herself, she will go on being tyrannized by interior indecision and external sexism. Unless the man who has been injured by the energies of stifling emotional connection and ambiguous, multilayered emotional relationship finds it in himself to embrace those very same energies in himself, he will be doomed to live his life in a drifting bubble of emotional isolation, unable to make deep and lasting connections with others, perpetually tortured with the secret feeling that he has made some sort of terrible mistake, even though his every important action seems rational, considered, and "correct."

In the metaphoric language of the myths and dreams looked at in this chapter, unless the fearful, ambivalent Izanagi in each of us can find the strength of character to approach and embrace the longed for Izanami sitting in the GTU Library, even under the accusing and disapproving eyes of the Navy officer gods and the feminist theologian goddesses of ideology and conventionality, then each of us, and society as a whole, will continue down the slippery road to self-destruction on which we are already so clearly embarked. Unless the fearful and ambivalent Persephone in each of us can find the strength of character to separate from her mother and from conventional femininity and class identity, learning to embrace the Hades/Vampire-Mosquito/Gorilla-Man of male energy, then each of us, and society as a whole, will continue to be painfully aware of the diseases and injuries that limit and threaten us and yet remain unable to mobilize the energies and ideas necessary to heal and cure them.

As we struggle to solve these interlocking problems in our personal lives and in our society as a whole, the ancient myths and sacred narratives are acted out again. Their symbolic forms are repeated in our dreams, dressed in modern costumes, amid contemporary sets, but acting out the same ancient psychospiritual dramas. The archetypes of authentic gender that animate and complicate our experience can be integrated more consciously into our lives. No dream, no myth, no sacred narrative has ever appeared to tell us that we have problems that we cannot solve.

To the very same extent that these ancient gender and class tensions manifest themselves again and again in our waking dilemmas and our remembered dreams, we can be sure that the symbolic shapes of creative, transformative solutions to our problems are evolving in us as well. Our myths and dreams continue to call us, individually and collectively, to acts of increasingly heroic self-awareness, compassion, strength, and responsible self-expression that will save and transform not only our own individual lives, but the lives of all the beings with whom we share the planet and the cosmos as well.

SUMMARY

The story of how the ancient mythical Japanese first parents, Izanagi and Izanami, were duped by the jealous and fearful gods into not making love after they were first married is another example of the universal symbolic language of archetypes shared by myths and dreams. The story addresses and gives specific symbolic/dramatic narrative shape to human anxieties and intuitions about sex and gender that transcend the particulars of culture and history.

The figures of Izanagi and Izanami, and the jealous gods and goddesses, are concrete examples of the gender archetypes Carl Jung called animus (the male energies in the psyches of women), and anima (the female energies in the psyches of men) respectively.

All authentic archetypal forms blend and merge into one another at their boundaries. The figures in the Japanese myth also represent archetypal energies of Shadow (the dark repugnant aspects of the unconscious that ironically always hold the greatest gifts) and Trickster (the transformative, creative, self-deceptive qualities of human consciousness itself).

Jung's original assertions about the inflexible gender links of animus, anima, and Shadow are simply not borne out in the actual encounter with dreams and myths around the world. There is a much wider range of normality than Jung's classic gender associations suggest or allow for, a range that corresponds to the natural diversity of physical body types, distribution of musical talent, and so forth.

Sacred stories from Australia, North America, Africa, and ancient Greece about the creation of the first human beings and their separation by gender expand and demonstrate the universal symbolic patterns of masculine and feminine and the archetypal linkage between sexual activity and death. In the course of this discussion, there is also an exploration of how the inherent human tendency to "split" complex and ambivalent archetypal forms into pairs of apparent opposites when these forms first surface into conscious awareness creates symbolic "twinning," "pairing," and "doubling" in myths and dreams.

Dreams of a man contemplating a change of career in his mid-fifties, a U.S. Navy chaplain on sabbatical returning to seminary for advanced studies, a woman struggling with sexism and class warfare in her life as a divorced single mother, and a woman reentering the work force after a midlife divorce reveal the same archetypal/mythological dramas in modern and uniquely personal form.

In the course of exploring some of the multiple layers of significance in these dreams, the myths of Demeter and Persephone, the murder of First Woman by First Man, and the global folklore of vampires are useful and significant. At one very important level, the abduction of Persephone by Hades is a metaphor of the difficulties women (and men) regularly experience in accepting their own masculine/animus energies for decisive action and separation from relationship. These archetypal energies are particularly distorted and injured in the contemporary social circumstance of oppressive sex- and gender-role stereotyping; and for that reason, they require particular attention, care, and healing. The vampire is an archetypal figure symbolically embodying the experience of repression and projection. The appearance of archetypally resonant figures of this sort in the dreams of contemporary people is a very reliable indicator of how they are dealing as individuals with these pervasive issues of postmodern life.

Chapter 4
THE COLLECTIVE REPRESSION OF THE GREAT MOTHER AND THE RESTORATION OF LOST WHOLENESS

It seems to me that in our time, this image of the goddess bringing to birth the resurrected sun—or Son—out of the womb of darkness, out of the burial cave of the earth, carries numinous power. For there can be no doubt if civilized humankind is to survive the dangers of this century of transition, when all the familiar landmarks are disappearing and the collective structures that used to protect us are crumbling, we must turn to the *goddess*, to the long-despised values of the feminine, to the feeling heart and the contemplative mind. Perhaps then our culture may see the rising of a new day.

Helen M. Luke

It is said that the Celtic/Welsh goddess Ceridooen, She of the Many Names and Shapes, Mistress of the Cauldron of Life and Death, once bore a son named Avgathi. By all accounts (and there are several), Avgathi was an exceptionally ugly child. Some even say that his name means "dark and frightening as the night." When Ceridooen beheld her son, she knew in her heart that the only hope he had for a happy and fulfilling life was for him to be as wise as he was ugly, for surely he couldn't thrive in the world on his looks (as so many of us do).

To help her son along on the way of wisdom, the Great Goddess decided to brew up a potion—a distillation of all intuitive knowledge of magic and the whole true hidden order of the cosmos. This brew required that every species of living thing (and for the ancient people who first wove this story, even the rocks and the clouds were alive) was required to give one of the best of its kind to be boiled and distilled into the elixir of Allwisdom.

Now to each thing there is a season of greatest potency, and in that season there is a particular moment of greatest intensity; so these representative offerings of all the world's living energies had to be gathered and collected over the course of a full turning year, each at the most propitious hour of day or night, at the precise moment of rain or draught, of wind or stillness, of sunshine or moonshine, of torchlight or lightning flash, of phosphorescence or total darkness that corresponded to its deepest hidden nature and its fullest power and strength.

And when they were thus collected, all these living energies had to be added in just the right amount and at just the right moment to the great cauldron in which the brew was being prepared. And that huge cauldron had to be kept perpetually boiling for that entire year and not allowed to boil dry or cool past a simmer for even an instant during that whole time, or else the whole magical effort would be in vain.

In order to accomplish this complicated and demanding task, Ceridooen acquired a bondservant, a boy known as "Little Gooyion." She set Gooyion to collect wood and carry water and tend the boiling cauldron with his full attention, under threat of the most terrible of punishments, both night and day, while she herself traveled about the world and accomplished the gathering and the blending.

Now Little Gooyion was no fool, and over the weeks and months of tending the perpetual fire and of watching Ceridooen's going and coming, and feeding the ugly infant, and grumbling to herself about his ill looks and all the trouble it was causing her, Little Gooyion figured out in his own mind what the great magic was all aimed at, and what the secret potion might do for the one who drank it...

In the many versions of this ancient tale, there are different details about just how Gooyion comes to drink the potion instead of Avgathi. In some, Gooyion simply steals a sip when he notices that the exhausted Ceridooen has nodded off to sleep after adding the last of the ingredients to the cauldron. In others, the cauldron overheats and bursts or boils over accidentally at the last moment, and the precious drop of hot distilled wisdom splashes out and falls on Gooyion's finger. As he instinctively sticks his burnt finger into his mouth to soothe the pain, he inadvertently sucks up the sacred potion. In some versions, it is three drops, echoing the great archetypal trinity, the three that are one, maiden-matron-and-crone, past-present-and-future, life-death-and-rebirth, found in sacred narratives all over the world and particularly emphasized in the Celtic tradition.

Whatever the details, in all the versions of the tale, Little Gooyion does come to drink the potion, and in that moment he acquires the immense magical knowledge and sacred wisdom Ceridooen had intended for her son.

Part of the knowledge he acquires in that blinding instant of revelation is just how angry and vengeful Ceridooen will be to have her carefully contrived plan to save her son frustrated by Gooyion's imbibing the potion. Filled with terror at this vision of her fury, Gooyion uses his newly acquired magical knowledge to transform himself into a swift hare and flees for his life.

Ceridooen comes to herself and sees in a flash what has taken place. In a consuming rage, she transforms herself into a greyhound and pursues him.

In desperation, sensing Ceridooen/greyhound gaining on him, Gooyion/hare leaps wildly into a stream and turns himself into a swift swimming salmon. Ceridooen/greyhound leaps in after him and transforms herself into a hungry hunting she otter.

Gooyion/salmon can not outswim Ceridooen/otter; so at the last moment, just as she is about to seize him and rend him, he leaps out of the water into the air, transforms himself into a swallow, and darts off into the sky. Ceridooen/otter leaps up too, transforms herself into a hawk, and presses the chase.

Gooyion/swallow flees with all his strength, but he knows it is not enough; so only moments ahead of his ravening pursuer, he plunges into a barn, transforms himself into a single grain of barley, and hides himself in a newly threshed pile of barley corn (Fig. 9).

Ceridooen/hawk flies into the barn an instant later and sees what Gooyion has done. She cannot tell which of the grains is Gooyion/barley corn, so she transforms herself into a gigantic black hen and pecks up all the barley, down to the very last grain.

But Gooyion has added his own wits to his new-found magical wisdom and has tricked Ceridooen one last time and won at least a momentary reprieve; because she has taken him into her

Figure 9. (Ancient Europe) Shape-shifting pursuit of Little Gooyion by Ceridooen.

body in the form of a seed, she becomes pregnant with him. Her own sacred law binds her—Great Mother and Divine Child have a sacred bond that cannot be broken.

Ceridooen is enraged to have been tricked in this fashion, and she broods and nurtures her fury for the nine long months of gestation. When she bears a second son, she does not look at him. She does not name him. Because he is now a child of her own blood and body, her own law forbids her to kill him; so instead, she sews him into a leather casket and flings him into the sea, cursed and nameless...

At this point in the many versions, the story shifts from the timeless world of the Goddess and the endless cycles of nature to the linear, historical world of human men and women:

Elffin, the ne'er-do-well son of King Gooyithno, has squandered all his father's wealth by gambling and entertaining while supposedly looking after his father's interests at the court of the High King. Elffin has returned home, penniless and with tattered honor, to his father's court.

In some of the versions of the tale, where the cauldron simply breaks and Little Gooyion consumes the potion accidentally, the parallel story of King Gooyithno's reduction to poverty is made even more dire. In addition to the losses incurred by his son at court, all Gooyithno's fine horses, known all across the land for their speed, endurance, agility, and tractable steadfastness in battle, have also been poisoned. When the cauldron broke, it was because the potion of Allwisdom was distilled and separated from the essence of all ignorance and evil. It was this essence of all evil that broke the sacred vessel, and the drop(s) of wisdom leapt forth to avoid being contaminated by the poison. The distilled magical wisdom fell on Little Gooyion's finger, and the poison spilled forth from the broken cauldron and was washed into the streams where Gooyithno's famous horses drank. When the esteemed royal herd came down to the stream to drink as usual at sunset, they were all poisoned to death by the evil residue of Ceridooen's potion.

When Prince Elffin returns to his unfortunate father, the young man has been scheming up a plan to recoup his own fortunes. When he enters his father's presence, the whole court is assembled. Prince Elffin approaches his father and asks him for the one thing his father has left of any monetary value—his right as king to take the first catch from the fish traps in the river on May Eve, the first night of the yearly salmon run. He boldly asks for this boon as a recompense for looking after his father's interests at the court of the High King, and his father grimly agrees...

It is important for modern readers to realize that when King Gooyithno grants this last gift to his son, he is not simply trying save face or appear magnanimous and generous in the eyes of his court. In most versions of the story, he is clearly aware of Elffin's lack of probity and of his spendthrift ways. The king has no doting parental illusions about his son, but because

Prince Elffin asks publicly, King Gooyithno is reluctantly forced to grant the boon as a *religious* obligation.

In the ancient Celtic realms, hospitality and generosity were legendary, not only because they reflected the necessary character traits of a leader who inspires confidence, trust, and loyalty, but because it was expressly in the unfailing generosity of the king and the nobility that the fertility of the land was magically renewed and ensured. Only as the king and the nobles gave unstintingly would the herds, the crops, the wild game, and the land itself be renewed and give their bounty to the people. Any failure or holding back in hospitality and generosity on the part of a king would lead to famine and infertility. The kings and nobles and even the simple crofters and householders were the "guardians of the land," not only militarily and politically, but in this even more important religious and spiritual sense.

When Prince Elffin makes his request, King Gooyithno fulfills his primary religious duty to ensure the continued fertility of the land and the life of the people. Despite the cost to himself of completing his impoverishment, he generously grants his son's request. Prince Elffin proceeds to the fish weir, gloating over the prospect of the renewal of his fortunes. Tradition tells us that the value and prestige of salmon as a food and as a "sacrament" was so great in ancient Celtic realms that a single good catch of the noble fish could equal a year's profit from all other activities.

However, when Elffin pulls in the weir, he can tell by how light it is that it is almost empty. He begins to bewail his ruination, for the only thing in the weir that night is a shrunken, salt-stained leather casket—the same casket that Ceridooen cast into the waves with the nameless reborn Little Gooyion sewn up inside.

The reborn infant hears Elffin's wails and speaks up from inside the casket. He tells Elffin to open it; it contains something worth far more than all the salmon he might have caught that night and many treasures more besides. Elffin tears open the casket expecting gold and jewels. Instead, he sees the infant. Dazzled by the light that shines forth from the infant's face, he exclaims in surprise, in Welsh, "Taliessen!" meaning "What a beautiful, shining brow!" By uttering this phrase, he gives the reborn Little Gooyion his new name for his new life.

"Let it be 'Taliessen' from henceforth," says the miraculous infant. He then rises from the casket and pronounces the first great magical poem, in which he tells his story as one "twice born" from the Goddess, possessing all magical knowledge and able to shape cosmic forces and human events with his magical words and wisdom...

The story continues with accounts of Taliessen's magical exploits and his loyal service to the house of Gooyithno and Elf-fin. I offer it here because of the insight it provides into one of the most important archetypes of the collective unconscious: the Great Mother.

The Great Mother

The Celtic/Welsh goddess Ceridooen is only one example of the archetypal figure of the Great Mother found in a myriad of different names and forms in myths and sacred narratives around the world, as well as in the psyches of even the most modern and sophisticated people. Whatever her name(s) and shape(s) may be in any particular society at any particular period of history, the Great Mother manifests certain basic traits and characteristics that remain the same and mark her as a single pattern of archetypal energy. She is always the "Mother of All." She gives birth to "the ten thousand things" out of her own being and body without any male impregnation or assistance of any kind. The rhythms of nature and the changing seasons define her liturgy; and at the appropriate season, she also shows a dark and terrible face that matches her bright and nurturing visage. As Great Mother, she not only nourishes all her children with her own body, but she also devours them all eventually and takes them back into herself at death, as corpses decay and return into the body of the earth. For those who love and accept both faces of the Goddess and give their lives to her without faint-hearted or selfish withholding, an eternal round of successively better lives is assured through the reward of reincarnation.

All of these attributes can be seen clearly in the figure of

Ceridooen, from her generous gifts of life and nourishment to all things, through her terrible inescapable devouring hunger, to her gift of reincarnation.

On the other side of the world, long before any sustained contact with Europe, the Mesoamerican peoples of Central and South America worshipped similar Great Goddess figures who exhibit similar archetypal traits: "Our Mother, Tonantzin, has mouths in her wrists, mouths in her elbows, mouths in her ankles and knees... When it rains, she drinks. When flowers shrivel, when trees fall, or when someone dies, she eats. When people are sacrificed or killed in battle, she drinks their blood. Her mouths are always opening and snapping shut, but they are never filled. Sometimes at night, when the wind blows, you can hear her crying for food" (Fig. 10).

Many contemporary Hindus practice a continuous tradition of worship of the goddess Kali that extends back into prehistoric times. She is another exemplar of the archetypal Great Goddess. She is often depicted in the very midst of her simultaneous act of endlessly generous giving of the gift of life from her

Figure 10. (Mesoamerica) Tonantzin, Mother and Devourer of All, the One to Whom All Paths Lead (after images in the surviving Aztec codices).

own body and substance, and her voracious feeding frenzy. She appears as a magnificent woman with blue-black skin and multiple arms. She is dancing, one foot raised, the other trampling on a corpse—often that of her erstwhile husband, the god Shiva. She is pictured in the act of decapitating herself with a sword and holding up her own dismembered head aloft to drink from the fountain of blood that spurts up from her severed neck (Fig. 11).

Many Westerners, particularly devout Christians, find this image horrifying, barbaric, and revolting in the extreme. The failure to recognize the beauty and profundity of this ancient image is in itself a symptom of the collective Western effort to

Figure 11. (India) Kali, in her ecstatic dance, drinks the blood that spurts from her own severed neck, while trampling on the corpse of her consort, Shiva.

suppress the archetypal image and energy of the Great Mother from consciousness.

From the perspective of the Hindu and other believers who worship her, this image of joyously embracing the inevitability of death and divinely promising the renewal of life in the midst of the dance is viewed as sublimely comforting and beautiful. Such believers often point to the obvious dream-like quality of this image as a proof that it should be taken symbolically, not as a literal horror. Many of the people who hold this view are themselves offended and appalled by the literalistic image of Christ tortured on the cross, precisely because it is so realistic and "pornographic," focusing attention on the literal horrors of physical suffering, and distracting attention away from the symbolic nature of the spiritual reality it is supposed to depict.

A growing minority of both Hindus and Christians understand that at a deeper level of archetypal symbolism, both self-decapitating Kali and crucified Christ are an exquisitely matched and similar pair in that they both give shape to the sublime pattern of Willing Sacrifice. The archetype of Willing Sacrifice is associated with the development and continuing evolution of human consciousness itself, both collectively and in each individual. As consciousness evolves, it must relinquish whatever self-image and self-awareness it has achieved in order to open to the evolving possibilities of change, growth, and developing maturity. Historically and psychologically, the first example of the Willing Sacrifice is the Great Mother herself.

The archaeological evidence is overwhelming. The earliest human intuitions of the divine were not of a masculine Father God, but of this feminine Mother Goddess. This deep intuition persists tenaciously in ideas and common phrases like "Mother Earth" and "Mother Nature" and (until recently) the habit of giving natural cataclysms such as tropical storms, hurricanes, volcanoes, and the like exclusively feminine names.

In the oldest magico-religious iconography from the earliest human communities of Neanderthal and Mousterian folk, even before the evolution of protomodern Cro-Magnon people, it is images of a goddess with a voluptuous, bear-like body and an uncarved face that mark the cave entrances and the burial sites.

Masculinist anthropologists and art historians have attributed the lack of facial features on these goddess images to "a lack of artistic and expressive skill" among "primitive carvers," but clearly the fact that the faces of these figures are *uncarved* is a positive symbolic statement that all of the physical world in its unmanipulated natural state is "the face of the Mother." The exquisitely expressive details of hands and arms and voluptuous folds of flesh on these faceless figures demonstrate to all but eyes clouded by prejudice what refined skills these ancient carvers possessed.

Reincarnation–the Promise of the Great Mother

The burial and other ritual treatment of the dead in matriarchal Great Goddess religions in all parts of the world involves interment or exposure of the deceased facing the east and the "reborn" rising sun in the same flexed fetal position of infants in the womb. The "passage graves" and "barrow tombs" of the British Isles, continental Europe, coastal North and West Africa, and the Mediterranean all exhibit this basic symbolic promise of rebirth in new physical form after death.

Burial in these tombs was carried out with great care and piety, but the tombs were regularly reused. The interred remains that were treated with such care just a little while earlier were regularly cast aside with seeming indifference, suggesting quite clearly that in the minds of the people using the tombs, the promised "rebirth" had taken place, making continuing exaggerated care for the physical remains of the dead no longer necessary or appropriate.

Patriarchal religions of God-the-Allfather have attempted to supplant and suppress this ancient psychospiritual intuition about the nature of the divine and to eradicate all official institutional religious interest in reincarnation. Despite the numerous biblical references and implications, official Christianity has succeeded in relegating the idea of reincarnation to the occult and nativist fringes. However, the banning and official suppression of the archetypal ideas associated with the intuition that the divine has a profound feminine form has not eradicated these archetypal symbolic forms from the human psyche; it has only forced them below the surface of conscious awareness.

Patriarchy and Economic Necessity

The transformation of the natural/physical world from "the Sacred Living Body of Our Mother" (to be touched and treated only with appropriate awe and respect) into a collection of "natural resources" (without any intrinsic worth or importance apart from their potential for "development" and exploitation) appears to have been a necessary step in the development of masculinist consciousness, technological innovation, and social organization.

For similar reasons of "progress," women had to be demoted from the status of goddesses (or representatives of the Goddess) to the status of mere property—chattel to be owned, bought, sold, and bartered. In the matriarchal spiritual worldview, the physical world of nature—and its archetypal correlative, the feminine realm of emotional experience and the archetypal intuition of the fundamental relatedness of all things as "children of the same mother"—was consciously alive with mystery and awe. With the imposition of the patriarchal worldview, both woman and world became instead a jumbled collection of disorderly possibilities, crying out for male domination and control.

In later patriarchal versions of the Taliessen story, this transition from matriarchy to patriarchy can be seen in details of the story that are altered over time. In these later versions, Ceridooen is demoted from "goddess" to "witch"; and in the process, she acquires "a husband," a shadowy figure named "Tegid" who never speaks and who appears in the narrative apparently for the sole purpose of asserting that Avgathi has a father, that he was not created by parthenogenesis as he was in the earlier matriarchal narratives.

Sexual Knowledge and Social Power

The final subterfuge with which Little Gooyion preserves his life in the face of Ceridooen's wrath is most significant in this regard. In the earliest matriarchal cultures, the ability of the

Great Goddess to produce children at will without male participation was believed to extend to human women as well. The
understanding that sexual intercourse was necessary for the production of children appears to have been either unknown or
"taboo." There is even some fairly compelling evidence that the
understanding that sexual intercourse was necessary to impreg-
nate was a "religious secret" reserved for female initiates into the
"mysteries" of the Goddess's cult practice.

In ancient Greece and Asia Minor, for example, the knowledge that women become pregnant *only* through intercourse with
men may well have been a religious secret given only to women
when they were initiated into the mysteries of the Goddess at
puberty. The few references we have to the actual content of these
initiation mysteries at the ancient Goddess sanctuary at Eleusis,
for example, suggest that they involved "seeds" and the renewal of
the promise of reincarnation after death. Coincidentally, ancient
Greek historians tell us that the Goddess's precincts at Eleusis,
where the mysteries were taught, were off-limits to all males, all
year round, and that any man or boy found within two miles of the
temple complex was summarily put to death without trial. When
Herakles eventually becomes the first male to be initiated into the
Mysteries (of the Mother) at Eleusis, it is an indication that the
ancient taboo on the "facts of life" has finally been lifted.

Evidence of this sort led the poet/scholar Robert Graves and
others to suggest that the "facts of life" with regard to sexual reproduction were a significant part of the mysteries taught to women
there in the course of their initiation into adulthood. He further
suggests that these basic facts were purposely kept secret from men
for religious and political reasons. When the Indo-European horse
riders appeared with detailed biological knowledge of the facts of
life in the male-dominated wild herd, they transformed the ancient
matriarchal/agricultural societies by spreading this information
around to one and all in the form of the original "dirty joke."

Male Sexual Desire and Castration Fear

The evidence is quite strong that what Freud called "castration fear" plays an important semiconscious role in this transition

as well. The image of the snake is "phallic" and has apparently always been so, even in the prehistoric period dominated by the collective worship of the Great Mother. The snake has always been the traditional animal companion of the Great Mother. The statuettes that have survived from the prehistoric matriarchal period on the island of Crete show the Goddess with snakes twined down both her arms as she holds them open in welcoming embrace toward the viewer/worshipper.

In the matriarchal world, the snake was a symbol of phallic energy on the one hand, and the penis on the other. But the penis itself was viewed as a female organ, only given to men "on loan" and therefore able to be "called back" at any moment, despite any conscious reservations the individual male might have. The proof was the seemingly independent will that penises appear to exhibit, straining to return to the "source" whenever the opportunity presented itself.

At this level, the fear of castration is born archetypically in the deep unconscious thought that the Great Mother can recall her "loaned" penis back to herself any time she wants, without any advice or consent from the individual man. The misogynist fury of newly established patriarchy can also be seen in the light of this ancient suppressed and taboo idea. The deposition of the Goddess meant at one level the acquisition of the penis as a male organ, but only at the cost of the lingering anxiety born of repression and denial of the knowledge that it had not always been so.

In modern times, Branislaw Malinowski's anthropological field investigations among the Trobriand Islanders prior to World War II revealed a twentieth-century society where males were apparently ignorant of their necessary role in procreation. Malinowski reported that Trobriand men told him they believed that women became pregnant when they were "chosen by the spirits of the ancestors" to reincarnate or when they undertook ritual exercises to attract these spirits to enter their bodies. In a stunning example of the all-pervasive quality of contemporary masculine sexism, Malinowski never even talked to women to see if they shared the same beliefs. It was only back in the United States, while was writing his book, *The*

Father in Primitive Society, that he even noticed this oversight. It was then that he was forced to ponder the implications of the apparent absence of unwanted pregnancies among Trobriand women. Malinowski concluded that "these natives have a well-established institution of marriage, but are quite ignorant of the man's share in the begetting of children.... My firm conviction is that the ignorance of paternity is an original feature of primitive psychology, and that in all speculations about the origins of Marriage and the Evolution of Sexual Customs, we must bear in mind this fundamental ignorance."

The fact that Ceridooen is confounded by Gooyion's "trick," his apparently newly found knowledge that if she takes a seed into herself she will become pregnant, may be seen as a clear symbolic representation of the knowledge of paternity imparted to males. It depicts one of the major turning points in that most ancient struggle for power, "the battle of the sexes." Gooyion's rebirth as Taliessen, with his memory of his previous life intact, is also a clear example of reincarnation, the Goddess's most ancient promise to her loyal children.

In order to transform society from matriarchy to patriarchy, the Western patriarchs also outlawed consideration of reincarnation. Without this alteration of theology, it is virtually impossible to make masculinist domination of the natural world in general and women in particular "stick." If rebirth in the womb of a woman is the ultimate fate of every just person (with the ever-present threat of rebirth in less attractive, "lower" animal forms for those who "sinned"), then women remain the inescapable arbiters of men's fate after death.

New Testament Hints of Reincarnational Belief

The official Christian churches have been most ferocious in their efforts to rid Christianity from any vestiges of reincarnationalism. Biblical scholars have tied themselves into awkward and complex knots to explain away the apparent acceptance by Jesus and his disciples of reincarnational ideas as evidenced by the Synoptic Gospels.

The gospels of Matthew, Mark, and Luke all recount that

after wandering around Judea for months, Jesus and the disciples approach Jerusalem. Jesus sends several of his men into town to gather news and report back what the people are saying. When his spies return Jesus asks them, "And who do they say I am?" He receives a number of answers: "Some say that you have been possessed by the spirit of John the Baptist after Herod had him murdered. Others say you're the Prophet Elijah come again."

To view these lines as having no reference to a general acceptance by the people of Jesus' time of reincarnation and the transmigration of souls after death into new bodies requires years of highly disciplined academic training and self-deception. The effort to pretend that these lines refer in symbolic terms only to the historical antecedents of Jesus' mission and prophetic preachments (John the Baptist and Elijah) and have nothing to do with a belief in reincarnation is a direct consequence of the patriarchal denial of the ancient religious intuition that the divine has a beautiful and terrible feminine face.

The Return of the Repressed

Here as elsewhere, the denial of the truth in no way alters the reality of the situation. Below the conscious surface of awareness, the banished archetypal energy of the Great Mother continues to exert her all-pervasive influence. As recently as 1956, the pope was writing letters to the bishops in Ireland chiding them about the disproportionate number of masses and feast days devoted to Mary and St. Brigid (a figure closely related to Bride, the Celtic/Irish Mother Goddess, an analogue of the Celtic/Welsh Ceridooen, assuming the "reincarnated" form of the medieval peasant girl/saint) as opposed to those dedicated to Jesus and all the male saints put together. Church officials regularly report the same "problem" among the peasant agrarian populations in Latin America and Asia.

In the folk traditions of Wales (the original home of Ceridooen), the Great Mother appears at Yuletide in the guise of the "Mari Lwyd" (Merry Lewis), a horse's skull on a stick, decorated and garlanded and carried from house to house to the accompani-

ment of boisterous singing. The bearers of the Mari Lwyd ask
rhyming riddles and make exaggerated boasts, inviting and chal-
lenging the householders to respond and solve the riddles and
"top" their remarks. If and when they fail to do so, the Mari Lwyd
and her companions are invited inside and offered food and drink.
The mythic tale that justifies these raucous goings-on is a story
about the Mari Lwyd being expelled from the stable before the
birth of the baby Jesus and thus being forced to wander the land in
search of hospitality.

Here is a particularly apt and relatively unambiguous
metaphor of the Great Mother (in her guise as the ancient Celtic
horse goddess, embodying death and rebirth, fertility and the
land, as well as the sacredness of the physical world in general
and the body in particular) being "expelled" by the patriar-
chal/masculinist Christian tradition, but "hanging on" in the
form of a holiday "horseplay" among the "lower classes" in agricultural societies where the relationship to the earth and to the
body are of necessity more immediate and conscious than in an
urban/industrial/academic context. The body is often symbolized by the horse in myths and dreams—the "animal" that the
consciousness "rides" through life. Here, the garlanded horse
skull has essentially the same symbolic weight and meaning as
the Hindu image of Mother Kali decapitating herself and drink-
ing from the ever-renewing fountain of her own blood.

Several years ago, a friend of mine sent me an art auction
catalogue that included a Punjabi folk figure that embodies the
entire theology of the Goddess in a simple and, to me, very moving form. The object being auctioned was acquired in Northern
India sometime in the 1950's. It consisted of a crudely carved
wooden torso, obviously female, with a metal rod through the
shoulder area to which two wooden arms are attached. This figure is driven upright into the ground, like a free-standing fence
post, at the edge of a farmer's field, next to a path to a nearby
shrine used by religious pilgrims. The metal rod through the
shoulders allows the arms to rotate freely. One arm is carved to
suggest that it is holding a baby. The mouth and groin area of
the torso are slotted so that when the arm is rotated, the arm

appears to pluck the baby from the figure's vagina, carry it up through the air, and devour it.

The story accompanying this description suggested that the farmer either carved or acquired the figure and set it up next to his fields so that devout Hindu passersby would be invited to pause, spin the arm of the Goddess figure, and pray for as long as the arms rotated, thus depicting the generosity of the Goddess in giving all life and her inexorable devouring of her children in an endless series of reincarnated lives and deaths. The farmer did this, the catalogue concluded, because of his conviction that the prayers uttered by the pilgrims would not only aid their spiritual development, but would also increase the fertility of his fields.

The tradition of rotating prayer wheels that energize and send forth their prayers by virtue of their spinning motion is very strong in that part of the world. I suspect that there is a blending of various traditions in the shape and use of this simple but eloquent figure.

The Great Mother in Dreams

Not only does the archetypal form of the Great Mother exhibit astonishing tenacity in these collective religious and folk traditions, but it also appears regularly at the level of individual experience. Men and women regularly dream figures that grow directly from the ground of this archetype, whether they are involved in worship or folk practices focused on her or not.

An American woman with highly independent feminist views, who is also locked in an ongoing emotional struggle with her father, dreams that she witnesses:

> a huge, terrible, naked woman with blue-black skin and horrible long sharp teeth and finger nails like claws, sitting astride her father's recumbent corpse, tearing his viscera out of his body with her bare hands and devouring them.

Here is the Great Goddess in her fearful devouring aspect as Kali, the Queen of Heaven and Hell. The personal drama of evolving emotional relationship with her waking-life father has reached archetypal depths where the details of her personal struggle reflect the timeless dramas of the Great Mother.

Whenever the details of individual human life and relationship become charged with emotion and significance that reflect the "timeless" repeating dramas of the archetypes, the stage is set for the appearance of archetypal figures and scenarios in that person's dreaming (and waking) life. It is as though "the gods" (archetypal energies) require living beings in order to manifest and live their own lives. When Georg Groddeck (the inventor of the term *id* as a name for the unconscious, the not-yet-speech-ripe) says, "We are lived by the 'Id,'" he is describing the same experience of intrusion of archetypal patterns into the mundane details of people's waking lives, at precisely the point where their individual emotional relationships and evolving dramas exhibit the same basic symbolic shapes as the myths and sacred narratives.

In this instance, the appearance of the Kali figure coincided with the dreamer's letting go of attachment to her father's judgments, both positive and negative, on her life and realizing that she had internalized many of his limiting views of how she should live her life in order to be a "responsible adult." For years, despite the conscious break with her father's generally conservative and sexist values, she still nurtured a longing for his love and approval. Largely through consciousness raising work in the women's movement, the dreamer succeeded in bringing these lingering unconscious yearnings to consciousness, and she was "rewarded" with this dream (among other things). The dream embodies the archetypal association of death with growth and transformation of personality and character. The image of "father" is well and truly dead, and the "corpse" provides "nourishment" for the Great Mother in the dreamer's psyche. Put in a more psychological way, the dream depicts animus energy, which was previously limiting and oppressive (internalized oppression born of growing up in a family that promoted strictly limited roles and possibilities for women in general and daughters in particular), being liberated and absorbed into a much greater understanding of the powers and creative/expressive possibilities of the archetypal feminine, the Great Mother.

Nor is the appearance of the Great Mother limited to the dreams of women, or to seeming negative or frightening images. A man struggling to make a success of life as both a husband and father and an independent freelance writer and teacher dreams:

> My Mother sends me on an important errand to visit my Grandmother and get some things from her. I have to go down into the earth and pass through several "levels" and "gates." When I get to her, she seems somewhat aloof, but still glad to see me. I don't have to tell her anything; she already knows what I am supposed to collect from her. She gives me a sheaf of glossy 8x10 publicity photos. I am amazed—they are photos of me, as I look now in middle age, even though my Grandmother looks the way I remember her as a boy, years before she died. She also gives me something else, some sort of "spell" or "curse" that I can use to "change my relationship to my enemies." I suddenly realize that I am "in the Land of the Dead." I wake up with a start...

Here, although the image is of the dreamer's own deceased grandmother, the deeper import of the image is clearly archetypal. The energies for "wealth" and creative "fertility" that the dreamer is seeking in his waking life are always held in the psychospiritual depths by the Great Mother in her guise as "Queen of the Underworld." They are essentially the same powers that Little Gooyion acquires when he drinks the magic potion from Ceridooen's cauldron. Like Psyche in the matrifocal Greek myth, the "journey into the depths" is undertaken at the behest of the Mother and leads to an even older and deeper feminine force. Contact with this deeper archetypal feminine energy results in renewed possibilities of creative action and success in the world.

Sedna: The Handless Maiden

In the native cultures of Alaska and the Bering Straits, Sedna, the Queen of the Sea, is a similar figure. In those traditional indigenous cultures, Sedna is believed to live at the bottom of the ocean and to have control of all the marine mammals, who were once her own fingers before her father cut them off. It all came about in this way:

Sedna was a beautiful young woman, much sought after by suitors from many different bands. They offered her father larger and larger "bride prices," but she would not accept any of them. Her father longed for the riches the suitors offered. In an effort to coerce her into marrying one of them, he took her out in his boat and threw her into the water, telling her he would take her back into the boat only if she agreed to marry one of the suitors and accept the bride gifts he offered. Sedna was clinging to the side of the boat, and each time she refused, her father cut off one of her fingers. She refused ten times, and when her last finger was severed, she sank to the bottom of the sea. Her severed digits became the whales and seals and otters and polar bears that the people of that ecosystem rely on for sustenance and survival.

Because she has no fingers, Sedna can not comb her hair or groom herself. When her hair becomes hopelessly tangled and full of lice, she is filled with anger and grief and calls all her parthenogenically created children to return to her and stay with her. The seas become empty, and the people starve. It is then that the spiritually gifted ones, the shamans and shamanas, have to take the archetypal spirit journey into the depths, to comb and groom the Goddess's hair and sing to her and restore her spirits so that she will release her children to feed in the seas again, and again become the living food of the people (Fig. 12).

The horrifying way in which Sedna loses her fingers places her clearly in the archetypal realm of "Handless Maiden," the feminine spirit dominated and subjugated, but not crushed or defeated, by the masculinist/patriarchal world-view. The shaman's journey into the depths in order to retrieve the gifts of life and continued survival from the Mother of All is undertaken in various forms in all cultures, even in the dreams of contemporary men and women living in urban industrial societies, as the dream of the freelance writer clearly exemplifies.

The details of the dream parallel other mythological accounts of heroic descent into the underworld to retrieve the lost treasure—like those of Innana, Persephone, Izanagi, Psyche, Hoder, and

Figure 12. (North Polar Region) A Shaman, riding his drum deep in trance, combs and smooths Sea Mother Sedna's tangled hair (a task she cannot perform for herself because her fingers have been cut off and transformed into all the sea mammals) while her dog-child looks on.

others—at least in part because in his waking life the dreamer has wholeheartedly undertaken his own unique and personal version of the archetypal hero/heroine's task. All people who make the courageous choice to live more consciously, creatively, and expressively must make a "descent into the depths" to seek the creative energies and ideas that lie deep within. When this choice is made along with a commitment to provide for a family at the same time, the energies released and sought are tremendous. It is the combination and blending of interior work and work in the world that always evokes these archetypal energies most clearly and vividly.

Holmes and Watson Sell a Mansion

When I was writing this chapter, I had a curious (and funny) dream giving metaphoric shape to the effort to talk, as a man, about the archetype of the Great Mother. In the dream,

I am both Sherlock Holmes and Dr. Watson. We have taken on the task of acting as the agents in selling an old mansion

filled with *objets d'art* from around the world, collected
when the British Empire was at its height. We negotiate the
sale to a very modern character—a very strong and professional black woman, who seems to be both an M.D. and a
Ph.D. She wears vibrant colors and big African gold jewelry.
She does not want any of the art or furnishings, and we have
to clear out the house before she will take occupancy. There
is some clue that we are seeking in the frantic stripping of
the house before she takes full possession of it—a clue to an
ancient crime that we wish to solve, and that apparently she
wishes us to solve as well, because she joins us, standing
around and offering friendly and firm encouragement as we
rush around removing the statues and paintings and tapes-
tries and displays of arms, etc. As we work to remove the layers of decoration, I am struck with the beauty and exquisite
workmanship of the building as a whole, a beauty that had
been obscured by the "Victorian clutter"...

Without suggesting that the meanings of this dream are
limited to those that I am aware of, I can say with the certainty of
the "aha" that at one level the "crime" is patriarchy and the
global oppression of the feminine in general, and individual
women in particular. The tremendously accomplished black
woman is, at one level, another image of the Goddess, the Great
Mother herself. The dream image emphasizes her immediate
contemporary quality in contrast to the historical quality of
Holmes, Watson, and the "spoils" of the British Empire that she
insists we remove before she accepts the house. At one level, it is
a metaphor of the effort to remove the artifacts of sexism from
my own psyche. At another, it reflects the desire that this book
will have a similar, collective effect.

"Holmes" is the "detective," the "investigator"; whereas
"Watson" is the "writer" (and being a "doctor," he is also the
writer concerned with healing). The black woman embodies the
energy of the Goddess herself—incredibly vital and contemporary, particularly in contrast to Holmes' and Watson's Victorian
quality. Despite the antiquity of much of the iconography and
other mythological evidence of the archetypal Great Mother, her
reality is completely modern (even postmodern).

The "ancient crime" that we are attempting to solve as we

remove the decorations from the house is, at one level at least, the murder of First Woman by First Man, alluded to in the previous chapter. Clearing away the distracting stereotyped images of masculinity and femininity that are most recently inherited from the period of European colonialism is a necessary step in restoring the Great Goddess to her rightful estate. In the process, the "great crime" of gender oppression must be uncovered and solved. Perhaps the best news is that when this is accomplished, the basic structure of the mansion (both human society and the collective, objective psyche on the one hand, and the basic pattern of the natural physical world on the other) is revealed to be beautiful and structurally sound. At another level, all the "art" is "decoration," cultural/intellectual distraction and a "cover-up" of the fundamental structure of the physical world—the realm of Maya, the sacred body of the Goddess herself. At that level, "cleaning out the house" is the symbolic equivalent of removing the veil of Isis, the ancient (and ultimately impossible) task of all initiates into the mysteries of the Great Mother.

Like so many actual black professional women in the industrial world today, the Great Mother has suffered tremendous oppression and has arisen from that oppression even stronger (and even less willing to play the game of polite deference and submission). Without her powerful nurturing and transformative energy, the patriarchal world is doomed to self-destruction. This self-destruction seems inevitable, like the "twilight of the gods," or the choking curse of the "wasteland" brought about by industrial pollution and mismanagement. However, it is the continued suppression of these energies that makes this approaching doom seem inevitable, and it is precisely in the archetypal energies and possibilities of the Great Mother that the solution to these seemingly insoluble problems lie.

It also strikes me that in the course of solving the mystery, Holmes and Watson must grow and change themselves, particularly in their "Victorian" attitudes about women. The tendency of the characters in Conan Doyle's stories to either ignore women or to hold them in exaggeratedly high regard represents tendencies in my own psyche that must change, as well as collective patterns of oppression that must be revealed and discarded.

A Gift for the Mother-in-law

Another dream that conveys a clear sense of the emergence of the archetypal Great Mother into the lives and experiences of contemporary people was shared with me in the summer of 1994, while I was attending the annual conference of the Association for the Study of Dreams, held that year at the University of Leiden in Holland. During the conference, I facilitated an afternoon training workshop focused on the group participation, "if it were my dream..." style of dream work that I regularly teach and practice. A woman currently living in Belgium offered a dream of her own as a concrete example for the group to work with to gain experience in applying the basic techniques that we had discussed in theory in the first half of the workshop.

> In her dream, she finds herself in a little potting shed behind her house. She experiences a great need to urinate, and is considering doing it right there in the musty old shed among the broken pots and rusting tools, when an unknown and officious man enters and tells her she has no business being where she is. This is very annoying to her, since this is her house and her shed, but she acquiesces without voicing her anger and resentment at his unwelcome intrusion into her supposedly "private" space. When she emerges, she is surprised to discover that she is no longer on her own property, but standing on a street in a little town in France where she once made a pilgrimage in waking life to visit a shrine of the Virgin Mary located in a nearby convent.
>
> As she recognizes where she is, she remembers in the dream that a charming old woman, the mother-in-law of an old friend of hers, is staying in a nearby bed and breakfast in the town. She remembers that she has purchased a little gift for the old woman, a little sachet made of dried aromatic herbs and flowers sewn into a pouch made from "ethnic," hand-woven cloth. She debates internally in the dream if her gift will cause her to appear "pushy," (after all, it's not *her* mother-in-law), or whether it may inspire invidious comparisons with the less beautiful, less thoughtful gifts that the daughter-in-law herself has given to her visiting mother-in-law. Upon consideration, she decides that this doesn't matter—"let the chips fall where they may."

As she walks through the town toward the bed & breakfast, she notices a bus coming up behind her. She decides to board the bus and ride the couple of blocks she has left to go to save herself from possibly tiring herself unduly with the walk in the hot sun. She boards the bus and tries to pay the nominal fare, but the driver refuses to accept her money and tells her that she has "the wrong change." She looks at the coins and tries to determine if she has made a mistake and mixed her French francs with another country's currency. She can't see anything wrong with the money, but she cannot tell for sure. She tells the driver that she's sorry and that she will get off and walk, but the driver tells her that she can't get off, and that the fare is constantly increasing the farther she rides. She is dumbfounded and angry. This is simply not fair, and crazy to boot! She awakens with these feelings of outrage and confusion uppermost in her mind.

As the diverse international group assembled for the workshop began to explore the dream, it became clear that the dreamer was a woman with deep religious and spiritual feelings. Raised a Catholic, in recent years she had become more and more concerned and involved with ecological issues, seeing in them the concrete expression of her deepening spiritual understanding of the sacredness of "God's creation," the natural world. She also expressed an increasing interest in the perspective of the ancient goddess-worshipping cultures that view nature as inherently sacred, as "the Great Mother's Physical Body," although she suggested that she had found little or no support for her explorations or for her evolving spiritual point of view in the liturgy and dogma of the institutional church of her youth.

With these details of her life revealed, the dream itself takes on the aspect of a symbolic comment on the unresolved tensions between her internalized religious restrictions and her evolving spiritual perspective. The dream gives symbolic shape to these tensions with the introjected values of the patriarchal church and how they "pop up" and interfere with her "private" spiritual life. In "the potting shed" (where seeds are planted and new seedlings are transplanted and made ready for outdoor life), she feels free to express her deeper, but less socially acceptable spiritual feelings (relieving her bladder), but her "officious" (intro-jected) male spiritual authority will not allow her to even think her own private thoughts through to their conclusion.

There is a clear relationship between the "officious man in the potting shed" and the "officious bus driver." One appears spontaneously as an unknown man in an intimate private space, and the other appears as a socially sanctioned authority figure in a public space. At one level, they are both symbolic representations of the same energy; and at another, they represent the difference between an *introjected figure* (an external energy adopted as an interior reality, even though it is not an authentic internal aspect of character) and a *projected figure* (an intrapsychic energy perceived as an external force). In this instance, they are both animus figures, associated with thoughts and feelings about religion and spiritual principle, each emphasizing the particular psychological dynamic of introjection on the one hand, and projection on the other.

The two men perform the same function, one "inside" and one "outside." The "man in the potting shed" prevents the dreamer from relieving herself, and the "bus driver" prevents her from reaching her chosen destination and making her desired connection with the "mother-in-law." This mother-in-law is a very important figure, even though she does not appear directly. She is, at one important level, the Goddess, the "Mother" in and of the "law of nature." From the point of view of the "bus driver" (an image of the actual patriarchal leadership of the church at one level, and of the dreamer's projected animus energies for order and discipline on the other), she is "making the wrong change" (of mind and heart and spiritual perspective). The internal struggle between spontaneous spiritual development and the internalized beliefs and religious habits of a lifetime are given shape in the imagery of the dream. At the same time, these personal issues are placed in the context of the largest contemporary archetypal dramas of ecology and global social change.

There is an ominous note in the symbolic formulation the dream is presenting: The "cost" of "staying on the bus," even though it is taking her farther and farther away from her chosen (spiritual) destination, gets greater and greater the longer she rides, and she is forbidden to "get off." In this image, we can see clearly a symbolic statement of the dilemma of so many people raised in authoritarian religious traditions as they struggle with the demands of their own evolving spiritual understanding and the old prohibitions against even thinking about leaving the tradition ("getting off the bus").

The "money" in our dreams seldom refers in any major way to our actual financial resources in waking life, but rather tends to symbolize our emotional energies and resources (the real medium of exchange we use in our important dealings with one another). The dream appears to be saying that "staying on the bus" (of the traditional European Catholic Church) is "costing" her greater and greater amounts of emotional and life energy without fulfilling her deepest spiritual needs. Once again, the bus, a vehicle for collective transportation, appears, at one level at least, as a symbol of the dreamer's relationship to a collective institution, in this case the traditional institutional church.

The "invidious comparison" she thinks about between her own natural, feminine gift of the hand-woven aromatic sachet and the unnamed but somehow inferior gifts of the friend who is "more directly related" to the mother-in-law raises interesting questions. As we explored these questions, it transpired that the dreamer has several non-Catholic, eco-feminist friends who have come to their sense of relationship to the archetypal divine Great Earth Mother from a more "political" and "secular" perspective, rather than being drawn to her by their deepening spiritual experience. At this level, the dream appears to gently address a question of "spiritual pride" rising in the very midst of the dreamer's change in attitude and relationship to the divine in feminine form.

The fact that the most problematic figures in the dream are men, and that the "daughters-in-law" are the ones bringing the gifts, is a clear implication in the dream that the dreamer is related to the "Mother" through the male principle—the son/husband. This marks the dream as related to the problem of the injured animus, just like the dreams of the "mosquito-headed boxer," and the "man in the gorilla suit." It is not only a psychological truth, but a spiritual reality as well, that integration of the despised "other" is a necessary hero/heroine's task on the quest for more complete and conscious relationship with the divine. It is the "officious men" that block the path to connection to the "mother-in-law," and it is, ironically but not accidentally, their very energies that are required in order to connect with her more fully.

There is an interesting implication in the fact that the supposedly inferior "gifts of the friend" are unspecified. The dream could easily have included a specific image for the "inferior or inappropriate gift"—an ash tray for a woman who doesn't smoke, or a gift certificate for a meal at a franchise hamburger chain for a vegetarian—but since the dream itself remains silent about the actual gift, the only evidence we have that the friend's gift is in fact "less thoughtful and appropriate" is *the unsupported opinion of the dream ego.* Whenever the dream fails to confirm an opinion held by the dream ego figure, it is always worth asking if this is another example of the dream suggesting that the dreamer holds an opinion in waking life that is in error, or is at very least in need of conscious reexamination and review.

Although we did not get to this question in our group exploration of the dream in Leiden (the limited time available for the workshop was insufficient to allow us to follow all the various threads of possibility—it always is), it has since occurred to me that in my version of the dream, there is also a gentle admonition to let go of the idea that my "spiritual" approach to the Goddess is somehow superior to the more "secular" approaches of my eco-feminist friends.

Dreams and the Selective Blindness of Waking Consciousness

When a person holds an erroneous opinion in waking life, the dream is faced with a difficult problem: It must depict the dreamer holding the opinion, and also provide a symbolic experience that invites the dreamer to reexamine the question and become more conscious of the truth of the situation. Even if my projection is in error with regard to this particular dream, it is still always worth looking for the generic situation where the only evidence that something is true is the unsupported opinion of the dream ego and asking if it is another example of the dream making use of this archetypal symbolic form to suggest that waking life opinions need to be reexamined and evaluated.

In actual practice, it is just this kind of image that the dreamer is least likely to be able to see on his or her own. The experience of the dream is that "of course" the gifts of the "the others" are inferior, and it doesn't even occur to me as dreamer to look for spontaneous confirmation of that opinion from the dream itself. The dream experience itself is a metaphor of the strength of my projections and the extent to which they warp and color my perceptions in waking life. It is precisely at junctures of this kind that the fresh eyes and fresh ears with which others see and hear my dream can be of greatest use and value to me, the dreamer. Even though I am not likely on my own to notice that the "inferior gifts" are unspecified and that there may be significance to that omission, it is quite likely to be noticed by someone else in my dream group.

The dream world does not often use the idea of "gift" lightly or casually. To the extent that it is "gifts" that are being offered and compared, it is quite likely that the dream is also coming to suggest to the dreamer that she has disparaging some of her own gifts without even exploring them or knowing what they are. This, coupled with the general indication that the masculine energies of the psyche are the most "officious" and "out of control," suggests that some of these supposedly "inferior gifts" may be gifts of masculine psychospiritual energy, and that their true worth may be much greater than she has presumed.

Once again, this dream demonstrates how the most ancient and archetypal mythic dramas of our individual and collective struggles regularly assume the costumes and settings of our mundane daily lives, while remaining rooted in our deepest individual and collective spiritual desires, intuitions, and longings. The dreamer had not imagined herself as a mythic heroine or a kind of modern Antigone, struggling to balance her responsibilities to support the official requirements of the state religion on the one hand, and her deepest loyalties to her blood and her most deeply felt spiritual intuitions on the other; but her dream takes her to that same universal drama of divided loyalty and self-awareness, and gently invites her to discern that same order of archetypal moral choice in her own life.

In this dream, the dreamer never arrives in the presence of the "mother-in-law," and we never actually catch a glimpse of her. There is some theoretical reason to imagine that if the dreamer had made it all the way into her presence, she might have appeared as black. In the dreams of many contemporary women and men, the image of the archetypal Great Mother is appearing with very dark visage, echoing the medieval tradition of the "Black Madonna" and the Hindu tradition of the Goddess with "skin as black as night." Often in contemporary dreams she takes the form of a very large black woman, who simultaneously befriends and scolds the dreamer for some omission. Once again, the archetypal association of "blackness" with "unconsciousness" is evident in these images. Like many black women in waking life, the Great Mother appears to be gaining power (in the psyche) directly from her outcast and abandoned state. The energies that are expended in suppressing a psychospiritual complex of feelings, ideas, and energies for creative/expressive action invariably "charge" and potentiate the suppressed complex with even more power and energy (which, in turn, requires even more energy to keep suppressed, so that the self-defeating spirals of neurotic behavior and frustrating energy waste are perpetuated).

The archetypal energies of the so-called Great Mother have been in this "pressure cooker" of repression and consequent energy build-up for thousands of years and are boiling to the surface in the escalating external collective crises of ecological disaster, as well as in the internal personal crises of more and more individual lives. Often when these archetypal energies appear in dreams, they appear in the form of the tremendously powerful and ambiguously feeling-toned "black woman."

Western patriarchal society was struggling with this terrible problem of the separation from the Great Mother even before the rise of industrial culture made the "wasteland" such a global reality. The "lost treasure" of the Grail in medieval legend is, at this level, exactly the same as the "lost treasure" of the enchanted frog story. It can only be recovered if the seemingly despised and down-trodden element of psyche and society is recognized and elevated once again to its proper position of honor, importance, and spiritual significance.

When this is accomplished, then even the terrible consequences of the destruction of the natural world, the extermination of whole species, and the genocidal warfare directed against parts of the human family can be reversed and healed. To accomplish this reconciliation, the disconnected and hubris-filled elements of psyche and society must be reintegrated into the whole; the intellect and the will must once again become the willing servants and friends of the heart and the spirit. The dominant powers of both psyche and society *for their own survival,* let alone the recovery of the "lost treasure," must become the protectors and guardians of the weak and the despised, rather than their haughty and unfeeling jailers and executioners.

As Carl Jung suggested on many occasions, the individual who accomplishes this task of interior balancing and self-awareness accomplishes something of tremendous social and collective importance.

To accomplish this, the dreams of contemporary men and women are revealing images of the Great Mother with more and more frequency and urgency at the same time that the planetary issues of ecological balance and biodiversity, and of social, economic, and ultimately spiritual justice, become more and more pressing.

All dreams come in the service of health and wholeness, which means that no dream ever came to anyone to tell them, "Nyeah, nyeah, you've got these problems and you can't do anything about them!" This is as true at the collective level as it is at the level of individual psychology. If a person dreams about an issue or a problem, it means that there is some possibility of creative response and transformative action, or else the dream would not have even been remembered in the first place.

To the extent that many of the dreams recounted and discussed here have implications for large collective issues of survival and growth, the dreamers of those dreams have a potential creative role to play in the collective transformation and solution of those problems as well. We as a species are responsible for generating the disasters that loom so ominously before us; and for that reason alone, we have a role to play in averting and transforming them. One of the most potentially powerful and useful sources of the creative energy and conscious insight necessary to transform our individual and collective circumstances is the archetypal complex that Jung called "the Great Mother." She is awakening in the collective psyche once again, and we continue to repress and ignore her only at our peril. To embrace her and give her her due is to release previously unimagined and unimaginable energies for growth, change, and reconciliation.

SUMMARY

The ancient Welsh myth of the Goddess Ceridooen (Ceridwen) and her furious pursuit of Little Gooyion (Gwion Bach) is a narrative revealing the basic shape of the archetype Carl Jung called "the Great Mother." This collective energy pattern is one of the most ancient to manifest itself in the human psyche. The archaeological evidence is overwhelming that the earliest human beings perceived the divine not as God-the-Allfather, but rather as the Great Goddess, Mother of All.

The suppression of her worship and the theological corollary of her worship, a belief in transmigration of souls to new bodies in "metempsychosis" and reincarnation, has done nothing to alter the fundamental power of this archetype in the psyche of contemporary people. The reacquisition of a more conscious relationship with this archetype, both individually and collectively, appears to be absolutely necessary if the consequences of oppressive global patriarchy and ecological destruction of the biosphere are to halted and reversed. Central to this effort is the restoration of a sense of numinosity and sacredness to nature and the physical world, which in the prehistoric matriarchal world were viewed with religious awe and reverence as the actual body of the Great Mother. Not only was the Earth revered as the "Mother of All," but she was also seen as the "Great Devourer, Death," and worshipped in her negative and destructive guises with equal spiritual fervor.

Inferential evidence is very strong that the prehistoric worship of the Great Goddess involved a belief that males had no central role in procreation and that sexual union was not related to pregnancy. With the arrival of the patriarchal, herd-tending Indo-Europeans, the agrarian, matriarchal Pelasgians were overthrown; and a new cosmological order was established that viewed the environment as "fallen" and unworthy of religious feeling–a confused collection of "raw materials" calling out to be "organized and exploited" by inherently superior masculine technologies. The desacralization of the physical world was also imposed on women, who ceased to be representatives of the Goddess on earth and became instead mere property and "raw materials" unfortunately necessary for the propagation of the species and the production of male offspring.

The suppression of the earlier intuitions of the feminine face of the divine has tended to make the spontaneous manifestations of this arche-

type appear fearsome and destructive, but in the same fashion that the "lost treasure" can only be recovered by "kissing the enchanted frog," so the "lost treasure" of ecological balance and healthy relationship with the physical environment and the deep unconscious can only be reclaimed through restoration and transformation of individual and collective relationship with this energy.

Several dreams of contemporary men and women are offered as specific examples of this important archetypal energy manifesting spontaneously in the interior lives of modern people.

In the course of discussing these dreams, it is noted that when a dreamer remembers a dream in which the dream ego figure holds a strong opinion or view of events that is not spontaneously confirmed by the images and events in the dream, it is always worth asking the question: Is the dream coming in part to suggest that the dreamer holds an equally strong view or opinion in waking life that it not in accord with the actual situation?

Chapter 5
HEROD'S TROOPS AND
THE PERPETUAL PLIGHT
OF THE DIVINE CHILD

One of the essential features of the child motif is its futurity. Hence the occurrence of the child motif in the psychology of the individual signifies as a rule an anticipation of future developments, even though at first sight it may seem like a retrospective configuration.

C. G. Jung

For most Westerners, the most familiar "Divine Child" story comes from the birth narrative of Jesus in the New Testament gospel of Matthew. There we are told that Joseph and Mary, the earthly parents of the as-yet-unborn Divine Child, must make the arduous journey from the town of Nazareth, where they regularly live and work, to the little village of Bethlehem, because the family must be officially enrolled on the tax ledgers at Joseph's ancestral and traditional/legal clan residence. The emperor in distant Rome, Caesar Augustus, has decreed that all the people in his world dominions, including the conquered province of Israel, shall pay taxes directly to him, instead of through local middlemen, as had been the case previously. By the time of these events, the once important town of Bethlehem, the ancient "City of David," has become a rural backwater, all but abandoned by history and commerce centuries earlier, long before the Roman occupation.

A number of factors arise that make the journey and the birth difficult. First, it is the middle of winter; the weather is inclement, and the roads are in bad shape. (T.S. Eliot imagines the difficult journey of the Magi toward Bethlehem "with the camels lying down in the snow...") The journey takes longer than Joseph had anticipated; and to make matters worse, when they finally do arrive, the unusual influx of travelers coming to register on the new imperial tax rolls has filled all the available overnight accommodations. There is no room at the inn, so the pregnant Mary must bed down in the stable. There, among the farm animals and beasts of burden, she gives birth to her child and lays the newborn infant in the trough where the cattle feed.

As though these difficulties attending the birth were not enough, Herod, the usurper puppet-king of conquered Israel set up by the occupying Romans, a superstitious and power-crazed man, has gotten wind of the fact that the birth of this unusual child has been "foretold in the stars." He puts his trust in seers and "psychic consultants," and they tell him that the newborn child in Bethlehem is destined to become "King of Israel"—the title Herod himself wants to hang onto as long as possible (forever, if he can manage it). If he does have to die and give up the throne and the title, the next best thing is to pass them on to his own son—definitely not to some low-born, unfairly favored upstart from the most backward and rural part of the kingdom. So in typical impulsive and imperial fashion, he orders his own household troops, the personal palace bodyguards allowed him by his Roman overlords, into the field to kill *all* the children born recently in and around the town of Bethlehem, just to make sure they get the child referred to in the prophecy.

Fortunately, Joseph is warned by an angel in a dream that Herod's soldiers are on their way with orders to kill all the children, so he and Mary and the baby flee southward toward Egypt to avoid the ferocious, royally sponsored pogrom. In the folk narratives that cluster around the canonical gospel stories of the "Flight into Egypt," there are many references to animals and dreams and the forces of nature coming miraculously to the aid of the holy refugee family. The animals and birds, the plants and trees, and the angels all conspire to feed and protect the infant and help the family get beyond the reach of Herod's assassins so that the child can grow to maturity and fulfill his destiny of revitalizing and resacralizing the entire world (one minor side effect of which is the eclipse of the House of Herod).

The "Herod" Within

"Herod" always gives his troops the same orders, because he is an example of the archetypal oppressive, imperial, inse-cure, power-crazed ego in its threatened, preemptive, defensive posture. Recently, at the collective level, Herod's archetypal orders were memorialized in the form of an illegal souvenir arm patch worn by some of the men of the 82nd Airborne celebrat-ing their tours of duty in Viet Nam. The patch depicts a grinning skull, wearing the distinctive black beret, with the words "Kill 'em all and let God sort 'em out!" emblazoned around the outer edge of the design. It is reported that the same sentiment was expressed by Soviet Russian soldiers as they followed Herod's orders to burn and "clean up" the countryside in Afghanistan.

In 1209, Pope Innocent III organized the infamous Albigen-sian Crusade to rid Southern France of the "heretical" Cathars. On July 22nd of that year, the Crusaders reached the town of Beziers, not far from the Spanish border. There they were faced with a mixed population of Cathars and loyal Roman Catholics. When the town council opened the gates but refused to point out suspected Cathars to the invaders, the soldiers turned to the papal legate accompanying the army, Abbot Arnold Amaury of Citeaux, and asked what means they should use to separate the heretics from the true believers. That gentleman is reported to have said, "Kill all of them; God will know his own."

I do not believe that either the black humorists of the 82nd Airborne or the grim Soviet "Afgantzi" veterans were secret scholars of the Albigensian Crusade. The spontaneous reappear-ance of almost precisely the same phrase in almost precisely the same set of circumstances is another grimly clear example of the way the inherent predisposition of archetypal energies and pat-terns manifests itself in essentially the same form, over and over again, in similar "generic" human circumstances. The inevitable repetition of archetypal forms is one of the main reasons why it is absolutely true that "those who do not understand history are doomed to repeat it."

The effort to abort genuine growth and change, both individual and collective, always takes a similar symbolic form. The actions and underlying motivations of "Herod's troops" are ever the same, no matter in what period of history they make their appearance, and no matter what political ideology they purport to represent and defend on either the collective or the personal level, because they are ever the same within the psyche. It is the "conservative" elements of human consciousness, the elements that prefer the pains and tribulations and injustices that are known and familiar to those that are only implied and hinted at by the possibility of individual and collective change, that always mobilize to prevent the birth of the archetypal Divine Child of creative new possibility. To the most conservative, *all* new possibilities must be rejected on principle, without exploration or analysis, in order to make sure that nothing "slips by" that might alter the "sacred," limited, "fundamental" vision.

The Cosmic Conspiracy to Protect the Divine Child

But the Divine Child also has *allies* in the collective, archetypal psyche. The cosmos itself seems to be secretly committed to the continuing experiment of evolution, particularly the evolution of conscious self-awareness that the Divine Child represents both in dreams and in the misplaced literalism of symbolic collective historical and contemporary events.

Taliessen, the reincarnated Little Gooyion introduced in the previous chapter as the re-born magician/poet son of the Great Mother in one of her Celtic guises, also exemplifies the archetypal Divine Child. He is able to speak poetry and wisdom at birth, and his poetic words transform the entire world of human possibility as he grows into maturity. In that version of the Divine Child mythos, the Goddess herself takes on the role of Herod's troops, pursuing and attempting to destroy her own offspring in vengeance for his evolving consciousness and independence from her control and domination.

Very similar stories are told about the difficulties attending the births of Krishna, Muhammad, Hermes, Herakles, Asklepios, and Horus—to name but a few of the more familiar figures who give specific shape to the archetype of Divine Child. All these divine children are persecuted at birth and miraculously aided by the forces of nature, and each grows up to establish a new "dispensation"—a renewed collective, social, and cultural form for economic, political, and, most importantly, spiritual life—one consequence of which is the overthrow of "the old order" that toiled so diligently to preserve its interests by preventing the infant from being born and growing up. In that sense, the jealous gods and goddesses who connive to prevent Izanagi and Izanami from consummating their nuptials represent the same archetypal conservatism.

On the Northern Pacific Coast of North America, there are innumerable stories of the difficult birth and miraculous gifts of Raven, yet another exemplar of the Divine Child.

Raven Steals the Sun

It is said that Raven was born first at a time when there was no Sun. Everything was in complete darkness, so nothing was able to grow. As a consequence, parents were forced to eat their children as soon as they were born because there was nothing else to eat. When Raven was born, he cried out in fear and protest as his mother reached out to devour him.

"Wait! Don't eat me! There must be another way to find food for the people to eat! Why is there no Sun? Why do the people starve in darkness?"

"Because the Old Man Who Owns the Sun keeps it hidden away in his lodge and will not share it with the people," his mother replies.

"Then do not eat me! I will find a way to steal the Sun and bring it to the people!" Raven cries.

Raven's mother is very hungry, but she does not want to eat her son. She pauses, struggling with herself and her hunger. Is it actually possible that someone might end this terrible darkness and bring light and food to the people?"

So, thinking that thought, and hearing her son's bold words, she controls her hunger and releases him.

Raven flutters off into the darkness. "Where does the Old Man Who Owns the Sun live?" he calls out.

"People say he lives far to the North," his mother's reply echoes in the darkness.

Raven searches inside himself for what North feels like and flies off in that direction. He flies on and on through the great darkness for a long, long time. Then, at last, the sky grows slowly brighter until Raven can just make out a landscape of trees and rivers and mountains. It is all indescribably beautiful, and Raven sees that there is food *everywhere!* He flies down and gorges himself on salmon berries and wild onions and grubs from a fallen tree. Finally, he flies on, a little more heavily, toward the apparent source of mysterious light.

Eventually he comes to a land that looks like perpetual dawn. The great trees drip with dew, and the breezes blow gently, carrying the scent of the forest and the ocean.

Raven lands on the bough of a great cedar tree and surveys the scene. The mysterious light seems to be coming from a huge lodge built all of cedar. It is imposing and grand, more like a mountain than a house. The pale dawn light seems to be coming from there, and Raven decides that it must be the lodge of the Old Man Who Owns the Sun.

He flies around it several times, but he can not find an opening, not even a smoke-hole. Then he lands and hops slowly around the great lodge, examining its foundations. But still he can find no means of entry. The great lodge is made of wood, but it is completely solid like a huge rock.

At last he hears the sound of a young woman singing. He flies back up to the cedar bough to watch and listen. A young woman with skin that seems to glow with its own light comes out of the lodge and walks to the edge of the beautiful clear stream that flows along beneath the tree that Raven is perching in.

As she walks to and fro, she sings a plaintive little song about her endlessly repetitive task of drawing the sweetest and best water for her father's meals and for his regular purifying sweat bath.

Sure enough, as Raven watches and waits, the young woman comes and goes, always at the same time, carrying water for her father and singing her work song. Raven also notices that after she fills her buckets, she always kneels down and cups her hands and takes a drink of water herself before she shoulders her yoke and returns to the lodge. Raven ponders all this carefully, and finally decides on a plan.

The next time she comes down to the bank of the stream, Raven changes himself into a salmon berry (in some versions, into a pine needle, another symbol of perpetual fertility) and drops down into the water just as the daughter of the Man Who Owns the Sun stoops down for her regular drink. In this form, she inadvertently swallows him. Like Ceridooen, having taken Raven into her body in this fashion, the daughter of the Old Man Who Owned the Sun becomes pregnant with Raven.

Soon her growing belly begins to show. Her father is enraged. How could this have happened? Who is the father? But the Sun Princess only weeps and swears that she has no idea how it had happened or who the father could be. As the nine long months of her pregnancy draw to a close, her father, seeing her misery and confusion are genuine, relents a little in his anger; and when Raven is born a second time as a shining little baby boy, the First Grandfather is totally charmed and won over by his new grandson.

The boy is perfect, and like his new mother and grandfather, he seems to glow from within with his own light. The little baby is very precocious, and as soon as he emerges, he starts crawling around and getting into everything. Of course, Raven is searching for where the Old Man has hidden the Sun. Newborn Raven/child plays briefly and experimentally with everything he finds, but only long enough to make sure that the new thing is not the hiding place of the Sun. Then he throws his new toy aside and cries and wails for something else. He cries and cries and cries, until finally there is nothing new left for him to play with except the Sun.

At first, the grandfather did not want to let even his adorable little grandson touch his most precious treasure, but the child cries and shrieks unceasingly, even pointing up into the rafters. Up there the Sun glows through the sides of the great cedar box where the Old Man has it hidden and out of reach. Eventually, just to get a little peace, the Old Man tells his daughter that she can retrieve the Sun from its hiding place and let her child play with it.

No sooner does his mother get the Sun down from the rafters for him to play with than Raven stops crying and begins to coo happily. The little boy Raven hugs the Sun and rolls it back and forth in front of the hearth pit, gurgling with delight, and singing a gentle, wordless song of pleasure over his new toy.

His mother and grandfather wait nervously for him to grow tired of playing with Sun and to start crying again, but he doesn't. He just plays happily and quietly, amusing himself with his new toy and singing his little baby song of contentment. The scene is suddenly so peaceful and so different from the endless howling and bedlam that had preceded it that in their relief, the Old Man and his daughter allow themselves to relax. They are both so tired from having had no sleep at all for so long that as they settle down and relax for the first time in ages, they both fall asleep.

Like Little Gooyion, as soon as Raven sees that the Old Man and his daughter have nodded off at last, he seizes the moment and grabs the long-sought prize. Reassuming his raven shape, he seizes the Sun in his beak and flies up toward the smoke-hole at the center of the high ceiling to escape with his prize into the sky. But the sound of his frantically beating wings awakens the Old Man and his daughter.

As soon as they see what Raven is doing, they both jump up and start throwing huge wet logs on the hearth fire, making billowing clouds of thick, black smoke to clog and block the smoke-hole and keep Raven from escaping. But Raven struggles on through the choking black smoke and wriggles and twists himself out the hole. He bursts forth into the sky with the Sun in his beak, bringing light to the world with the First Sunrise.

Before he stole the Sun, the Northwest native storytellers say, Raven was completely white, like all the creatures that live and die in darkness without ever seeing the light. But the smoke from the Old Man's hearth fire covered him and stained him completely black while he was struggling to push the Sun out through the smoke-hole. And that is why all ravens are black now in the world where light has come at last and the Sun rises and sets every day (Fig. 13).

Figure 13. (Pacific Northwest) Raven, freshly blackened from his passage through the smoke-hole, releases the Sun into the sky.

The Never-Ending Task of the Divine Child

The parallels to the Taliessen story are many and significant. There is the devouring of the shape-changed child in seed form (at least in the versions where Raven changes himself into a salmon berry), the pursuit, the devouring mother, the bringing of a whole new way of life as a result of the Divine Child's escape from the powers that seek its destruction. In this story, the ancient archetypal symbolism of "light" as consciousness demonstrates itself again. The world is "dark" because it is unconscious, and the task of the Divine Child is to bring the light in the midst of darkness, to cause new consciousness to awaken in the depths of the psyche and make its way to the horizon of waking awareness and illuminate the new day of conscious possibility and action.

Of course, one consequence of this "dawning" (of new conscious self-awareness) is the overthrow of the old order of "dark" (unconscious) habit and precedent, "the way it's always been," before the new idea or new creative energy emerged into consciousness. The conservative forces of the status quo, both individual and collective, always mobilize, like Herod and the Old

Man and his daughter, to attempt to prevent the Divine Child from growing to maturity and bringing about this overturning of the old order.

Because the archetypal energy of the Divine Child is always focused on the overthrow of the old, prematurely closed, and limited frame of reference and possibility, it always exhibits qualities of the Shadow and the Trickster as well.

From the point of view of the established social order on the one hand, and the dominant pattern of waking ego consciousness on the other, the promise of the Divine Child to "make everything new again" is inevitably perceived as "a death threat." This guarantees that from the perspective of the conventions of my society—always remembering that those conventions may obtain only in the subculture that I identify with and may appear to be quite unconventional from the perspective of the dominant culture—the Divine Child will always appear as a negative "Shadow figure," a miscreant or a juvenile delinquent, or even more frequently as "an impossible burden."

Because the archetypal energy of the Divine Child is always associated with new ideas and emotions coming into conscious awareness, it will also always bear a deep connection to the archetypal Trickster as well. (We will examine Trickster in more detail in chapter 8.) Briefly, the Trickster is an archetype of human consciousness itself, with its "tricky" propensity for self-deception on the one hand, and tremendous creativity on the other. Since the Divine Child always heralds the possibility of new consciousness, it presents the image of a seemingly weak and unthreatening figure that is also capable of creating disruption and havoc through deception and totally unexpected, creative behavior.

The Death of the Divine Child in Modern Myth

Most of the mythic narratives that come down to us from the ancients are stories about the survival and success of the Divine Child despite the forces that are arrayed against it at its birth. Our ancestors were aware that their own human societies existed because the infant culture hero/heroine had survived to bring about the changes in conscious self-awareness that separated the humans from the other animals in the first place, in spite of the great weight and inertia of the world of nature to repeat herself and keep things ever the same.

In modern times, we have been given another set of myths, grimly describing the consequences of the failure to allow the Divine Child to grow into maturity and fulfill its world-shaping destiny. Jung himself was impressed with the science fiction story by John Wyndham, *The Midwich Cuckoos,* (twice made into a motion picture, once in England and once in the United States, and called *The Children of the Damned* both times) as an example of such a mythic narrative in which the archetypal Divine Child (or, in this case, children) are eventually slain by Herod's troops, once more played by the forces of government and officialdom.

In the John Wyndham story, unseen space invaders land in the rural community of Midwich in rural England, cutting off all communication with the outside world for a night. By morning the space invaders have disappeared, but it transpires that all the women in the community are pregnant. And nine months later they all bear unusually gifted and beautiful children, all of whom look distressingly alike and do not get along with the other children. Because of the unusual circumstances surrounding their collective conception and birth, the British government monitors the development and progress of the children as they grow unusually quickly into preadolescence. During this period, the secret government security agency in charge of monitoring the children discovers that similar events have taken place, and similar children have been born, all over the world.

The increasingly nervous government begins to view the children as a potential "national resource" and takes over their care and education directly, taking them away from their terrestrial mothers and foster fathers. They start to interest the children in the design of weapons, only to discover that all the children are in deep telepathic rapport with each other all over the planet. This "breach of national security" is too much for the government officials to bear; so one by one, each government makes the same decision—to kill the children before they grow up and become too powerful to be manipulated and controlled.

Sometimes people fail to heed the warning dreams, and Herod's troops arrive in time and succeed in exterminating the dangerous threat that the Divine Child always poses to the established order of life, both individual and collective.

The Divine Child in Dreams

The motif of "discovering the neglected/abandoned infant" is one of the most common manifestations of the archetype of the Divine Child in the dreams of contemporary people. Like the danger from which Little Gooyion flees after imbibing the elixir of Allwisdom, or the flight of the Holy Family from Bethlehem to Egypt to avoid the murderous soldiers sent by Herod, or Raven escaping from his original dark cannibal mother, and later from his rebirth mother and grandfather, the archetypal Divine Child is always born amidst trouble, with all the forces of the established world arrayed against it. But the promise is also always the same: If the child grows to maturity, the new creative energies and new conscious awareness it brings will transform and bring "new light" to the whole world.

The reports offered by the growing number of women "space alien abductees" about being impregnated by their captors and later having their fetuses removed resonate, at one level, with the archetypal pattern of the Divine Child myth. These "hybrid babies" have both an earthly parent and an unknown "sky parent." These children are said to be part of an effort to "save the earth" from the ravages of short-sighted human exploitation by forcing an evolutionary change in humankind itself through the blending of human and alien characteristics and intelligences. In this way, this postmodern sacred narrative developing out of the testimony of "abductees" carries forward the basic pattern of the Divine Child archetype. The Divine Child always comes amidst trouble for the purpose of transforming the human task of living in the entire world into a more "holy," integrated, and meaningful experience.

Some time ago, a woman shared a dream at a dream group I was facilitating:

> She opens a drawer and discovers a baby. In the dream, she remembers that she put the baby in the drawer *twenty years ago!* She is filled with shock and horror—how *could* she have taken responsibility for this baby and then neglected it in this way? She is filled with fear and shame, but to her amazement, the infant seems fine, virtually the same as when she forgot about it in the drawer twenty years earlier. As she stares in disbelief and horror at the tiny child, it makes eye-contact with her and says, "I'm dehydrated!"

As we worked with this dream, the dreamer shared with us that, yes, this was an actual drawer in her waking life, a drawer where twenty years ago she put an unfinished manuscript away "for safekeeping." Once again, in a very dramatic way, the dream demonstrated that the figure of the Divine Child is fundamentally connected with the energies of creativity and new possibility in the dreamer's life, in this case with the novel she had set aside when she decided to become pregnant and start a family.

The archetypal "neglected dream baby" usually appears in the dreams of particularly active and responsible people, people who have busy schedules filled with good works and activities that help others. For this reason, the people who have this generic dream are often particularly ashamed and appalled to dream themselves as so "irresponsible" as to take charge of a baby and then forget all about it. In these dreams, the neglected dream child almost never has a name, and therein lies an important clue to its significance. The active and responsible people who dream of the neglected baby generally have filled their waking lives with activities and priorities that all have names that can be written in appointment books and have left no time for those nascent possibilities of creative development that don't even have names yet—the "divine children" of creative intellectual, emotional, and spiritual possibility that always lie asleep in our psyches.

These possibilities may be neglected for long periods of time, but they do not die. In the course of working with the dream mentioned above, the dreamer said that she stopped working on her manuscript when she hit a particularly difficult writer's problem, and she decided to try to get pregnant "instead," because it was one of the only things she could think of that had "equal weight." She left the difficult manuscript in the drawer for twenty years while the tasks of parenthood took priority. Apparently her unconscious concurred in the shift of priorities to parenthood, but her children were now almost grown and leaving the house. The dream came when she realized that it was time to find a new central focus and organizing principle for her life. The neglected dream child is clear about what is necessary; it's "dehydrated," parched and thirsty for the waters of life and emotion that were "diverted" (from the point of view of the dream child at least) to the task of parenting.

The Guru's Drink of Water

There is a charming Hindu "framing story" that addresses the inevitability of returning to the postponed task of creative psychospiritual development. A young man apprentices himself to a guru and follows the old man on his wanderings, serving him as an acolyte. At one point, they find themselves in the middle of a deep, hot forest. The old man sits down on a rock and tells his apprentice to go and find water and bring him a drink before they can go on. The young man departs and searches for a pond or a stream.

Eventually he finds a stream, but as he is dipping the water to take back to his master, he looks up and sees a beautiful maiden in great distress. It turns out that she is the daughter of a king who is fighting for his life against a powerful magical enemy and is losing. Her father's last command to her was to flee for her life and seek a hero to protect her. The young man offers to help her, but she rejects him as a weakling and nobody—nothing like the hero she is seeking. The young man has fallen in love with her, and despite her rejection, he rises to the occasion. After a series of amazing adventures, he succeeds in overcoming the demonic usurper and winning the love and respect of the beautiful princess.

When the evil usurper is overthrown and the old king released from bondage, the young man marries the princess and becomes king. He takes up the life of a monarch and fathers several children and regularly goes hunting in the forest. One day he becomes separated from his retinue, and to his amazement, he comes upon the old man, sitting exactly where he left him so many years ago. The old man is a little put out and tells the young man that he certainly has taken his time finding the water, and that in the interim, the old man has become even more thirsty...

It is in this fashion that the deepest callings of our psychospiritual lives wait for us to mature and find "the waters of life" with which to nourish ourselves.

A man dreams:

> He is walking through the woods, carrying a suitcase, on the way to catch a train. Several children and their parents walk along with him, headed for the same train. The dreamer is annoyed that his pleasurable anticipation of a solitary ramble down the path in the forest is disappointed. His mild disappointment deepens into consternation as he realizes that now night is falling, and the adults have all disappeared leaving him alone with the children. He is now responsible for the children by default. He had never intended to take responsibility for these children, but he can't abandon them alone in the forest at night either. He walks on, casually talking with the children and asking their names so as not to communicate his upset and anxiety to them...

Here again, the children represent possibilities for creative expression and psychospiritual growth that do not yet even have names in the dreamer's waking life, but he realizes in the dream that he has "no choice" but to take responsibility for them, even though it is clear to him that looking after them will necessitate that he change the whole way he leads his life.

In dreams, as in mythology and sacred narrative, the Divine Child often reveals him/herself by the precocious abilities to speak, sing, communicate telepathically, levitate, tame wild animals, and perform other miraculous feats. The particular examples of the Divine Child's miraculous abilities in the dream(s) are often clues to the nature of the creative gift that has lain neglected in the dreamer's psyche and that is now calling for recognition.

Most often, it is a creative energy and possibility in the

dreamer's life that is the specific occasion for the archetypal energy of the Divine Child to take concrete shape in the dream world. Creativity itself is often symbolized by the image of "levitating" or flying without mechanical assistance. In this way, dreams of flying are often the "answer" to the dreams of the "neglected baby." The basic archetypal association between creativity and flying appears to constellate up around a symbolic association of gravity with conventionality; gravity/conventionality holds all but the creative few to the same level or plane of possibility. The creative person defies conventionality/gravity by levitating or flying. The style with which a person flies in dreams is often a symbolic indicator of that person's style of creative expression.

Dream Flying and Creativity

I once worked with a woman who was completing her training for her teaching credentials in an internship under a very strict and conventional supervisor. The intern student teacher, who was very intuitive and creative, kept dreaming that she was flying, but trying to disguise the fact by skimming along just an inch or two above the floor lest "other people" notice her unconventional behavior. The dreams clearly reflected, at one level at least, her solution to the dilemma of student teaching, where she feared that if she let her creativity flow easily into her teaching, she would receive a poor evaluation from her super-conventional internship supervisor.

The metaphor of defying gravity, particularly by vertical ascent, is also deeply associated with spiritual longing and achievement. It is another way in which creativity and spiritual development are archetypally linked. Obviously, elevators and helicopters are much too recent inventions to be archetypal images in and of themselves, but since they both give concrete manifestation to the ancient symbol of vertical ascent, they do have a strong tendency to be connected with the evolving spiritual issues in people's lives when they appear in their dreams.

I have taught for many years in a number of programs in the San Francisco Bay Area focused on spiritual development.

My particular specialty is, of course, dreams and dreaming, and the psychological, emotional, and creative energies they mobilize and release in the course of serious psychospiritual development. One of the common dreams that people in these programs report is of

> getting on an elevator, expecting to rise to a higher floor, and discovering that the elevator goes sideways and zooms around, and often ends up in a totally different building, or not in a building at all, but somewhere out of doors...

These dreams very often turn out to reflect the dreamer's expectations about what the spiritual development promoted by attending the programs will be like ("traditional" vertical ascent, what one naturally expects from an elevator), only to discover that the actual development of psyche and spirit takes them to totally new and unexpected places, often places outside of and beyond the structures of organized religion and traditional religious dogma.

This unexpected transformation of conventional thoughts and expectations through deep psychospiritual experience is what the Divine Child always brings. These dreams of flying and levitating, and taking wild unexpected rides in transverse elevators, are all fundamentally associated with one another. The ancient symbol of vertical ascent infuses the images of modern technology. When the Divine Child survives the efforts of Herod's troops to exterminate it, the result is often an unexpectedly wild ride in a dream helicopter or a dream elevator.

In the lives of most contemporary people, the dramas of psychospiritual development do not involve heroic struggles with evil, but rather the struggle to stay authentic and alive and growing, and not to succumb to the seductions of mechanically convenient life. The most responsible and busy people fill their waking hours with scheduled activities and commitments, so that there is no conscious time or energy left to nourish the Divine Child of new, evolving possibility that does not even yet have a name. It is the people who find themselves in this archetypally repeating predicament who will most often discover the image of the neglected, abandoned baby in their dreams. When they do, the quality of self-recrimination and anxiety, along with the unwillingness to accept the grotesque inconvenience that looking after the Infant Self of New Possibility inevitably entails, gives the most accurate indication of the state of that person's psychospiritual development at that moment.

"I Forgot I Was Enrolled in This Class–and Now It's Exam Time!"

There is also a deep and close association between the dreams of the "neglected and abandoned infant" and the dreams of the "forgotten class." Many people are familiar with their own versions of this classic "anxiety dream":

> I suddenly realize that I have been officially enrolled in a class since the beginning of the semester, but I have forgotten all about it. Now it is final exam time, and I realize that not only have I never attended class or done any of the reading, I have also forgotten to drop the class, and now I must take the final exam. I don't even know where the exam is being administered. I awaken in panic and dismay...

In my experience, this generic dream also reflects the dreamer's spiritual predicament. It is as though every person were automatically enrolled in an ongoing "class" at birth called something like "What Is Really Going On Here Below the Surface of Mere Appearance." Over the course of living our lives, we "forget" that answering this question is one of our primary commitments and obligations (symbolically reflected with exquisite emotional accuracy in the metaphor of "forgetting that we were enrolled in the class to begin with"). Every once an a while, the fact that we have neglected this psychospiritual inquiry and that a "final exam" is coming up (at every developmental milestone and ultimately at death) shakes our conventional attitude, and we tend to have some version of this dream.

This generic dream is most common among people who have attended college or university, although versions of it also occur to people whose formal education is minimal. I strongly suspect that the frequency and wide distribution of this kind of dream offers a strong collective criticism of Western formal education, as well as a

symbolic emotional commentary on the psychospiritual development of the individual dreamer. The widespread appearance of
this dream theme points clearly to a promise made and betrayed
by formal education, in both East and West, a promise to address
and answer our deepest and most existentially pressing questions
about the meaning and value of life. The regular recurrence of this
generic dream serves as a criticism of higher education in general,
as much as it indicates the individual dreamer's "forgetting" his or
her own deepest desires for spiritual knowledge and experience.

In fact, the promise of the Western intellectual tradition to
investigate and even resolve the most ancient existential questions of humanity's relationship with and to the divine, the problems of good and evil, of suffering and joy, of love and
indifference, of progress and stability, has been betrayed by the
failure of academic institutions to search for a continuing synthe-
sis of the ever more specialized and separated bodies of knowledge and information that the so-called Enlightenment
spawned. Every person who pursues "higher education" has this
promise somewhere in mind; and as we become increasingly specialized and higher education becomes increasingly compart-
mentalized, we become disillusioned about the possibility of
understanding, let alone solving, any of these issues. We "forget
that we are enrolled in the class," and are taken by surprise each
time there is an intimation that "a final exam" is in the offing.

However, the continuing good news is that all dreams really
do come in the service of health and wholeness. Whenever such a
dream appears that is focused in any recognizable way on some
issue in the dreamer's life that appears to be unsolvable, the fact
that the dream has occurred and been remembered at all is an
absolutely reliable indication that the dreamer has it within his or
her power to respond to the problem in some new, creative, transformative way. The dreamer may not be consciously aware that
these creative possibilities exist, but that is one of the reasons why
the dreams come with such emotional force and persistence—to
overcome the prematurely closed ideas and conventional formulations of what is possible. No matter how blasé and cynical we
become consciously, the hidden depths of creative energy in the

psyche are still there, ready and able to come to our aid in the resolution of even the deepest psychospiritual dilemma.

The Divine Child is the patron of all such changes in consciousness and creative possibility. The Divine Child is the part of our psyche that knows how to pass the exam in the forgotten class, how to bring light to the habitually darkened world, and how to transform the dreamer's individual life and collective society into a more accurate and true reflection of the (unconscious) Divine Source from which it ultimately springs. The forces of "the old order," Herod's troops, are always on guard at the crossroads with orders to kill the Divine Child and all those who would give aid and succor to the fugitive. But the forces of Nature herself are also secretly arrayed to help and protect the neglected infant, so the outcome is always in process—a process reflected in our dreams, both individually and collectively.

SUMMARY

The stories of the birth of Jesus and the adventures of infant Raven as he goes to steal the Sun are offered as specific examples of the archetype of the Divine Child. This archetype is always associated and intertwined with the archetypes of Shadow and Trickster. Reference is made to Gooyion Bach/Taliessen also being a specific example of the Divine Child archetype.

A number of dreams are also presented, particularly examples of the "neglected baby" and the "unprepared for the final exam" motifs, to illustrate the parallel between the mythic narratives and the spontaneous dreams of contemporary people.

The Divine Child symbolizes the possibilities of total transformation and development to new and previously unimagined levels of consciousness and authentic expressive awareness. The "neglected baby" is one of the most common archetypal symbols in dreams of this human possibility. The "unprepared for the final exam" motif in dreams also refers to the possibilities of making deep spiritual sense of the anomalies of contemporary life–a task all human beings are drawn to, and one we are all too likely to forget and neglect, particularly when the shining possibility of resolution of our psychospiritual difficulties and confusions through higher education and participation in conventional institutional religious practices proves to be a hollow promise. The cynicism born of frustrated and disappointed spiritual desire is the single greatest enemy of the archetypal energy of the Divine Child.

Through this set of connections, the archetypal qualities of dreams of flying without mechanical assistance (a primary metaphor of creativity), dreams of vertical ascent (even in such relatively modern conveyances as elevators and helicopters), and the classic dream of suddenly remembering the final exam of a class in which the dreamer has been enrolled all semester but has forgotten about until this moment are all related. These last two dream motifs tend to relate most directly to the unfulfilled (in many instances unconscious, and thus unacknowledged) spiritual longings of the dreamer–longings to live a life with deeper meaning and significance than mere waking comfort and convenience.

Chapter 6
OEDIPUS THE KING:
THE FOUNDATION MYTH OF
WESTERN PATRIARCHY

There must be a voice within us which is prepared to acknowledge the compelling power of the fate of Oedipus...and there actually is a motive in the story of *King Oedipus* which explains the verdict of this inner voice. His fate moves us only because it might have been our own, because the oracle laid upon us before our birth is the very curse that rested upon him. It may be that we are all destined to direct our first sexual impulses toward our mothers, and our first impulses of hatred and violence toward our fathers; our dreams convince us that we were.

Sigmund Freud

The story of Oedipus has been presented in several slightly different versions by several different ancient authors. The basic story is fairly consistent.

Laius and Jocasta are the king and queen of Thebes, in Greece. An oracle predicts that Laius' and Jocasta's first child will be a boy who will grow up to murder his father and sexually defile his mother. Their first child *is* a boy, and driven by fear of the oracle's prediction, Jocasta and Laius decide to have the infant killed in order to thwart the prophecy.

The man charged with doing the actual killing (like the

Huntsman in "Snow White and the Seven Dwarfs," an archetypal figure in his own right) cannot bring himself to kill the innocent newborn child cursed by the oracle and instead leaves him to die "naturally" of exposure, having taken the precautionary step of piercing the infant's foot and staking him to the earth so he can not escape. It is this wound that is the source of Oedipus's famous limp. It is also this injury which gives him his name *Oedipus*, which translates to "Swollen Foot" or "Swell Foot" in English. The soft-hearted servant (as always) can not bear to watch the infant's death agony, so he departs.

A shepherd comes by soon afterward and finds the nameless, tortured infant. This "good shepherd" takes the boy and presents him as a "divine gift" to the childless king and queen of Corinth, who in turn raise him into manhood as their own child.

The curse pursues Oedipus, and he hears it when he reaches adulthood. In order to escape the possibility that he will fulfill the dreadful prophecy, Oedipus, believing that his kindly foster parents are his real parents, flees from Corinth.

Once away from Corinth, Oedipus believes he has escaped the prophecy. When he encounters Laius, his real but unrecognized father, Oedipus kills him in an argument over the right-of-way at a crossroads.

Oedipus then goes on to Thebes, where he faces the riddle of the Sphinx. A monster, half-human, half-lion, with the wings of an eagle and a snake's tail, she guards the road to Thebes, asking each passerby the same riddle: "What walks on four legs in the morning, two legs in the afternoon, and three legs in the evening?" and killing all who fail to solve the riddle (Fig. 14).

Oedipus answers the riddle: "Man" (who crawls on all fours as a baby, walks on two legs in adulthood, and hobbles on a cane or a crutch in old age). This is the right answer, and the Sphinx throws herself off a cliff in frustration and despair when he solves her puzzle. (In her petulantly self-destructive behavior, the Sphinx reveals her archetypal kinship with other frustrated riddlers, like Rumplestiltzkin and Tom-Tit-Tot, who also destroy themselves when the puzzle of their correct names is solved.)

Having defeated the Sphinx, Oedipus is hailed as a hero and marries the widowed queen, Jocasta. They have several children and live quite happily for several years.

Eventually, a terrible drought and famine comes upon the land, and Jocasta and Oedipus call on the blind seer Teiresias to divine the cause of the problem. Teiresias explains that Jocasta and Oedipus are in fact mother and son, as well as wife and husband, and that this is the source of the infertility of the land. Faced with this ugly revelation, Jocasta commits suicide and

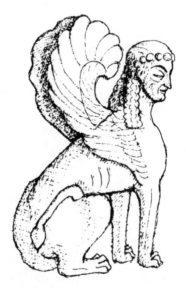

Figure 14. (Ancient Greece) The Sphinx (after a sculpture in the Museum of Corinth, 14' high, tentatively dated 4th century B.C.E.).

Oedipus blinds himself in shame and remorse. The hero Theseus, home from his adventures with Ariadne and the Minotaur and now king of Athens, takes the blinded Oedipus under his protection. Because of his ordeal, Oedipus has the power of healing touch and the ability to prophesy.

After his death, the twin sons of Oedipus and Jocasta become involved on opposite sides in a civil war over the rightful succession to the throne of Thebes; and all of the children except the youngest daughter, Ismene, are killed in the ensuing struggle and its vengeful aftermath.

Oedipus and Modern Thought

Immanuel Velikovsky argues that the Oedipus story is actually Egyptian and was only transposed to Greece late in its development. He suggests that the original Oedipus was an actual historical figure, the great apostate king Akhenaten, who attempted to impose monotheism on the traditionally polytheistic Egyptians. At one level, Velikovsky's argument is another example of how the deep, collective, archetypal resonances of some particular mythic symbolic narrative will echo and invite the feeling that it applies to more than any one particular local situation or example in which it appears. All archetypal narratives give the impression that they "originated elsewhere." Velikovsky says Oedipus originated in Egypt; Freud says Oedipus originates in the deep psyche. In one sense, both men are saying the same thing, offering their unique, individual testimony to their compelling experience of the universal, transpersonal, archetypal resonance of the story.

In this self-consciously tragic tale, Freud saw the basic repeating shape of the human (male) unconscious mind. The whole of human history becomes, for Freud, a tragically projected metaphor of the sexual struggle to "possess" the mother as a "primary object."

Freudian metaphors aside, the Oedipus story also gives symbolic shape to the inevitable struggle over the equally inevitable transfer of power from one generation to the next and the endless battle of the younger generation of male leaders to succeed the older generation of patriarchs before the older men are prepared to relinquish power. To this historical/political/economic picture, Freud adds the element of deeper, unconscious, psychological, emotional motivation—the sons always wish to murder and displace the fathers, not only because they long to wield power directly for themselves, but also because they harbor the terrible desire (secret, even from themselves, except for the hints and clues offered by their troubled dreams) for sexual union with their mothers.

When pressed, Freud also proposed a kind of ironic "gender parity" for women in the myth of Electra, who wants to murder her mother (recruiting her brother, Orestes, for the task) so that she may be in primary and exclusive (albeit posthumous) sexual relationship with her father. Despite the fact that the Electra myth does give compelling symbolic shape to at least one aspect of archetypal relationship between daughters and fathers, the notion of the "Electra complex" never achieved the same kind of celebrity or general acceptance as the famous "Oedipus complex."

Freud insists that the fundamental psychological/emotional conflict embodied in the myth of Oedipus is the foundation of *all* human society, because *all* male children are inherently and instinctively predisposed to fixate on their mothers as "objects of desire" and to resent and hate their fathers for taking up mother's time, sexual attention, and energy when the baby boys want it all for themselves.

Geza Roheim, an early twentieth-century intellectual and financial supporter of Freud and an anthropologist of note in his own right, even went so far as to propose a symbolically Oedipal model of sleeping and dreaming itself. Roheim proposed that since the unconscious itself is essentially "feminine and maternal"–being the source that "gives birth" to and nurtures individual conscious awareness—the very act of falling asleep and dreaming is a symbolic acting out of the Oedipal desire to "return to" and "achieve (sexual) union with" the mother. Roheim did a great deal of primary research among aboriginal peoples of Australia, particularly in the area the European invaders called "Arnhemland." He found in their myths and the details of their ritual/communal lives ample demonstrations of the essential truths of Freud's Oedipal analysis of the panhuman psyche.

The evidence of contemporary dreams and dreamers confirms that there is great truth in Freud's formulation, but this same evidence from the dream world and the world of waking emotion also indicates that the Oedipal explanation is not as all-encompassing and all-explaining a truth as Freud imagined.

Oedipus in Prehistory

The tale of King Oedipus is indeed an archetypal narrative. The Oedipus drama has legitimate claim to being the foundation story of Western society, not only because it depicts certain archetypal tensions in the emotional dynamics of the human family, but in even larger measure because it reflects in symbolic form the social and political structures and, even more importantly, the deepest religious convictions of ancient patriarchal Indo-European society.

The basic social and religious structure of Indo-European culture appears to be modeled on the recurring dynamics of the life of large herds of wild animals in nature, which in turn always reflects the "Oedipal" generational conflict of father and sons over sexual dominance and possession of the reproductively active females in the herd. It is the great wild herd that was the source and guarantee of life for the humans who first followed its seasonal migrations; it is the herd, dominated by the "alpha male," the strongest, most aggressive bull, that is the fundamental "book of nature" in which the prehistoric, patriarchal Indo-Europeans originally read "the will of God."

As discussed in more detail in chapter 4, the matrifocal/agrarian societies of the Mediterranean basin focused on the Earth herself, with her ever-renewing cycle of vegetative life, living, dying, and being reborn through the seasons of the ever-turning and ever-repeating year, as the primary revelation, the primary natural metaphor of the Divine Plan, "the will of the Goddess." This is a very different view from the patriarchal, nomadic, hunting and herding societies of central Eurasia which saw and experienced the land only as an unreliable and inadequate pasturage over which the herd and the people who followed it were forced to roam ceaselessly in order to survive and sustain themselves.

The herd in nature was, for the patriarchs, the primary revelation of God's divine law. For the ancient Indo-Europeans, God and the gods are like the "old bull"—unquestionably male and tragically doomed. God is the Strongest, and shows his divine favor to only the strongest. In this ancient patriarchal tradition, might not only *makes* right—it *is* right.

The conflict between these two fundamentally different views of the divine, of nature, of the physical world, and of the experience and social/religious place of women in contrast to men, lies at the unconscious heart of much, if not most, of the conflict and oppression with which we are still struggling at the close of the twentieth century. Anything and everything that the patriarchal world calls progress was and is predicated on the overthrow of the matrifocal worldview (in which nature, the physical world, and women are all seen as sacred and thus untouchable) and replacing that ancient view with an understanding that nature, the physical world, and women are mere property, disorganized "natural resources" crying for ownership, organization, development, and exploitation. The basic natural model for the desacralized physical/feminine world is to be dominated and controlled by the "alpha male."

For the matriarchs, the natural social order observable in the beehive is the divine model that human societies must emulate. All effort is focused around the queen bee; and the purpose of life is to follow the seasonal cycle through to the harvest, to "make honey," reproduce, die, and be born anew, all in harmony with the monthly cycles of the moon and the endlessly turning seasons. For the patriarchs, it is "God's will" that human society should mirror the herd. Life is dominated by the strongest male, who determines the direction of the herd's hungry wandering and fights off challenges to his dominance until he is eventually defeated, and the cycle starts over again.

In nature, the alpha male is inevitably doomed to be overthrown by his own male offspring. Even the gods of the Indo-Europeans can not escape this larger divine law. The gods themselves are destined to follow this Oedipal pattern of inevitable rise to power and equally inevitable fall from dominance, only to be replaced by the next generation of younger, stronger gods, who in turn are governed by and suffer the same fate.

The Germanic myth of "Ragnarok," the inevitable "Twilight of the Gods" is a prime mythological example of the essentially tragic worldview of the masculinist Indo-Europeans. The gods themselves are inescapably doomed; and in their final death struggles, they will destroy the battlefield on which they fall, which is the world itself. Nothing can be done to prevent the final outcome, but endless struggles are justified in the effort to post-

pone it. This is Oedipus writ even larger, in spiritual and cosmological "script." It is a tragedy that continues to haunt us today.

This repeating pattern of struggle for dominance of the
herd in nature is essentially Oedipal, involving as it does a violent conflict between fathers and sons for the sexual control of
the mothers. To the extent that the Oedipus mythos reflects and
grows out of this fundamental, archetypal situation, it is the
foundation myth of Western, male-dominated, technological
society, because it is these ancient patriarchal Indo-Europeans
who have given their collective stamp both to our Western psyches and to the institutions and mores of contemporary indus-
trial/technological society.

As the Indo-European hordes swept across Europe and Asia
at the beginning of the historical period, overwhelming and conquering the in many ways more sophisticated and developed matri-
focal/agrarian/Goddess-worshipping societies, they brought with
them this fundamentally tragic religious worldview and imposed it
on the conquered populations, laying the archetypal foundations
for technological civilization today.

Freud and the "Collective Unconscious"

Like all archetypal patterns, the structure of the Oedipus
drama resonates with and reflects the basic shape and pattern of
other archetypal energies. Jung himself, on several occasions,
said that Freud should be credited with "discovering the first
archetype." On most of these occasions, Jung went on to chide
his former mentor for stopping there, as though there were no
more archetypal patterns to be discovered.

Early on, Freud himself talked about a realm of unconscious life that was clearly collective, suggesting that the Oedipus
drama was a primary component of this "archaic heritage" of
the psyche:

> Dreams may bring to light material which could not origi-
> nate either from the dreamer's adult life or from his forgot-
> ten childhood. We are obliged to regard it as part of the
> archaic heritage which a child brings with him into the
> world before any experience of his own as a result of the

experiences of his ancestors. We find elements corresponding to this phylogenic material in the earliest human legends and in surviving customs. Thus dreams offer us a source of pre-history that is not to be despised.

What might the history of psychology and archetypal studies be like today if Freud had not abandoned his interest in the further exploration of this "phylogenic material" that appears in everyone's dreams, and if he and Jung had cooperated and supported one another in their investigations of the collective unconscious?

As has been noted earlier, the archetypes have the distressing tendency to "flip over," "dissolve at the edges," and change their shapes into one another at precisely the moment when we think we have nailed them down and finally succeeded in defining them in mutually exclusive terms. Another reason for Freud's ability to see Oedipus everywhere and in everything is that *any* truly archetypal form may be seen as the center, with all the others radiating outward from it as "variations on a theme." At one important level, which archetype one chooses to put at the center and use as the benchmark from which all the others are measured is an aesthetic question. Freud chooses as the foundation of his psychology the demonstrable force of sexual attraction/repulsion and desire that can be observed in the behavior of all animals, including human beings. Jung proposes as his fundamental principle the apparently uniquely human desire for an ever-increasing awareness of meaning, significance, and purpose—a fundamental desire for awareness of greater and more far-reaching patterns of energy exchange and relationship.

In many important ways, both men were addressing the same psychospiritual reality, Freud from an assumed position of "abstract scientific objectivity," and Jung from a more conscious acknowledgment of inevitable human involvement in the process of observation itself. In that sense, the historical dispute between Freud and Jung may be viewed as a specific case embodying the larger tensions of the gradual movement of Western culture away from the scientism, objectivism, and positivism of the industrial age to the relativism and deconstruction of the postmodern, electronic era.

The Indo-European Invasion

After the close of the last ice age, the innovation of agriculture (by the Goddess worshippers) led to the development of stratified, increasingly specialized urban life. In that early period (approximately 7000 B.C.E. to 1500 B.C.E.), the two great social/spiritual perspectives of settled agrarian matriarchy and nomadic herding patriarchy were kept ignorant of and separate from one another by the barrier of the mountains we call the Caucasus. Descendants of the Indo-European invaders are called "Caucasians" today because their ancestors invaded Europe across those mountains, sometime after 1500 B.C.E.

Apparently there was a great environmental upheaval (most archaeologists and paleo-environmentalists posit a terrible drought), an ecological disruption of proportions unprecedented since the last ice age, that caused the great wild herds to break out of their ancient, seasonal patterns of natural migration back and forth across the great plains that lie between the Caucasus and Ural mountains and to cross the mountains in their increasingly desperate search for pasturage. The roving bands of male-dominated, horse-riding pastoralists that relied on these herds for their survival followed the dwindling herds in their desperate migrations through the high mountain passes. When they emerged onto the fertile plains on the far side, the riders fell upon the first great agricultural civilizations with unparalleled ferocity.

When the nomadic, pastoralist Indo-Europeans came upon the ancient city of Mohenjo-Daro in the valley of what is now the Indus River, for example, they found a great city with running water available to all its inhabitants through municipal aqueducts. It was a city *without walls,* open to the vast fertile fields that surrounded it. The only storehouses for harvested crops were in the temples to the Goddess. An inescapable inference is that this is a picture of a great beehive/commune organized on matriarchal religious and social principles, where the fields were tilled,

planted, and cultivated for the Goddess, the crops were offered to
her at harvest time as gifts of gratitude, and her priests and priestesses doled out the harvested food to the populace in the form of
rations—"gifts" from the Goddess to her faithful subjects.

In the archaeological remains of Mohenjo-Daro and her sister city of Harrapa, which also fell to the invading pastoralists, we
can discern the social shape of agricultural Goddess worship, a
static world in which every act has its prescribed time and place,
and the repetition of the liturgy of planting, tending, and reaping
becomes the all-pervasive meditation on the mysteries of consciousness, life, death, and reincarnational rebirth. The lack of
fortifications strongly suggests a lack of organized intercommunal conflict and war—or at very least, a system of ritual combat
for settling intercommunal disputes that involved contests
between "champions" rather than mass conflict involving armies
and whole populations (not unlike the ritual combat between
David and Goliath described in the Old Testament or the series
of single combats the Irish hero Cuhoolan fights with a succession of champions, one each day, chosen from the invading army
of Queen Maeve, as recounted in *The Cattle Raid of Cooley*).

When the invaders from the North arrived outside
Mohenjo-Daro almost four thousand years ago, it had just rained.
The fields and the streets were muddy; and from the traces left in
the mud, it is fairly clear that the city offered no resistance to the
invaders. The evidence is that people came forth with gifts of surrender and submission for the wild riders, but it is equally apparent that the invaders were not interested in surrender. They were
interested in the joys of pillage (and not even plunder). The fact
that the populace did not resist or fight back made no difference
to them (except, perhaps, for a mild disappointment?). The men
and women I know who take joy in violent combat relish worthy
opponents and take less joy in easy victories.

In the course of that day of terrible slaughter, the city caught
fire and burned to the ground. The heat of the conflagration
baked the wet, muddy streets into hard clay, capturing innumerable "snapshots" of the last moments of the great city's fall. People came forth, offering submission; and the riders galloped and
trotted through the streets, striking the people down without dis-

mounting, leaving their shattered corpses and rejected offerings scattered in the muddy streets. The impressions of the fallen city dwellers, along with the hoofprints of the invaders' horses, were baked solid and covered with ashes, waiting for German archaeologists to discover almost four thousand years later.

In this (to our modern sensibilities) barbarous and surprising lack of interest in conquest, in their apparent total absorption in the moment of slaughter for its own sake, the Indo-Europeans appear remarkably like the wild horsemen who exploded out of central Asia in historical times: the Mongols, Huns, and Tartars. All three of these groups were highly traditional, nomadic, patriarchal pastoralists. For millennia they followed the migrations of the great herds that wandered over the grassy plains of their native Asia. They used alcohol as their primary recreational drug and as their sacramental consciousness-changing means of communing with their rough collection of sky, weather, and thunder gods. When they burst forth into Europe, they swept all before them, burning and pillaging without particular interest in collecting anything but the most portable plunder and without any abiding interest in the administration and continued exploitation of conquered peoples.

These later Asiatic invaders of Europe from the North and East in historical times exhibited almost exactly the same worldview and understanding of the relationship between divinity and power as their Indo-European predecessors. For them, the earth was indeed feminine; but it represented the inadequate and always insufficient pasturage of the herd, rather than the unlimited bounty of the Goddess.

They too had great difficulty maintaining alliances and agreements, because like the original Indo-Europeans, they lived under a religious obligation to obey the will of God and take the cattle from the one who was not strong enough to hold them. For men living out this archetypal pattern (clearly not a racial pattern per se, since it recurs in Europeans, Asians, Africans—in fact, in nomadic, masculinist, pastoralist societies, wherever they appear), God only favors the strongest. And when a ruler ceases to be the strongest, even his own sons have an ultimately *religious* obligation to preserve the deepest traditions of their forefathers and overthrow the weakened leader and take his herds.

This nomadic, conquering (but not staying in one place to live as conquerors) way of life can only be sustained as long as there is a horizon to ride over each spring when the weather improves. When this conquest (actually more of a greatly prolonged and extended raid) reaches the shore of an ocean, it faces a crisis. A decision must be taken either to alter the ancient fundamental cultural/religious forms, give up the nomadic life and settle in one place (supported by a "new" peasant class that practices agriculture), and take on the task of the administration of the lands and peoples that have been conquered; or to remain true to the old ways and keep up the endless nomadic conquest.

If the more conservative and traditional position prevails, then the whole army must turn around and ride back across the "scorched earth" that they themselves created, facing the rising generations of young warriors who have been raised on stories of what inhuman monsters they are. Men living out this ancient archetypal pattern do not have the skills or the inclination to carry their endless raid out across the trackless ocean, where their beloved horses can only travel as cumbersome and helpless cargo.

The deeply conservative Mongols, Tartars, and Huns chose to remain true to their ancient way of nomadic life; and after sweeping to the shores of the Atlantic and the Mediterranean, they ebbed back across Europe, leaving almost no lasting imprint on European culture (except for the long-denied but obvious genetic strains of Asian blood in the children fathered on the local women who were not massacred along with their fathers, brothers, and sons). There are no Asian loan-words in European languages, no remnants of Mongol religious practices in the folk traditions of European peoples, no Hun recipes, no Mongol architectural forms, no remnants of Tartar legal practices. The only lasting legacy we have in the West is the persistent memory of the "barbarian hordes" and their inhuman ferocity. These stories are, ironically, accurate reflections of the barbarism of the ancient Indo-Europeans themselves; and they offer another example of the way repression and projection function at a collective level.

Like their Indo-European predecessors, the Asian horse riders were also uninterested in lasting treaties and alliances, since they too believed that the "god is only with the strongest" and that even the strongest inevitably grows weak with the passage of time. Like the Indo-Europeans, they were held together in a single army only by the strength of personality of a "great leader"; and with his death or defeat, his hold over his vassals evaporated into endless struggles over succession, not just because it is "human nature" to vie for power, but because it is a deeply intuited religious obligation. These are people who prize loyalty highly, but for whom loyalty must be offered to the highest authority; clan over immediate family, king over clan, and the demands of God above all—even above the king.

The Masculinist Myths of Conflicting Loyalties

For this reason, one of the deepest archetypal narrative patterns of nomadic pastoralists—Asian, African, and Indo-European—is the story of the great warrior who must discern his way through increasing dilemmas of conflicting loyalties, loyalties that become ever more complex and mutually exclusive as time passes, until at last there is no clearly "honorable" solution and the warrior must die in dubious battle, fighting against his own sons and/or against men who were once his closest allies and friends. There is clear evidence that this conflict of loyalties has its ancient roots in the fact that for the patriarchs, even the gods are destined to be overthrown and killed by their sons.

The reputed ferocity of Yahweh in demanding the death of Jesus to expiate the original sin of Adam has particular appeal for the Indo-European psyche. The gods of the Indo-Europeans have been requiring the deaths of their sons as they reach maturity for a great deal longer than the general Indo-European embrace of Christianity. The reappearance of this ancient archetypal pattern in the Judeo-Christian scriptures certainly played a part in the conversion of the royal families of pagan Europe to Christianity after the time of Constantine.

These archetypal patterns are visible in a great many more ancient Greek myths than Oedipus. The habit of each generation of ancient Greek gods to eat their children is a direct reflection of the effort of the divine to hold onto "dominance of the herd" as long as possible. When the male Divine Child escapes this incestuous cannibalism, he grows into maturity, defeats (and often castrates) his father, and becomes father (marrying his mother, the Great Goddess in her ever-renewing youthful form). He also takes up the family tradition of eating his children in a vain attempt to prevent his own sons from growing up and displacing him.

Unlike the conservative Mongols and Huns, the Indo-Europeans made a different choice when they reached the sea; they chose to restructure their deepest religious traditions to accommodate their new circumstances. They devised a sacred narrative justification for the transfer of the ownership of cattle through means other than ritual combat (commerce), and for maintaining alliances through agreement on mutual interest rather than brute strength (diplomacy).

Hermes, the Thief

The figure most responsible for this extraordinary transformation of Indo-European culture is the god Hermes. The archaeological evidence offered by icons carved in stone is unequivocal: Hermes (like his Hindu brother, the elephant-headed god, Genesha) is much older than the patriarchal birth narratives that come down to us in the sacred narratives of the invading patriarchs.

There must have been Pelasgian birth stories of Hermes (in which he was almost undoubtedly born, like Genesha, from his mother without male assistance) that were outlawed and replaced by the narratives found in Hesiod and the Homeric hymns.

In the later propagandistic narratives (comparable to later versions of the story of Taliessen where the figure of "Tegid" appears, apparently solely for the purpose of providing the goddess Ceridooen with a father for her children), Hermes is born to the nymph Mia as a result of one of Zeus' extramarital dalliances. The moment he is born, Hermes rejects his mother's breast and toddles off to steal some of his uncle Apollo's "sacred cattle of the sun." In Indo-European lore, such a theft of cattle can only portend a changing of the gods, in accordance with the old Oedipal pattern. Apollo has not only lost property, but his position as dominant god of the sun has also been openly challenged.

Apollo returns, detects the theft, and with advice from Hecate, Goddess of the Night, discovers that Hermes is the culprit. He takes the infant Hermes up to the court of Father Zeus to receive the inevitable judgment of death for his crime; but on the way up the mountain, baby Hermes cobbles together the first lyre, made from the entrails of the stolen cattle, and gives it to Apollo as a gift. Apollo accepts the newly invented musical instrument and appears before Zeus to demand ancient justice with the prototype of the lyre in one hand and the blood-smeared infant in the other.

When Zeus offers his precocious son an opportunity to speak in his own defense, Hermes points to the lyre and says that since Apollo has already accepted it as a gift, and since it was made from the very bones and sinews of the cattle that Hermes is accused of stealing, he has "received payment for goods received," and that it isn't theft at all—it's *commerce*. Zeus, vastly amused, throws the case against Hermes out of court, appointing Hermes the divine patron of commerce, commercial travelers, diplomats, messengers, and thieves but allowing Apollo to remain the divine patron of music and the arts in general, and the lyre in particular (Fig. 15).

Amusing and relatively light as this narrative may appear to be to our contemporary eyes, it is this story that provides the sacred narrative justification for the transformation of the most ancient and fundamental principles of traditional Indo-European nomadic pastoralist life and that allows the invaders to settle permanently and exchange wealth and power by diplomacy and commercial agreement, rather than by ritual combat to determine who is the strongest. We Western, postmodern, technological folk are still living off the archetypal energies of commerce and statecraft released by this story, which has a clear claim to being the second most important founding myth of Western culture, right after Oedipus.

The story of the birth of Hermes and his "trickster" invention of a new way for cattle to change hands without declaring religious war allows the ancient power struggles of Indo-European nomadic life to be resolved in a new and more civilized way. This transformation of basic religious worldview is absolutely necessary for the further development of Western culture in the form that we know it. Without it, or something very much like it, the Indo-Europeans would have melted back

Figure 15. (Ancient Greece) Apollo drags the infant Hermes off to face the judgment of Zeus, while Hermes cobbles together the first lyre, made from the remains of the stolen "cattle of the sun" (in the style of "white ground" Attic vase paintings).

the fastnesses of the Eurasian plains, just as the Mongols, Huns, and Tartars did many centuries later when faced with a similar archetypal dilemma.

In the ancient archetypal structure of Indo-European myth, "progress" is defined by the generational overthrow of the old divine regime and its replacement by the new. At a deep unconscious level, much of our collective obsession with progress, as against the more responsible and human idea of sustainability (a modern term for the ancient religious idea of mutually agreeable and respectful relationship with the Goddess of the Earth and with the physical world in general), is in large measure a reflection of this ancient tension.

When the Indo-Europeans overran the matrifocal agrarian societies of the Mediterranean, they did so in part because they *rode* horses, whereas the matriarchs appear to have used horses only to pull carts and chariots. Anthropologists have argued that it is this "superior energy-use technology" that ensured their victory over the more sophisticated and developed civilizations they conquered, proposing (in archetypical Indo-European fashion) that it is a "law of culture" that societies that consume more energy more efficiently will always supplant and replace societies that produce and consume less energy. This, at one level, is simply another symbolic example of the deep archetypal religious belief that "might is right," in the sense that it is an inescapable "law of nature" (and is therefore a situation in which we may read "the will of God").

The great prehistoric agrarian civilizations do seem to have collapsed before the "barbarian hordes" with surprising ease. I have become convinced that not only was the superior technology of horse riding versus drayage partially responsible for this collapse, but that there were also other, less obvious, but nonetheless crucial psychospiritual factors contributing to the demise of these great civilizations.

The Precession of the Equinoxes, the Collapse of the Prehistoric Matriarchies, and the "Original Dirty Joke"

As mentioned earlier, another crucial factor seems to have been the "original dirty joke," the common knowledge in the possession of the cattle-herding nomads that sexual intercourse was the single and only reason why females become pregnant. The matriarchal conviction that the Goddess bore her children without male assistance and that human women and female animals could do the same was, I believe, "laughed off the stage" by the invading patriarchs, causing deep and lasting scars in the collective psyches of both men and women.

But I suspect that destructive as this wide dissemination of "the facts of life" must have been to the old matrifocal socioreligious culture, there was an even greater factor contributing to the upheaval and collapse of the old Goddess-worshipping agrarian societies, stemming from the failure of their religious traditions to predict the precession of the equinoxes. This failure to foresee the eventual disparity between the body of oral sacred lore and the cyclic events in the heavens those sacred poems were supposed to predict shook the ancient matriarchies to their very core. The tradition of sacred poetry was the foundation on which those societies depended for their ultimate sense of rightness and order. The failure of the old hymns to the Goddess to predict the changes in the sky over millennia engendered a failure of nerve and vision at the highest levels of leadership in the matriarchies themselves.

Every two thousand years or so, the background of seemingly fixed stars can be observed to have slowly shifted one-twelfth of the way "backward" along the parade of constellations that mark the path of the earth around the sun (the so-called "houses of the zodiac"). The ancient poetry and stories that survive in various states of purity from around the time of the Indo-European invasion all tend to have imbedded in them the same story of "destruction of the cosmic order" by the "mill of the gods" being thrown off its axis. Instead of grinding out prosperity and order and happiness for all, as it has done since "the beginning of time," the mill of the gods "tilts" or "falls" or "tumbles" and continues to turn, grinding out "salt tears" and "the salt of the sea." (See the discussion of the sources for this chapter in Appendix II for a more complete description of the celestial phenomenon known as "the precession of the equinoxes.")

Georgio de Santillana and Hertha von Dechend, in their monumental work, *Hamlet's Mill,* catalogue in great detail the stories from around the world (with particular attention to relatively "uncontaminated" Polynesian sources) that appear to have this same story woven into them. They argue (and their argument convinces me) that this story of the fall of the mill of the gods is a symbolic reflection of the existential crisis that the precession of the equinoxes precipitated all over the world. In the great agrarian matriarchies of the Mediterranean world, religious, political, and economic life were one fabric, defined and delineated by a body of sacred oral poetry that predicted events in the sky from season to season. These societies used those celestial predictions, reliable for the past thousand and more years, as constant "proof" of the divine revelation and ordination of their way of life. This agrarian way of life included the absolute necessity of religious sacrifice, particularly sacrifice of the "first fruits," including (in many carefully archaeologically attested instances) the sacrifice of a woman's firstborn child.

Harvest Guilt

My own strong suspicion with regard to religiously inspired human sacrifice is that it is an archetypal consequence of the transition from nomadic hunting and gathering to settled, urban, agrarian life. For lack of a better term, it might as well be called "harvest guilt."

Hunting and gathering, even when amplified by the use of increasingly sophisticated and effective fabricated tools and weapons of the hunt, are still activities easily discerned in "the book of nature." All animals hunt and forage; humans are simply a little more conscious and organized about it. Hunting and gathering do not fundamentally alter humanity's relationship to the Goddess; hunters and gatherers still "follow the way of the Goddess," as do all living things.

Agriculture involves the inevitable "sacrilege" of tilling the earth, of planting and cultivating and harvesting, of touching the Mother's sacred body to make it produce even more in a more orderly and predictable fashion. This activity, even when undertaken with the crudest wooden tools, does alter the fundamentally "natural" relationship with the Great Mother. Symbolically, it is distressingly like rape. In return for these agriculturally coerced "gifts," something must be given back; and our ancient agrarian ancestors decided that "first fruits" (of both the harvest and the womb) were the only appropriate sacrifice to atone for the "crime" of mistrust and coercion of the Goddess in her unmanipulated and natural state. The first *opus contra naturam* ("work against nature") is not language, but agriculture. Hunting and gathering are simply variations on the theme of "life feeds on life" or "nature red in tooth and claw." Agriculture ushers in a whole new relationship with the divine in which (necessary) "sin" must be paid for with (necessary) sacrifice.

The Goddess grants the predator the right to the prey. She grants the bees the right to forage and harvest the pollen and the nectar. In this way, the life of the beehive becomes the natural justification for hierarchical matrifocal society, just as the wild herd becomes the natural model of hierarchical patriarchal culture. Close to the center of the sacred justifications for the settled life of agriculture is the expiation of harvest guilt through the sacrifice of first fruits.

When the justification for one's entire way of life (including child sacrifice) rests on an oral tradition of "revealed truth," constantly confirmed by the predictable correspondence of events on earth with events in the sky, any obvious disruption of the "Divine Plan" creates a crisis of faith. When it became progressively clearer and clearer that the celestial events no longer corresponded to the predictions in the sacred songs and poems, a crisis in the whole matriarchal social structure was inevitable. At precisely the moment when the starving Indo-European nomads were descending into the fertile plains of the Mediterranean basin, the elite of the matriarchal societies must have been in the grips of such a crisis because of the precession of the equinoxes. As de Santillana and von Dechend document so thoroughly, the world's myths from this period all reflect the agony of a religious vision "tipped over" and a perfect order "overturned and ruined."

The increasing lack of correspondence between earth and sky would be most obvious and undeniable to the most highly placed leaders and religious officials, those who were most educated and who had been fully initiated into the "mysteries of the Goddess." These would be the women and men who understood both the exoteric and esoteric meanings of the sacred narratives most deeply and fully, and for whom the obvious failure of the poems to predict the observable events would be the most disturbing and distressing. I believe that, in the words of the contemporary Greek poet Cavafey, "for them, the barbarians were a kind of solution."

An elite that is struggling with barbarous invaders, while losing faith and confidence in the very ideas and institutions it was born and trained to uphold, may provide the kind of leadership that wins battles, but not the kind that wins wars. When the inevitable observable consequences of the precession of the equinoxes became too obvious to ignore, there must have been a crisis of confidence in the entire matrifocal religious worldview that also contributed in a subtle but overwhelmingly important way to the collapse of those societies in the face of the Indo-European invasion.

This crisis of faith and confidence also played a role in the subsequent accommodations and blendings of the newly arrived patriarchal worldview with the more sophisticated and organized worldview of the conquered farmers.

In the ancient Irish *Book of Invasions,* the story is told of the tyrannical half-breed king Bres, who bargains for his life with the (Indo-European) invaders of his (matriarchal) island, using the religious secrets of the agricultural calendar, the all-important knowledge of how to read the sky and know when to plant in the spring, as his main bargaining strength. In this story, I believe, we have an accurate depiction of actual negotiations between the two great cultural and religious traditions in the late prehistorical period. This is not only an accurate account, but also a symbolic rendition of the whole process of accommodation of the conquered matriarchs to the religious and spiritual worldview of their new overlords. Like the story of the birth of Hermes, it is a story of the negotiations of a conquered race with their conquerors, in which the conquerors themselves are changed as much as the conquered.

We are *still* struggling over the details of those accommodations and negotiations. We struggle with them in the projected forms of all the social and cultural issues that plague us at the end of the twentieth century. We fight what is crudely known as "the battle of the sexes" in the shape of all the problems we face, ranging from the personal struggles of sexual relationship and marriage, on through the progressively larger questions of earning a living and finding "right livelihood," through issues of local community conflict, to the even larger issues of social, economic, political, and cultural change. We experience them in the controversies over institutional and psychological sexism and male dominance as reflected in issues like providing truly equal education to girls and boys; in controversies over the ordination of women and gay men into the ministry and priesthood; in issues of contraception, abortion, and women's rights to control their own bodies; and in the ongoing problems of local and regional intra- and inter-communal conflict, always undertaken in the threatening shadow of escalation and degeneration into global war.

We struggle with these archetypal issues projected into our efforts to preserve the balance of the natural environment necessary for our continued survival as a species. We struggle increasingly to control our voracious appetite (like Raven's mother) as we devour other whole species in our efforts toward economic expansion and "progress."

The Struggle Continues in Dreams

All of these questions grow out of and reflect the archetypal tensions inherent in the clash of masculinist and feminist archetypal/religious worldviews. The ancient matriarchs and patriarchs met and clashed at the dawn of recorded history, directly and intensely embodying these archetypal energies in their struggles. As a result, we now live embedded in "history," where truth always has to have a prior source in a written text; while deep in our psyches, prehistory still lives and shapes our lives in the form of archetypal symbolic predilections toward feeling, opinion, and behavior.

A man in his late forties dreams:

> My brothers and I are all students in an oriental martial arts school. The school is run by our waking-life father, an extremely harsh man (both in the dream and in waking life when he was alive—he has been dead for many years). Every day there is a fierce and bloody ritual combat among the brothers to determine our "rank" and "pecking order." The "Old Man" observes and supervises these battles, and

confirms the victor. We all know that by fighting this way among ourselves we will never be free of the Old Man's domination, but we always enter into the combat in the hopes of being "top dog," at least for the brief period before the next fight.

I try to organize a secret meeting of us brothers to plan the overthrow of the Old Man, or at least a mass escape from his domination, but one of the brothers betrays me, and the Old Man captures me with their help and hangs me up in a cage outside where all of my brothers and sisters can laugh at me and mock me... I awaken with a deep sense of anger and despair.

In waking life, the dreamer has many struggles making a living despite his unusual intelligence and great creative gifts. At one level, the dream symbolically depicts life in his family of origin, right down to the mother's mysterious but unquestioned absence from the scene. At another level, it depicts the Oedipal internal conflicts in men created by the collective demands and oppressions of patriarchy itself. Men are separated from "their brothers" by the very structures of competitive male dominance that are supposed to support and empower them. This is true collectively, regardless of the particulars of any man's individual upbringing. When the structure of the family of origin is as oppressive and patriarchal as the society itself, then there is a double pressure placed on the individual man, as is the case with this dreamer.

Men raised in harsh, competitive, male-dominated families often have difficulty finding their authentic selves and their creative energies because these energies have been "devoured by the father," both personally and collectively. Sometimes the death of the individually oppressive father releases the previously suppressed energies; and sometimes it takes even more effort on the part of the man himself to free himself from the habits of a lifetime of defense and competitive aggression, even when consciously that is what he desires most.

One of the most important things about this dream is the fact that the dreamer remembered it at all. When such a seemingly bleak and hopeless dream is recalled, it means that the dreamer is able to respond creatively and transformatively to all the issues the dream raises. The more blunt and symbolically clear the dream is about the issue(s) in the dreamer's life, the surer he or she can be that those very issues are evolving to a point of transformation and change.

In many ways, this dream can be viewed as a "post-traumatic stress dream," like the recurrent nightmares of rape victims and survivors of particularly horrifying combat encounters in war. When such dreams are recalled, they often transpose the original experience into a symbolic analogue—in this case, the depiction of the interior drama of childhood memory and current emotional struggle as an endless ritual combat in a martial arts school. This transposition of the drama into a symbolic analogue often has the effect of reframing the original dilemma or struggle in new terms, so that the seemingly stuck and frustrated energies for growth and change can find a new avenue of expression within the implied structure of the new symbolic "frame." In this dream, the use of an oppressive martial arts school to stand symbolically for the drama of the family of origin, the oppressive masculinist competitive society as a whole, and the dreamer's own internal emotions suggests that in the symbolic framework of "martial arts training" there are implied possibilities of growth and change.

In this particular dream, the Oedipal drama is clear. Ironically, one result of being "betrayed" is that the dreamer has been removed from the repetitive ritual struggle with his brothers. He is "out of the game"; and even though that is what he wanted in the first place, it makes him unhappy and miserable. The dream depicts him as "hung up," an object of ridicule and rejection; however, the primary desire expressed in the dream, to be free of the repetitive combat, has been achieved. What has not been achieved is the sense of freedom and autonomy that was supposed to result. The dreamer still has work to do to recognize his true stature and creative gifts; but his "secret meeting" (a metaphor at one level at least of changing emotional energy dynamics below the surface of waking awareness) has accomplished its task. It's just that the dreamer still wants to *win* the old game before retiring from it—an understandable, if not particularly wise, desire that leads to his sense of being "hung up" and "trapped."

The dream clearly suggests that a feminine element has entered the psychological picture; the previously unmentioned "sisters" join the crowd of people mocking the dreamer hanging in his cage. Eventual escape from the cage seems much more likely with their appearance. It is easy to imagine in the symbolic circumstance that the dream evokes that there is at least one "sister" who, though she may appear to be joining in the degradation of her caged brother, may be as interested in escape as he is. She now knows she has an ally, even if the dreamer is as yet unaware of it. The appearance of the "sisters" suggests that the very emotions that seem to paralyze the dreamer and make him feel stuck also have the potential of freeing him and liberating his creative energies in new directions.

The nightmarish quality of the dream is unequivocal; there is a survival issue depicted here. The feelings of anger and upset that the dreamer is left with upon awakening may in fact be the very feelings necessary to motivate the deep life changes in attitude and secret desire that are needed to accomplish his liberation.

As Jung pointed out on numerous occasions, in order to be successful, the unconscious energies for transformation and change must be as strong and energetic as the forces of habit and neurosis that they must overcome. The intensity of the pain and frustration that the experience of the dream evokes may in fact be precisely what is needed to motivate the dreamer to positive action in waking life. The dream sets up the situation and evokes emotional energies sufficient to motivate waking action, but the dreamer—like all of us—remains free; the decision to act and change his life must be made consciously, in waking life. The dream comes to support and facilitate that choice.

Another implication of the transposition of the family of origin into a martial arts school is that the transformative power of imagination and symbolic form itself has been awakened in the dreamer's life at a very deep level, the level of memories of childhood and adolescence. Whenever a difficult and traumatic memory is recast into another symbolic form, it is a clear indication that the "magical" transformative power of the creative unconscious has been activated.

A further implication of the oriental martial arts setting is that the issue is not just personal, but also has important collective "traditional" elements at work in it as well. It is very easy to feel misery and despair in life situations like the one that forms the waking background to this dream. There is an insidious invitation to take it all completely personally, and to see his continuing but momentary failure to "solve" the neurotic dilemma as a purely personal failure. The transmutation of the family of origin into a martial arts dojo suggests that the immense, conservative, institutional forces of sexism and male supremacy have as much to with the dreamer's seemingly "personal struggle" as his unique character and personality. There is also an implication at this level of the other side of the Oedipal drama, the inevitability of the overthrow of the fathers by the sons. The implication is that, like continuing training in martial arts, there is a gradual increase of skills and self-confidence that the oppressive process itself promotes, and that eventually the dreamer will free himself from the drama.

Once again, the levels of the dream, from the uniquely personal to the compellingly collective, all point to the possibilities for solving these problems through the embrace of authenticity and the transformation of habitually prejudiced views, all of which the dream points to in the midst of the frustrating and unfinished struggles for liberation in the waking world.

We cannot hope to solve these pressing contemporary dilemmas, either in our intimate personal lives or in our institutional struggles with one another, unless we allow ourselves to realize the extent to which the forces that drive and shape these problems are unconscious, archetypal, and collective.

Our greatest problems continue to reflect the shape of unconscious archetypal forces. These forces, lurking just below the surface of appearance, reveal themselves both in our dreams and in our largest collective efforts and dilemmas. Those who are ignorant of the prehistoric forces that shape our lives do appear to be doomed to repeat their seemingly inevitable patterns. The felt sense of the inevitability of these struggles and their predictably unsatisfactory outcomes is in itself a very reliable indicator of the extent to which the archetypal energies fueling the drama(s) have not yet been raised to consciousness.

SUMMARY

Freud asserted that all male children feel an instinctive sense of attraction to their mothers and a concomitant competition with and hatred of their fathers. He believed that this instinctive "Oedipus complex" is the symbolic and psychoenergetic basis for all personal neurosis on the one hand, and all of "civilization and its discontents" on the other. Freud also proposed a corollary mythic pattern in the unconscious lives of women emphasizing their instinctive incestuous desires for union with their fathers, but this "Electra complex" never achieved the same kind of currency and acceptance as his famous formulation of the "Oedipus complex."

In addition to the personal, psychosexual levels of the Oedipus story explicated so extensively by Freud and his followers, the Oedipus myth also gives symbolic shape to other ancient, collective, archetypal patterns of patriarchal Indo-European thought. The Oedipus story is the story of the life of the wild herd on which the nomadic pastoralists depended for their existence and survival.

Just as the beehive is the most important natural symbol of matriarchal, agrarian, Goddess-worshipping culture, so the migratory herd is the natural model for the archaic patriarchal, nomadic, "God-fearing," Indo-European society. The herd in nature is dominated by the "alpha male," who for a while in his prime fights off all challenges to his dominance, but who is ultimately doomed to be overthrown and replaced by his own offspring when he becomes too old and decrepit to defend his exclusive claim to the fertile females. This natural pattern of the life of the herd is obviously fundamentally "Oedipal"; and it marks the Oedipus myth even more clearly as the foundational symbolic drama of contemporary Western culture, because it is from these patriarchal Indo-European pastoralist warriors that we today inherit our most fundamental concepts, convictions, and deep unconscious predispositions to particular patterns of archetypal symbolism.

For the ancient Indo-Europeans, even their lusty, drunken, male, lightning-wielding gods are doomed to be overthrown, just like the old alpha male bull, by their own male offspring, when the older males grow too old and weak to maintain their dominance. For them and their gods, might does not just make right, it is right. Any experience of weakness inevitably means that it is "God's will" that his earthly representative be overthrown and replaced by the strongest competitor. The Germanic myth of "Ragnarok," the "Twilight of the Gods," is an example of this tragic Indo-European worldview in symbolic/narrative form. Even the gods themselves are doomed; and in their death struggles, they will also destroy the battlefield on which they fall, which is, of course, the earth itself.

For these wandering, horse-riding Indo-European pastoralists, the earth is also feminine. But far from being the inexhaustibly fertile Goddess of the agriculturalists, she is the unreliable and inadequate pasturage that can not support the herd and that forces them to wander endlessly in search of fresh fodder.

Around 1500 B.C.E., apparently forced by extensive drought to break out of their traditional patterns of nomadic migration back and forth across the trans-Caucasian plains, the Indo-European pastoralists followed their starving herds across the mountains and invaded the settled agrarian matriarchies around the Mediterranean and the Indian subcontinent. They quickly overran the Goddess worshippers they found on the fertile plains and imposed their essentially tragic religious worldview, symbolized by endless generations of gods endlessly overthrowing one another and destroying the earth in the process, on the conquered agriculturalists.

When faced with the problem of administering the conquered agricultural societies, they modified their fundamental belief that God gives his approval only to the male who is physically strongest. They allowed cattle and property to change hands by treaty and agreement, rather than by ritual combat, which had always been required. The mythic narrative of the birth of Hermes played a crucial role in this fundamental transformation of archaic Indo-European culture.

The matrifocal, Goddess-worshipping, agrarian societies that fell to the invading Indo-European horsemen around 1500 B.C.E. were apparently already in a state of existential crisis before the invasion because of the failure of their sacred oral tradition to predict the precession of the equinoxes. Events in the sky no longer matched the predictions in the ancient verses.

This, together with the more efficient use of horse power by the Indo-Europeans and their dissemination of "the facts of life" (the general knowledge among the nomadic pastoralists that intercourse with a male was necessary for a female to become pregnant), spelled the end of the millennia of state-sponsored Goddess worship and its official replacement with state-sponsored and enforced worship of masculine forms of the divine.

These ancient, unresolved archetypal struggles are still discernible in the dreams of contemporary people and in the ongoing collective struggles over such questions as reproductive rights, the role of "progress" as against "sustainability," the symbolic structures of inter-communal conflict, and so forth. Examples are offered of the mythic narratives that give the clearest view of the archetypal patterns of these ancient conflicts, and a dream is examined in depth with emphasis on the ways in which it too reflects these archetypal patterns.

Chapter 7
QUEEN JOCASTA: A MYTHIC NARRATIVE OF THE TRANSITION FROM MATRIARCHY TO PATRIARCHY (WITH AN ASIDE ON "CHANNELING" AND SPIRIT COMMUNICATION)

> "Whenever we give up, leave behind, and forget too much, there is always the danger that things we have neglected will return with added force." The fullest possibilities of human life, therefore, are to be realized in conformance with grand, overarching shapes found in all mythologies, a conformance that is "neither a question of belief nor knowledge, but of the agreement of our thinking with the primordial images of the unconscious."
>
> *Frederick Turner*
> *(quoting Carl Jung)*

In the spring of 1972, I wrote an article entitled "More on Matriarchy" for the now defunct feminist/pagan journal *Nemeton*, published in Oakland, California. In that article, I laid out in detail the researches that led me to the conclusion that public revelation of the necessary male role in procreation, together with the failure of the old matriarchal, agrarian cultures of the

Mediterranean to predict the precession of the equinoxes, should be listed among the most important causes of the collapse of the Pelasgian Goddess-worshipping cultures before the Indo-European invasion (see chapter 6 for more details).

When the article was published, I felt a sense of completion and satisfaction. Even though the audience that read *Nemeton* was relatively small, it was a sophisticated audience, quite capable of assessing my arguments. I had the satisfying sense that the ideas I had worked so hard on had gotten out into the world and would receive a small but fair hearing. I thought I was done with that phase of my research into the prehistoric patterns of archetypal energy still alive in the deep psyche and was now free to move on to focus on other issues related to the collective nature of our human predicament.

Well after midnight one Friday night late in November 1972, I was driving my ramshackle VW bug home over familiar Marin County back roads made oddly strange and new by my tiredness, by the darkness, and by the lateness of the hour. I was going over in my mind the multileveled and fascinating events of the regular weekly extended-family dream group that had taken place earlier that evening, when suddenly the voice of an old woman started speaking from the back of the car.

I was tingling with surprise and fear. I had thought I was *alone!* No one was visible in the rearview mirror. My first wild thought was that since I hadn't bothered to lock the car for the space of time it took to walk the baby-sitter up to the door of her home, some old homeless woman must have crawled into the back of the car in that brief moment.

I took my foot off the gas and turned my head to look directly into the back seat area. As I turned, I realized that the voice was apparently turning with me, keeping its same relative distance and position, behind me and a little to my right. That could only mean that the voice was *in my head!* But without that clue, all my other perceptions told me it was a *real* voice, physically speaking into the air in the closed space of the car.

I now believe it was the years of remembering dreams and cultivating the meditative states of mind that writing and other creative work require that allowed me to hold onto my feelings and my sense of myself that night. I realized that the "old woman" was reciting—chanting really—a narrative of ancient Greece, set at the end of the era that I had been researching so intensively for the past few years. She was a muse! She was giving me a poem!

My surprise and disorientation transformed almost immediately into excitement—and apprehension. I remembered Coleridge and the "person from Porlock" who interrupted him while he was in a similar state, composing (if you can call it that—it's more like taking dictation) "Kubla Khan," and how poor Coleridge could never recapture the inspiration, and thus the poem remains for us today only in the form of the inspired fragment.

I didn't want to let the inspiration slip away the way Coleridge's had. My first impulse was to stop right there under a streetlight (the dome light on that old car was broken when I bought it, and I had never bothered to repair it) and write in the notebook/journal I always carry. But Southern Marin County is one of the most well-patrolled communities in the country, and I knew that it would only be a matter of minutes before a police car or a private security patrol came by. I could imagine the exchange all too easily:

"Having trouble, Sir?"

"No, thank you, Officer. Everything's fine. I just got an idea for a poem, and I don't want to lose the moment of inspiration."

"Can I see your license and registration please, Sir?"

"Certainly, Officer..."

"And would you step out of the car, please..."

It would be worse than the person from Porlock! I realized that I had to get home and just hope that I could recapture the first words when I got back into a space where I could work uninterrupted.

In fact, the voice graciously started over when I got home. I sat at the kitchen table, staying up all night scribbling frantically, trying to keep up with the steady flow of her words. Around 3:00 A.M., my wife, Kathryn, got up and inquired after my well-being. Since she too is a writer and dream worker, she immediately appreciated the value and potential importance of such a compelling inspiration. She blessed me and went back to bed, leaving me to it.

For the next couple of days, I wrote hurriedly and continuously—on the airplane to and from Los Angeles, during breaks in my scheduled lectures and workshops, and in my motel room late at night—falling asleep exhausted when I could no longer sustain the effort.

Each time I had the opportunity, I went back to the writing, fearing that the voice might be silent. As I read over what I had already written, filled with wonder at the unfolding process, the voice would start speaking again, and I could pick up the narrative and write onward from the place where I had been forced to stop, without any sense of discontinuity or break in the flow of the story.

This is the only piece I have ever composed in this fashion. Reading personal accounts of the creative processes of other writers and artists, and talking with friends and acquaintances who have had similar experiences, I have come to the conclusion that I might as well call *Queen Jocasta* "a channeled piece."

The voice of the old woman never identified itself, but for the whole period of the four days that she recited to me, I never lost my interior sense of her being a separate entity, even after it became clear that she was speaking inside my head. She told the story in her own words (I never imagined, except for that first electric moment in the car, that anyone else could hear her), and then she departed.

When it came time to publish the piece, I really wanted another name to put on the flyleaf, to formally acknowledge my more distant relationship with this poem in comparison to my other work; but my efforts to raise her again and get her to communicate with me, if only to give me her name, met with no success.

Over the ensuing years, I have allowed myself to harbor the thought that the unusual manner in which the inspiration for this piece came to me is a kind of spontaneous "confirmation" from beyond the personal unconscious that my more scholarly researches into the collapse of the matriarchies were essentially correct. There are two moments early in the story where there seem to be references to the failure to predict the precession of the equinoxes: when the old woman says that "the stars fell into a confusion," and when she makes reference to Jocasta's mother being "plagued by secret doubts." But those are the only moments where there seem to be direct references to the conclusions drawn from my research. I still suspect that doing that research prepared me in subtle as well as more obvious ways to "receive" this piece.

The simplest thing I can say about the process of composition is that I was so interested and involved in that research that even after I thought I was done, my unconscious continued to shape the material I was working with into more emotionally interesting and compelling narrative form. On the face of it, that certainly is what happened; but I have had many versions of the experience of "unconscious incubation" over the years, and none of them were as complete or as "other" as the voice of that old woman, and I reserve the right to suppose that there is more to it than that.

Any way you look at it, there is the "simple" fact that the creative imagination is always working, making dreams and making art, even when the conscious mind is focused elsewhere.

There is an implication, also early on in the narrative, that the women of the great prehistoric matriarchies may have known all along that sexual intercourse with a man was a necessary act in order to invite new life into the world, but that it was kept secret, as Robert Graves suggested. The old woman says, "The secret of the seed was not spoken..." It appears that this is an accurate statement, even without the implication of feminine conspiracy, since by all accounts the deepest mysteries of the grieving Mother and her reborn Daughter at Eleusis were revealed without words, with the psychopomp simply holding up an ear of grain in silence.

My friend Bob Trowbridge, who has had many channeling experiences himself, has a wonderfully sane and matter-of-fact attitude toward "spooks," as he calls them. Bob says, "There's no more reason to believe a spook than anybody else sitting next to you on the bus." And even more to the point: "Just because you're dead doesn't mean you're smart!"

I know he's right. The experience of "inspiration directly from the muse" is most compelling and real, but it does not necessarily confer any superior status to the ideas and opinions that are "channeled" in this fashion.

With those caveats clearly in mind, I offer the following "revisionist" narrative of the Oedipus myth. To the best of my knowledge, all the details in the following narrative have some precedent in the scholarly literature and the archaeological record.

Queen Jocasta is an aural piece. It came to me in an auditory form, and it has its greatest impact when spoken out loud and listened to.

Queen Jocasta

The night is warm.
The men are in their cups
Roaring drunken boasts and clattering
Their shields upon the stones.
We shall clean the ewers and trays
Outside, rubbing them with reeds
Under the autumn stars.
They will not hear us, or if they do
They will dismiss it
As the meaningless mumble
Of women at their work.

I am old. My fingers are gnarled
Like the roots of oaks.
You berate me
That I cannot scrub your pots
But I will earn my keep
And tell you something
That will widen out your nostrils
Like the scent of musk,
Open up your languid eyes
Like votive lights
Flickering in a grotto,
And fill you with shame
For the scraps you feed me.

You laugh! But that is good.
They will think that we are sporting
And talking of the barnyard—
When I was just a girl
I saw my Mother spitted on a stake
Giving up her soul in pain
Because some man
Overheard her tell this story
And called it sacrilege.

You do not laugh.
That too is good.

In my Mother's Mother's Mother's time
Things were not as now.

Men still were children, and the Earth
Gave forth her gifts,
But people loved the Mother
And paid her homage.
Queen Kallista ruled this land
By Mother-Right
And when a child was born
Men trembled
At the Goddess's beneficence.
The secret of the seed
Was not spoken.
Each year we walked
To Delphi, Athens, and Eleusis
To celebrate the sacred silence.

But the Goddess turned away her face.
The stars fell into a confusion.
Dust blew from the North
On hot, dry winds.
Crops were meager
And rains washed gullies
Through the land
'Til the Gulf of Corinth
Was as brown as a sow's wallow.
Out of the towering amber clouds
Centaurs appeared
Casting fear into the heart.
There were battles—
Many women died in armed resistance
But our fields and vineyards
Were overrun
By men on horseback.

When they reached this valley's mouth
Up there where the acacias
Crowd close around the stream
And no grass grows,
Queen Kallista and her eldest daughter,
Jocasta, Princess and Queen-to-be,
Together with the Palace Guard
And Temple Servants of the Goddess
Arrayed to meet the bearded warriors,

The old Queen borne upon a litter,
Jocasta, resplendent in her purple cloak,
And others, some dressed for battle,
Some bearing jars and baskets—
Torn
Between resistance and submission.
Kallista, burdened with her years,
Plagued with secret doubts,
But filled with passion for the Goddess
Still urged resistance—
Supporting her, the warrior women,
The heads of clans, the older women
Of the sacred colleges.
But Jocasta chose a milder course,
Rallying the farmers, acolytes,
And younger daughters—
Appeasing her Mother
With warlike preparations
But hoping
For some compromise.

Into this grove old Laius came
Covered with the dust of battle,
Tired from the months of struggle,
He too prepared to fight, but open still
To some negotiated settlement—
Laius, the sow-butcher,
Laius, the tamer-of-horses,
Laius, lusting for his own kingdom
And an end to hungry wandering.
They spoke through surrogates—
Laius employing a blind poet
Captured in battle to the North,
Jocasta speaking through the voice
Of an acolyte
Born in service to the Goddess,
While Queen Kallista mumbled angrily
Surrounded by her armed escort.
They spoke all afternoon
With ceremonial silences.
They came to an agreement:
Laius would permit spring planting,

No woman would lose her home,
Male slaves would have the choice
Of changing masters,
And Laius would be King—
Marrying Jocasta in public ritual.
Kallista raged, but Jocasta
Carefully considered and agreed.
Laius made it clear
That he was no corn-King
Born for butchering—
The rites would be observed
But Laius would live out his years
A King.

How much Jocasta was moved
By his pride and power,
His clear, unflinching eyes
And shiny, flowing hair
I do not know.
He was the first man
She had ever met
Who was not awed by the Dark Mother,
Who talked with careless ease
Meeting her eyes with open curiosity
And lust,
Not bowing,
Or looking deferentially away
With the acolyte's
Practiced, politic politeness.
Perhaps it was the vision
Of her Daughter's awakening desire
That drove Kallista to despair—
She cried out once
And fell back on her couch
Ordering her guards to bear her
Away to the Goddess's sanctuary,
Vowing never to set foot
In her own ancestral grounds again.
The old Queen's heart had failed.
She died before the sun had set
But not before she poured the wine
Upon the stone

And spoke the curse
We all inherit—
That the first child
Jocasta had by Laius
Would grow to murder him
And restore the Goddess
To her full rights in sunny Thebes.

This curse came to Laius
As a prophecy
Whispered
By the Pythoness at Delphi
Before his marriage.
This message tried him sorely
For he had conceived a passion
For Jocasta almost as strong
As his lust for land and power.
On their wedding night
He demanded and received
What Jocasta freely gave
But interrupted their coupling dance
And spilled his seed upon the sheets
Denying Jocasta the culmination
Of her pleasure.
For nine long years he used
His horse-taming wit
To master his own passion,
Never giving fully
Husband's duty
But siring many children
Among the palace servants
In open mockery
Of Queen Jocasta's right.

At last, upon returning from
Some petty thievery
In Sparta to the south,
Seeing shrines to Zeus and Hermes
Everywhere,
Believing that the Gods
Had overthrown their Mother,
Rendered rash and swollen

With his celebrations,
He entered Queen Jocasta's chamber
And worked his will inside her belly
To the end.

Jocasta felt the Goddess-gift
Of new life stirring in her loins
And was afraid.
Laius too was struck with fear.
Eagles nested in the tower,
The earth trembled
And springs broke forth
Through the paving stones
Flooding the palace courtyard.
Jocasta struggled with herself,
Considered flight, remembered
Stories of the women
Who had not succumbed,
Like many of Kallista's guard
Who fled across the sea
To Africa,
There establishing themselves
An armed camp,
Loyal to the Goddess,
Poised and pledged to armed invasion,
But failed in her resolve.

When the child was born a son,
Jocasta felt released—
How could a son
Restore the Mother-Right?
The prophecy must fail!
But to her shocked surprise
Laius was driven almost mad with fear
And would have killed the boy,
Drawing his sword, and swearing
A bloody horseman's oath,
If she had not embraced the child
And invoked the Mother's Mysteries
Within the dark confines
Of the House of Birth.

For one full week
Jocasta kept the baby by her side
Within the women's precinct
Refusing either
To give him up
Or name him.
Laius raged and threatened.
His men grew uneasy.
There was talk of insurrection
And many women were raped and tortured
In the mad search for secret leaders.

Queen Jocasta's deep confusion
Spoke to her in sleep
With many voices.
She would sometimes jerk awake
And wander through the halls
Falling exhausted in some corner
Like a slave.
The babe grew stronger
And Queen Jocasta's secret wish
That he would die
And absolve her of her choice
Grew stronger too.

Her best advisors,
Respected since her Mother's time,
Came secretly to her
And urged her
To feign a peace with Laius,
To lure him somewhere all alone
And poison him, or drive a dagger
Through his ribs.
But still Jocasta wavered.
They argued passionately
For the sanctity of Mother's
Blood
Over blind, male raging—
To kill a husband
Is like cutting wheat,
But to kill a child of your own blood

Is to set yourself against the Mother
Forever.

At last Jocasta made a fumbling choice—
The child would be exposed upon a hill,
Pinioned to the Earth—an offering
To the Mother. She would reclaim him
With her own cold touch
So his blood
Would not be on Jocasta's soul,
Or so she reasoned in her blind despair,
As though the Goddess
Were some foolish merchant
To be cheated by a clever contract!
In her deepest heart
She knew her effort was a sham—
To placate her husband
She sent a man
To do a woman's business.
The child was given
To one of Laius' lieutenants
And was staked upon a snowy hillside,
A tent-peg through his heel.
And when his wailing stopped
And his tiny body ceased to twitch,
That foolish prick-puller returned home
To the warmth of wine and fire
Presuming that something
So small and fragile
As a newborn child
Must be dead in that bitter cold,
Ignorant of the Mother's strength
That lives inside a child
That close to birthing.

A passing shepherd found the child
And knowing more of the Mother's ways
Than Laius' lazy lackey
Saw life flickering still
In the blue and rigid body.
He took him home
And gave him to the woman

Who nurtured and increased
The flocks he tended,
Making of the boy
A second, living offering.
Together they raised him
In the Mother's ways
Until he grew
To strapping, limping youth,
Calling him "Oedipus,"
Because he had no other name.

During those years Queen Jocasta
Came once again to rule
As old Laius slowly found
That he had spent his zest
For wielding power, fucking,
Fighting, and the phantom lure
Of tomorrow's unspent riches.
For a while he wallowed
In wine and reminiscence,
But that too paled in his burning eye
And he took to wandering again
With a small armed escort
In search of oracles and seers
And a glimpse beyond the veil
The Goddess wears
Woven of our vain illusions.

When young Swell-Foot grew
To an age where he left milky come
Scattered in his sleeping place
After dreaming of his mirrored mind,
His surrogate Mother cast the stones
And asked the Goddess for a sign
Of his future life and destiny.
Kallista's curse rose mute and menacing
In the silent shapes she saw.
That wise one knew too much
To make vain opposition
To the Mother's Will.
She gathered up her mantic stones
And paused to set her heart

In grim acceptance
Of a Mother's endless pain,
Then banished her surrogate son
To face his fate
Alone.

At first young Oedipus rebelled,
Demanding reasons
For his sudden fall from favor.
But when she told him
She had read the stones
And that he had a destiny
Larger than their rough-hewn walls
And rocky, rolling pastures,
He laughed and left home
Willingly, blessing them
With youthful arrogance,
Heedless of the silent sorrow
Shining in his Nurse-Mother's eyes.

For many months young Oedipus
Stepped forth as boldly
As his crippled foot allowed
Until one day he faltered
On a narrow path along a bluff,
Tired of the daily search for food,
Cold nights, and the
Loneliness of his desires.
He paused and leaned upon his staff
To watch the ocean snarling far below
Restless from a storm just passed
Writhing in cloud-strewn sunlight.

It was thus that Laius came upon him
Standing staring at the sea.
The old King was on his way
Yet again to Delphi
Riding in a two-horse chariot
Together with an armed companion.
This charioteer reined roughly in
And ordered young Oedipus
To scramble down the bank

And clear the path for them.

Oedipus called loudly back
That he stood aside
For no
Man.

Old Laius was consumed with rage.
He seized the spear
Slung underneath his shield
And hurled it at his Son
Ordering his man to gallop on.
His throw was long
And Oedipus lunged toward the horses
Striking at them as they passed.
He struck again
And caught the chariot wheel
Causing the whole conveyance
To veer off the narrow track
And plunge down the stony bluff
Tumbling and turning as it fell.

Oedipus scrambled to the edge
And panting
Watched it fall,
A single tangle
Of horses, men, and billowing capes
Fluttering like failed wings
Until the image shattered
Scattering into sudden, still,
And separate shapes
Strewn among the rocks below.

Once discovered,
The news of Laius' death
Spread outward like a ripple
Reaching Jocasta here in Thebes
And spreading South across the sea
To reach the remnant of
Her Mother's army.
That, together with the news
That there was war
Among Laius' lieutenants

And bastard sons
Loosed them from their years of waiting
Like an arrow from a full-drawn bow.
They sailed North, returning home
Receiving messages along their route
From fisher folk
Still loyal to the Goddess
Regarding battles, deaths,
And the bloody course
Of civil war in Thebes.
They landed on a promontory to the South,
Striking at the city
At the moment when the raging forces
Of contending men
Were at their weakest,
Butchering the invaders
And Laius' bastard sons together
In a bloody offering
To the Dark Mother.

With Jocasta
They made an uneasy truce—
Many blamed her still
For their earlier defeat.
But her lineage was
Undeniable
And when she walked
Across the darkened battlefield
Surrounded by her torchbearers,
Dressed in the glittering garments
Of the Goddess,
Her trailing hems
Soaked slick and shining
With spilled male blood,
Carrying
Both fruit and flowers
In her upraised arms,
The warrior women
Hailed her as their Queen.

Kallista's aging generals
Grudgingly agreed

But retained control
Of the women under arms.
They set up a shrine
On the heights before the city
And began an inquisition of all men,
Sacrificing those
Who failed to pay
Proper homage to the Goddess
In her guise as Sphinx,
Clothed in lineaments of
Lion,
Woman,
Snake,
And eagle—
Four-fold guardian
Of the four-fold year—
The embodiment of life in death
Held in balance
Between her soft and taloned paws.
Many men were slaughtered
At the feet of her mighty image
While Queen Jocasta looked calmly on.

News came to Oedipus as well
That the man he tumbled down the cliff
Had been the King of Thebes
And that returning forces
Of the old Queen
Had seized the land,
Disposed of Laius' many heirs,
And were demanding
Homage to the Goddess
As the price of passage
To that realm.

Having spent his life among shepherds
Guarding flocks consecrated
To the Goddess,
He well knew
the rhythm of her round.
He knew the Queen
Would soon be seeking a male consort

To act in the repeating ritual
Of coupling and planting.
And who more likely
For that regal role
Than the hero
Who had overthrown the King?

Oedipus slowed his progress
To pace his journey
To the turning stars
And arrived the day of
Vernal Equinox
Before the Sphinx.

Word of his coming
Had gone before him,
And at the end
His path was flanked
With crowds of silent Thebans
Well aware of the possible significance
Of his arrival.
They eyed his limping bold approach,
So different
From so many other men
Who had been dragged struggling
To face the Sphinx's deadly
Double questions.
Jocasta watched him climb the hill,
Briefly took his youthful measure,
And thought again
Of the disturbing news
That came to her from
Neighboring invader-kings,
Uneasy on their fresh-won thrones
Who watched the Goddess's return
And rapid retribution
With great alarm—
The taking of a consort-king
Might thwart the threats
Of armed invasion
That daily reached her ears.

Oedipus stood tall
Before the terrible image
Towering before him—huge wings
Outspread, paws
At his chest, huge breasts
Surmounted by the giant face
Staring with star-flecked eyes.
Close at his side
An aged woman stood
Peering at him sharply.
He expected her to speak
But a voice rang forth
Resonant and loud
From within the giant figure,

"WHO IS YOUR MOTHER?"

Oedipus was tingling with surprise
But found his voice and spoke.
For a moment Queen Jocasta met his eyes
And felt the same unflinching gaze
That Laius once had had
And heard him ringingly proclaim,
The four-fold Mother of us all—
First, as curling ocean wave
Embodied in the woman who bore him
And nursed him as a babe
Creeping on all fours,
Now, as Sun and fire
Nourishing and warming all men
Standing on two legs,
Then in his future, final years
As Moon,
Mistress of the winds and tides,
When he would hobble on a staff,
And finally, as Earth herself
Who would cut him down
Devouring her son
To bear him through the dark
And back in life again.

The test was passed, but Oedipus spoke on,
Demanding ancient honors
As the instrument of Laius' sacrifice.
He described the scene, as I have told you,
Where he slew Laius on the road
To justify his claim as consort
And dropped at last upon his knees
Before the silent statue of the Sphinx
Fore-acknowledging
Whatever choice she made.

Queen Jocasta savored
The barely breathing silence
Together with the pleasures
And the dangers of her choice.
She sensed the crowd's acceptance
And stepped forward to meet his gaze
And place her outstretched hand
Upon his head.

That evening
When the sun touched midpoint
On the horizon to the West,
They made a great procession
In the dying, orange light
Bearing the Sphinx upon their shoulders
Down
Into the city.

Queen Jocasta took her unknown son
As consort a few nights later,
Coupling with him
In a regal tent
Set up upon the recent battlefield
While her subjects
Reveled noisily outside
With flutes and torches
Endlessly repeating
Her royal act
Naked on the bloody ground.

Nine times the Moon repeated
Her monthly miracle of death and birth
Before the Queen gave birth to twins—

Two boys, an event of evil omen
That set the restless nation in a panic.
The oracles urged
That one be put to death
According to the ancient custom
And to assure a clear succession,
But Queen Jocasta cast all such advice
Contemptuously aside,
Saying she had had enough
Of prophecy.

Crops failed. The rains were harsh
And many blamed the Queen.
When she gave birth to a daughter
There was great rejoicing.
The Goddess had been reborn again—
Surely Earth must mirror to that
Miracle, and bear herself anew!
A second daughter
Made it seem
Inevitable
But still the crops were small.
The royal granaries were opened
Not for profitable trade
Or celebration
But to feed the famished populace.
There was a brief renewal of the ritual
Of inquisition by the Sphinx,
But Queen Jocasta was not willing
To risk for little reason
Her fragile truce
With worried, warlike neighbors
By loosing zealots on the land.
She forbade it
But the ritual continued,
Repressed
Into the writhing shapes of rumor—
Someone had a vision
That a single sacrifice was called for.
A sown-man, claiming lineage
From the time of Cadmus
And the Dragon Mother's teeth

Hurled himself
From the city's shining walls.
Another dreamed the Goddess as a cat
Weeping blood
And devouring her kittens.
A third that Laius had returned
To sow the land with bitter salt
In vengeance for his
Ignoble death.

Young Oedipus stayed much indoors
Fearing that some other man
Might repeat his famous exploit
And play Swell-Foot to his uneasy Laius,
But Queen Jocasta forced him to go out
And preside with her
Over a public ceremony
Devised to crush the rumors
And restore the shaken faith of people
In their Goddess
And their Queen.

Many people crowded to the square
To proclaim their troubled sleep
And visions—
Groups of women, thin and ragged
From purifying rituals
Held in the mountains
And by the sea,
Men still bloody
From ecstatic rites
Of self-castration
All afire with their fervor
For the Mother,
Worried peasants
Holding children close
Speaking haltingly of strange plants
Growing on ancestral graves
And monsters briefly glimpsed
At dusk among their flocks.
The babble of their many voices
Rose to drown the mutter of the sea

While Queen Jocasta listened
Glittering and silent
And Oedipus moved restlessly
Upon his throne
Like a yoked ox
Plagued by buzzing flies.

A sudden silence fell upon the crowd
When fabled, blind Teiresias appeared,
He was dressed as was his wont,
In a harlot's fringed and flowing dress,
Bedecked with ornaments,
His blind face rouged and painted
In grotesque parody
Of a woman's beauty,
His long beard oiled and glistening
Falling like a nest of newborn snakes
Across his naked breast.
The crowd drew back
In deference, disgust,
And awe,
Making a path before the dais
Down which Teiresias passed slowly
Gently guided by his young companion.
When he sensed that he had reached
The center of the gazing space
He stopped
And struck a studied pose
And at last began to speak.

He began a rambling story
Of how he had once chanced to see
Two great, golden serpents
Coupling on Mount Ida
And how the Goddess had then
Struck him blind
For viewing her
In such a fashion,
Later granting him the gift
Of second sight and prophecy
In a grim joke,
The kind she likes the best,

Lighting up his darkness
With terrible true visions,
Making of her gift
A double punishment
For his unwitting
Sacrilege.

Oedipus broke roughly in
Demanding that he speak of
Current Theban woes and troubles
And leave his stories
For another time,
But Queen Jocasta raised her hand
Silencing his interruption.
In his darkness, Teiresias
Was momentarily confused
By Oedipus' unfinished admonition.
But then he laughed like
A coquettish courtesan
And tossed his head
Continuing his speech
With an account of how
He had been captured long ago
By Laius and forced to play
His interlocutor
In the initial parlay
With Jocasta.

He spoke of Queen Kallista's curse
And the many, bitter years
Jocasta had spent watching
The invaders settle onto Theban soil.
Often he would break off
Demanding food and drink
Before he would continue
All of which Jocasta silently commanded
While Oedipus stirred restlessly
And the people watched and listened.

At last the old man grew a little drunk
And proclaimed that all the Theban woes
Were caused by simple ignorance

Of the Goddess's desires—
That she brought
These troubles on the land
To force an understanding of her Will—
Had she not inspired Kallista
To cast her curse?
Had she not filled Laius with desire
To make a child against
His will and better judgment?
And had she not preserved the child
Cast out upon the mountain
To play his part
In her predestined drama?
And now she brought this famine
On the land to force all ignorant
And doubting people
To fall in awe and wonder
Before her endless
Miracle.

Jocasta had begun to guess—
She first grew pale
And then leaned forward in her seat
As though to catch the old man's words
Before he spoke them.
But Oedipus lashed out
Unwilling to be silent longer.
He railed at old Teiresias
Threatening him with banishment
Or even death
For his pointless, rambling narrative
And adding that when he stood
Before the Sphinx
He spoke more truly of the Goddess
In a few short lines
Than all Teiresias' rantings.

The old man answered angrily
That Oedipus was both a fool and fraud,
Sitting on a throne he'd never won
Having failed to give true answers
To the Sphinx's simple question.

Oedipus sprang forward with such rage
That it might have silenced any man
Who saw it,
But blind Teiresias spoke on
Proclaiming that Oedipus was
Queen Jocasta's firstborn child,
Son of Laius,
Sleeping in the bed
Where he had been conceived,
Siring children who were at once
His sisters and his brothers,
Living consort of the Living Mother
In full but witless harmony
With the Dread Goddess's commands.
Oedipus was frozen in midstep,
His hand raised to strike the seer,
His face flattened to a mask of rage
And horror at the words he heard,
Filled to bursting with contending passions
But finding
No release.

Queen Jocasta too was overwhelmed
With conflicting feelings and regrets.
In that instant the entire sky
Seemed to poise and pivot
On her pounding heart.
She clutched the rampant lions
That formed the armrests of her throne
And remembered that the universe
And all that it contains
Is but a finely polished mirror
For the Mother's fair and
Fearsome face.
She looked at her trembling husband-son
And at Teiresias' empty, staring eyes
Which saw it all
So clearly
And felt the pathos
Welling up within her
At the cosmic jest
That is our little life.

She threw back her head
And laughed
While the people murmured
Many falling to their knees
In horror, awe, and wonder
At the unfolding knowledge
Of their fate.

Jocasta's laughter struck Oedipus
And made him
Stagger.
He turned from old Teiresias
And took two tottering steps
Until he wavered over Queen Jocasta
Sprawled upon her throne.
He cried out once,
An awful, piercing sound
That echoed from the palace walls
And sent the seagulls wheeling overhead.
He seized her upturned throat
In both his hands
And throttled off her
Voice and
Breath.
Jocasta's guards were on him in an instant
But not before he sent her soul
Into the Mother's dark embrace.
They would have killed him
On the spot
But Teiresias spoke out again
In a voice possessed and
Magnified—
So strong it stopped their blood
And paralyzed their will to act.
The old man burned
With a prophetic fire
As he forbade them
To harm Oedipus
In any way.
His blind eyes
Blazed
As he proclaimed

The Mother's Will—
Oedipus was but the instrument
Of her design. He acted
To exact just punishment
For Queen Jocasta's violation
Of the Mother's Law
And turning from her ways.
Although he could not see
He pointed straight at Oedipus
And commanded him to obey
The voice that spoke within him
For it was
The Goddess's command.

Oedipus stood still,
Head cocked a little to one side,
Chest heaving with his labored breath.
Then he stepped again
Toward Queen Jocasta's
Limp and silent form.
He gently touched the double golden snakes
That twined round Queen Jocasta's
Still-warm breasts
And raised these serpents high
Above his upturned head
So that they glinted in the sun.
Then he dashed them down
With all his strength
Into his open, staring eyes.
Blood spurted forth
As from a fountain,
And Oedipus fell heavily
Without a sound
Backward at his Mother's feet.

The voiceless crowd dispersed
Slowly, and in great confusion,
Too shocked and horror struck
To make
Any lamentation.

That night the city throbbed
With screams and torches
As news of the monstrous horror spread.
In the morning the populace discovered
Their city under siege
By forces of King Theseus of Athens
Whose spies had sped the message
Of Queen Jocasta's death
Swiftly to him by signal fires
In the anarchy of darkness.

Thebes fell without resistance,
And Theseus set Jocasta's clever cousin Kreon
As his puppet-ally on the Theban throne.
He took blind Oedipus
Under heavy guard to dry Colonus
Where he lived a while
In the Goddess's sacred sanctuary
Consumed by an insane, prophetic trance,
Uttering fevered oracles of the age to come
And curing illness with his touch.
The Goddess spoke through him before he died
Of a future cursed with fear and fire
When all women would be slaves
And the Earth burned black and barren
By male ignorance and war.

All that she spoke has come to pass.
She rules us still, but is not seen,
Withdrawn behind her veil,
Always a mystery,
Hidden
By her daily
Miracles.
You have heard me out
But still you do not understand.
You dream of shaping destiny
Only through your lovers, sons, and husbands—
Or worse,
You do not dream at all—
You paint your faces
And forget
Yourselves,

Blind
To the Goddess
Who is in
Us
All!

One yawns; another is asleep.
Your memories are dulled
By lack of thought and practice.
You will remember my fierce words
No more than you recall a dream
That nags your conscience on awakening.

I am resigned.
I accept
The Mother's Will.
Until you weary of the slavish life
And awaken to the Goddess once again
This story must die here
Under the chilly autumn stars
With me.

Chapter 8
SHADOW, TRICKSTER, AND WILLING SACRIFICE: THEIR EVOLVING ENERGY IN ANCIENT AND MODERN LIFE

> Trickster is at one and the same time creator and destroyer, giver and negator, he who dupes others and is always duped himself....He knows neither good nor evil yet he is responsible for both.
>
> *Paul Radin*

In the Oedipus story, the blind soothsayer Teiresias plays a pivotal role. One crucial aspect of that role is fulfilling the function of the archetypal Trickster.

He is the same Teiresias who, prior to his involvement in the Oedipus narrative, played a similar ambiguous, archetypal trickster role in the Olympian battle of the sexes by getting himself transformed into a woman for several years, and then back into a man again. This transformative experience makes him the ideal person to settle the argument between Zeus, the king of the gods, and his wife, Hera, over which partner generally derives the greatest pleasure from sexual intercourse, the man or the woman. Zeus summons Teiresias to offer his unique testimony on this question, and Teiresias answers (I assume honestly) that "if the pleasures of lovemaking be divided into four parts, then three belong to the woman, and one to the man." Zeus is annoyed by this answer, and in this version of the myth, it is Zeus who blinds Teiresias for his impertinent candor in answering the god's question.

230

In that moment of meting out this punishment, Zeus himself assumes the mantle of spurned Trickster, preferring his own opinion and the power to enforce it over the truth, even after the larger truth has been clearly revealed. Stubbornness in the face of overwhelming evidence is another classic hallmark of the energy of the archetypal Trickster, as it is of human consciousness itself.

When it comes time to answer the questions that Queen Jocasta and King Oedipus ask about the reasons for the famine that has overtaken the land of Thebes, Teiresias does it again; he reveals the suppressed truth that has always been there, lurking just below the surface of conscious awareness. His answer "upsets the apple cart" and brings the whole regal assumption of power, moral superiority, and unquestioned righteousness crashing down in ruins. This overturning of arrogant assumption and being the agent of "poetic justice" has always been a major part of the archetypal Trickster's task.

When Coyote follows Earthmaker around, amending and undoing his work (see chapter 3), he too is playing the archetypal role of the Trickster. He restores a kind of precarious "balance" in the cosmos. He reminds everyone, including Earthmaker himself, that the unknown is still stronger than the known. In performing this part of the archetypal Trickster's task, he lays claim to the new territory of human conscious self-awareness and choice in the larger landscape of divine creation. At a very deep level, *the Trickster is an archetypal symbol of human consciousness itself.* In reflection of the simultaneous strengths and weaknesses of human consciousness, Trickster always goes about performing the ironically sacred tasks arrogantly and clumsily, but with amazing tenacity and creativity.

When the jealous and apprehensive gods and goddesses trick Izanagi and Izanami into abstaining from sexual intercourse even after they are officially married (see chapter 3), they too are assuming the energy and role of Trickster. When Little Gooyion shape-changes into the single grain of barley and tricks the angry Great Goddess in her momentary guise as Ceridooen/Hen into eating him (see chapter 4), he too fulfills this aspect of the archetypal role of Trickster. He brings to light by his actions the truth that had previously been unconscious, but was always present just below the surface of conscious assumption and awareness. He reveals the implications of that previously unacknowledged truth. At one important level, newly conscious Gooyion/Trickster reveals the truth that male "seed" is instrumental in the creation of new life and sets the stage for a whole new cycle of human civilization, characterized by male domination of religious, economic, and political life.

When the infant god Hermes presents his uncle, Apollo, with the first lyre, made from the remains of the very cattle he has just stolen (see chapter 6), he also assumes the role of Trickster. Hermes embodies Trickster in the very midst of fulfilling his destiny as Divine Child. In this particular narrative, the two roles are synonymous. The Divine Child brings the gift of new consciousness and new collective awareness. The full range of consequences stemming from this new awareness are not yet known, and it is this "tricky," not-fully-aware quality of evolving human consciousness that Trickster always reflects in his/her unique and inevitably ambiguous behavior.

Like the actions of tricksters everywhere, Hermes' actions blur the academic distinctions between archetypal forms and make it clear once again that they all blend and merge into one another in practice. Hermes sets up the arrogant God of the Sun for the previously unimaginable and unthinkable overthrow of his most cherished and unquestioned assumptions of power and omnipotence and tricks Apollo into participating voluntarily and unwittingly in his own downfall. At the same time, Baby Hermes is also a clear examplar of the archetype of Divine Child, born amidst trouble, yet surviving to create a new dispensation, a whole new way of relating to the divine and to the world.

Despite the general preponderance of male trickster figures, the archetypal energy is (once again) not gender bound. We have inherited a smaller but significant number of sacred narratives in which the archetypal trickster pattern is embodied in female form. It seems reasonable to suppose that there were probably many more mythic narratives with females playing the archetypal Trickster in the ancient matrifocal/agrarian world. Many of those stories have come down to us as folk tales, where the clever and resourceful heroine tricks and cunningly defeats the seemingly all-powerful ogres, kings, demons, magicians, and the like, and offers "comeuppance" to the arrogant characters who exhibit the greatest hubris.

In the archaic mythological tradition of the Japanese archipelago, for example, comes the following story about the conflict between Ama-terra-tsu, (the Goddess of the Sun, "Mother of the Earth, due all honor and respect") and her younger brother, Susan-o-wo ("Swift, Strong, Impetuous Male").

The Anger of Ama-terra-tsu, Goddess of the Sun

The story begins by telling us that Ama-terra-tsu has been given the task of creating the world. (In some versions, it is given by the mysterious God-Beyond-Naming; and in others, by Izanagi and Izanami, whose children she and Susan-o-wo are said to be.) She is sent to perform her divine mission in the company of her brother, with whom she does not get along. Like most sidekicks in creation narratives of this sort, Susan-o-wo initially plays an archetypal trickster role himself, accompanying his sister everywhere and infuriating her with his clumsy imitations of her primordial creative acts, just as Coyote follows Earthmaker around and infuriates him with his clumsy, boisterous imitations of divine creativity. But Susan-o-wo's imitations produce nothing of worth in his sister's eyes, "nothing that lives."

This is always the archetypal matriarchal/feminine criticism of male energy and activity, reflecting at one level at least, the contempt of the archetypal feminine for the masculine, which does not physically bear and bring new life into the world. Obviously, such criticism has tremendous weight in a world where the Goddess (and all women, indeed all female organisms) are believed to reproduce parthenogenically, and male participation is not perceived to be required in the creation of new life. In such a world, the males are always expendable. Male consciousness is unable to achieve full commune with the Great Mother until and unless it is reborn in female bodily form, in an ironic precursor of the masculinist/patriarchal assertion that only men can truly commune with God the Father.

The echo of this archetypal criticism of "barren maleness"

is one of the more stubborn and pervasive remnants from the archaic period in the collective development of human consciousness and spiritual awareness when the divine presented an almost exclusively feminine face. When this particular criticism of the male characters appears in a mythological/folk narrative, it is most often an indication that the story has roots that extend back into the prehistoric, matrifocal world, even as it echoes the ongoing gender tensions in contemporary society.

Eventually, Ama-terra-tsu becomes so exasperated with Susan-o-wo's dogged and unredeemably masculine interference in her essentially feminine task of creation that she banishes him from her presence. Since she is the sun, the source of all warmth and light, she is condemning him to "outer darkness" by exiling him from her presence.

This punishment causes Susan-o-wo to become most distressed and disconsolate. He wanders in the darkness of his exile, bewailing his cruel and undeserved fate and promising to mend his ways, but all to no avail. Eventually, he comes up with the idea that perhaps he can worm his way back into his divine sister's good graces again if he gives her a gift. However (like Ganesha, St. Michael, Hephaestos, and so many other divine and semi-divine males who faced the same problem), he soon realizes that *everything that is* was originally the gift of the Creatrix of the world in the first place, so nothing (no matter how grand, beautiful, intricate, or elaborately reworked it might be) can possibly serve as a unique and adequate gift in return.

Faced with this seemingly unsolvable problem, Susan-o-wo realizes that the only place where such a new and unique gift might be hidden is in the as-yet-unexplored depths of his own interior being. Making use of his "swift, strong, impetuous male" energy, Susan-o-wo plunges his fingers into his chest at the level of the heart and tears it open. (This "rending the chest open with bare hands" is the primary archetypal gesture of Willing Sacrifice in the act of self-exploration.) Inside, he discovers a horse—the first horse—the essence and epitome of swiftness, strength, and loyal impetuosity—a figure born of, and reflecting, his own deepest being.

Filled with pride and renewed self-assurance, Susan-o-wo

brings the newly-called-forth horse to the palace of Ama-terra-tsu to present it to her as a gift. Ama-terra-tsu, however, has left strict orders with her door guards not to allow Susan-o-wo to enter or even approach her palace under any circumstances. Susan-o-wo and his "gift horse" are turned away by her warrior maidens. Refusing to be put off so easily, Susan-o-wo turns on all his charm and powers of persuasion (which are considerable) and shows them the horse, explaining to them that it is a special gift for his divine sister, their mistress—a new and unique thing, a thing of stunning grace and beauty, a thing that she has never seen or even imagined before.

The horse is indeed beautiful, and the guards are so moved by it that they decide to risk Ama-terra-tsu's wrath and tell her that her brother is waiting at the gate with a most marvelous gift for her. They bring the news to Ama-terra-tsu where she is sitting in her garden weaving, surrounded by her household women. She is unmoved by their story of the marvelous horse. She knows her brother all too well, and she is completely convinced (in an archetypal act of hubris) that he is incapable of creating anything of interest or importance to her. She angrily strips her guards of their rank and authority as punishment for disobeying her explicit orders, and sends them back to drive Susan-o-wo away once and for all.

The guards, enraged that Susan-o-wo's smooth talking has caused them to fall from their mistress's favor, attack him and drive him and the horse away with great ferocity and bitterness.

Bruised and beaten, Susan-o-wo is filled with misery and frustration. It a fit of impetuous rage, he cuts off the horse's head with his sword and flings the bloody decapitated head over the wall of the palace in a last impotent gesture of despair and defiance. The severed head comes whirling over the wall into the garden where Ama-terra-tsu is sitting at her great loom, weaving the orderly succession of the days and nights, the procession of the moons and seasons, with all the colors of the rainbow and the sunset. The bloody severed head comes sailing over the wall into the tranquil garden and crashes down into the loom and shatters it. Ama-terra-tsu is enraged anew—not just at her brother, but at all the gods and goddesses who have allowed these impertinent sacrileges to continue.

In her divine rage, Ama-terra-tsu calls to her entire entourage and commands them to follow her. She leaves her palace and stalks off to the great mountain. She faces the mountain and commands it to open and receive her and her servants. The mountain trembles and obeys, and the Goddess of the Sun and all her minions enter the depths of the mountain, closing it tight behind them. Ama-terra-tsu withdraws her shining presence from the world, condemning all—animals, gods, and goddesses alike—to a lingering death in the cold and the darkness created by her total and absolute absence.

Word spreads quickly, and the gods and goddesses light torches and gather in front of the mountain, weeping and tearing their beautiful robes and scratching their faces in ritual gestures of submission, grief, contrition, and supplication. Inside the mountain, the Goddess of the Sun can hear their weeping and cries for forgiveness, but her heart is hard. There is no forgiveness in her.

At this point, Uzume, washerwoman to the gods, the most lowly and despised of all the gods and goddesses, appears on the torchlit scene. She has been down by the river, washing the clothes of the gods and goddesses. She thought the sun went down unusually early, even for the middle of winter, but she did not give it any thought. Now she arrives, carrying her basket of clean laundry, and finds her divine masters and mistresses all in the most extreme attitudes of distress and supplication. She is surprised and asks what is going on.

The gods and goddesses can hardly be bothered to tell her. (The tendency of the figures of established power to ignore and demean the trickster is one of the hallmark archetypal elements of the repeating trickster story.) Eventually, Uzume is able to piece together the story: Susan-o-wo has finally gone too far. He has cut off the head of the first horse and smashed her divine loom with it, and now his divine sister has withdrawn her divine and necessary presence from the world, and all who remain are doomed to a horrible, lingering death.

Uzume is incredulous. "Really?"

"Really!"

"We're all going to die?"

"We're all going to *die!!*"

"Even me?"

"Even you!!"

"Well then," Uzume looks around, "there's only one thing left to do!"

"What's that? What can there possibly be left for us to do? Don't you understand? We're all *doomed!*"

"In that case..." Uzume puts down her load of divine laundry and tips the basket over on the ground so that it becomes a makeshift platform. She climbs up onto the overturned laundry basket in the flickering torchlight and takes off her obi, revealing her bare breasts. "Let's party!"

The gods and goddesses are stunned. Uzume starts to sing a ribald little song. She takes her breasts in her hands and pretends that they are gigantic eyes. She makes them look to the right, and then to left, as she sings. She prances and dances on top of her overturned laundry basket/podium. Then she causes her breast/eyes to look cross-eyed.

Despite their misery and despair, the gods and goddesses are moved to laughter. They roar and hoot as Uzume performs her comic, seductive striptease.

Inside the mountain, Ama-terra-tsu hears their laughter and is confounded and amazed. What have they got to laugh about? They are all doomed! What can they possibly find funny in the face of their inevitable and ignominious demise? She presses her ear against the rock to see if she can hear what the cause of their merriment can possibly be, but all she hears is a little high-pitched singing and increasing gales of laughter. Slowly her divine curiosity gets the better of her, and she parts the rock like a curtain and takes the tiniest peek into the darkened landscape to see what can possibly be so amusing in the face of inevitable slow and lingering death.

But since she is the Goddess of the Sun, when she parts the wall of the mountain to steal a peek at the incomprehensible merriment, a ray of golden sunlight shoots forth into the darkened scene. Uzume sees this one ray of light, and with unaccustomed authority, she commands the God of War to hold up his endlessly polished shield and catch the beam of light and reflect it back at the mountain.

When Ama-terra-tsu peeks out of the mountain, the first thing she sees is her own divinely radiant image, reflected in the mirror-smooth surface of the shield of the God of War. She has never seen herself before, and she is convinced it is another goddess. In that instant, she is utterly dismayed and entranced. The gods and goddesses must have somehow created and called forth another goddess of the sun to take her place—one that is so unbelievably radiant and beautiful that even Ama-terra-tsu herself cannot tear her eyes away from her shining beauty. Uzume calls out triumphantly, ordering the God of War to walk backwards, carrying his mirror/shield, so that the reflected image of Ama-terra-tsu begins to recede in her gaze. Ama-terra-tsu comes forth, slowly following the magnificent receding image, entranced by its luminous grace, power, and beauty.

When she emerges, Uzume calls out to the rest of the gods and goddesses to close the mountain behind Ama-terra-tsu and turn it into solid rock, so that the Goddess will never be able to withdraw from the earth in that way again (Fig. 16).

Trickster as Archetype of Evolving Consciousness

In this story, Uzume, the goddess of washerwomen, plays the same Trickster role as Coyote, Hermes, and the rest. She expresses the instinctive wisdom of the body and the irrepressible archetypal energy of evolving human consciousness, which is not defeated, but rather is spurred on to new levels of creative activity by the desperation caused by inevitable misfortune and death. Once again, Uzume, like all archetypal tricksters, embodies human consciousness itself—bawdy, trivial, and venal on the one hand, and simultaneously capable of the greatest acts of courage, invention, and creativity, on the other.

As Paul Radin points out, the Trickster "knows neither good nor evil, yet is responsible for both." This is a symbolic formulation of ever-evolving human consciousness itself, responsible for the greatest good and the greatest evil simultaneously, yet blindly and foolishly unaware of the consequences of its actions in any given moment.

Figure 16. (Ancient Japan) Ama-terra-tsu, Goddess of the Sun, is enticed from her cave by curiosity about the hilarity of the gods and goddesses at the comic/erotic dance of Uzume, goddess of washerwomen.

In story after story, the Trickster is the seemingly unlikely savior, like Uzume, the lowly and despised one who turns the seemingly hopeless situation on its head and transforms it completely. Over and over again, it is the Trickster who is responsible for the creation of language (that most ambiguous and "deceptive" of human inventions) as well as all the other artifacts of culture—cooking, singing, dancing, praying, kinship terms, clothing, commerce, writing, tattooing, and rituals for all purposes.

The Trickster is also the inventor of *conscious deception*. The moment the strategy of conscious deception has been invented, the Trickster inevitably deceives him- or herself, and performs the most gratuitous acts of stupidity and self-destruction. In story after story (as exemplified in the narrative of Coyote and Earthmaker in chapter 3), Trickster is the one who brings Death into the world, always unaware of the full impact and significance of his/her act. The archetypal Trickster simultaneously reflects the best and worst qualities of evolving and always-less-than-complete human consciousness, with all its foolishness and grandeur.

Jung and Trickster

Jung formulates the Trickster as an essentially "archaic" archetype. He assesses the Trickster to be of diminishing relevance to contemporary, "civilized" mentality and social structure:

> [T]he trickster obviously represents a vanishing level of consciousness which increasingly lacks the power to take shape and assert itself.

Unfortunately, like his assertions about the "unbreakable" gender links in animus/anima and Shadow, subsequent experience demonstrates that this formulation is overly arbitrary, incomplete, and prematurely closed. Of course, one aspect of the archetypal Trickster presided over the "primitive" emergence of human consciousness "at the beginning of the world," but since Trickster is a primary archetype of evolving consciousness itself, it informs the shape of human activity in *all* periods of history.

In fact, the archetypal Trickster is alive and thriving in contemporary, postmodern Western society. Trickster asserts itself with depressing regularity, delivering the eternal comeuppance to overweeningly proud individual and collective consciousness in the midst of its hubris—its arrogant assumptions of intellectual/cultural superiority and invincible technology. The moment the builders of the *Titanic* announced that it was "unsinkable," the Trickster yawned and stretched and looked around for an iceberg.

All the archetypes are "archaic," "timeless," and regularly "take shape and assert themselves" *as repeating patterns* in our contemporary lives and circumstances. The Trickster in particular, far from being a "vanishing" archetypal energy, dominates the course of contemporary life. As an archetypal constellation representing the evolving potential of human consciousness itself, it stands at the center of the conflict over prematurely closed worldviews and the role of increased conscious manipulation of the global environment, which (like all trickster manifestations) reflects stunning technological cleverness on the one hand, and increasingly self-deluded and self-destructive behavior on the other.

By attempting to relegate the Trickster to the "nursery stage" of human development, Jung has unfortunately done us a great disservice, potentially distracting us and turning our attention away from one of the most important archetypal dramas of our individual and collective lives. Ironically, the Trickster gains in power and significance even more because it is repressed and denied, as Jung himself goes on to say in the very next sentence:

> Furthermore, repression would prevent it from vanishing, *because repressed contents are the very ones that have the best chance of survival.*" (emphasis mine)

Academic/theoretical relegation of the Trickster to an element of "primitive" psychology and social organization *is* a very real form of collective repression, and has contributed to the continued "underground" influence of trickster energy on the dilemmas of postmodern life.

The repeating pattern of the trickster archetype is discernible in many of the most seemingly endemic and intractable problems of contemporary life. For example, if one were given the task of designing a system of publicly financed education, the purpose of which was to take relatively young and inexperienced criminals and turn them into hardened and remorseless ones in the minimum amount of time with maximum efficiency, one could do no better than the current penal system in the Western world. The penal system is *itself* "a bumbling trickster," creating and making worse the very thing it is trying to control. The escalating failure of the prison system to protect society continually shows the hubris-driven leadership that its basic assumptions are flawed. Fear and coercion do not create law-abiding docility; they create more fear and coercion in response.

Like Zeus blinding Teiresias for speaking the truth about the pleasures of sexual intercourse, the Trickster of incomplete administrative consciousness prefers the arbitrary exercise of power to any admission of failure. Collectively, we prefer "to throw good money after bad" rather than to voluntarily face the possibility of real growth and change in our most cherished assumptions and institutions.

Trickster in Contemporary Guise

Another distressing example of the archetype of Trickster at work in contemporary society is the failure of the Forest Service to actually increase the productivity of our timberlands. The basic unquestioned assumption of the Forest Service—its hubris, if you will—has been, until very recently, that "a managed forest" will, by definition, be more productive than "a wild, unmanaged forest." To the end of increasing the productivity of the forests, the Forest Service has carefully watched for the last sixty years or so for the first signs of fire in the forests and made prodigious efforts to put out every fire it saw as quickly and efficiently as possible. The result is that the natural cycle of forest burning, which tended to serve the function of "pruning"—burning the smaller trees and the brush, but not "topping out" and killing the older, larger trees—has been interrupted, so that now *every* fire has the potential of becoming a holocaust and destroying millions of acres (to say nothing of board feet) of timber. The national effort to control forest fires has contributed greatly to making them even more dangerous and destructive.

Recently, the Forest Service has been reluctantly forced to the conclusion that a certain amount of fire in the national forests is a good thing, and it has even instituted a program of "controlled burns" in national forests like Yosemite, in an ironic effort to "reproduce the natural cycle." These efforts have led to tremendous public outcry, primarily because the basic assumption of our collective, cultural hubris has not been addressed. The "public relations problem" of the Forest Service in winning public approval for controlled burning is directly linked to the archetypal energies of the Trickster/Shadow/Divine Child that (once again) challenge our deepest collective assumptions about the superiority of conscious manipulation and control over the unconscious/natural/spontaneous energies of life.

King Herod sends the household guards to slaughter the

innocents with the same contradictory sense of desperation and arrogant certainty as the legislatures show in allocating more and more money for building and maintaining prisons. Trickster is alive and well and thriving in postmodern society, and pretending otherwise only makes the task of dealing with our true dilemma more difficult.

The primary symptom of the negative (Shadow) aspect of the archetypal Trickster is *failure of imagination.* Whenever a person believes he or she has no choice but to do some less-than-desirable thing (like cutting financial support for public education so that there will be money available to build yet another prison), the Trickster is manifest. Whenever an individual, or a society as a whole, begins to seriously entertain the notion that everything that needs to be known *is* known and that the only remaining tasks are "refinements of administration," that is *hubris,* and the inevitable consequence of the constellation of that order of hubris is the activation and energizing of the archetypal Trickster.

The Monkey's Paw

The modern story of "The Monkey's Paw" offers an exquisitely accurate symbolic narrative of how the energies of Trickster continue to operate undiminished in the modern world, despite the "vanishing" of the trickster figure, per se.

In the story, a rich industrialist decides to throw a party to show off his power and beneficence to the world. His wife plans the details of the event and invites an old Gypsy fortune-teller to come to the party to provide entertainment for their jaded guests.

The fortune-teller makes use of a shriveled, mummified monkey's paw as a magical talisman, a "prop" in her "act." She tells people that if they can overcome their squeamishness and hold the paw in their hands, the paw has the power to grant three wishes. The old woman goes on to warn the guests darkly that they should ponder carefully what three wishes they really want to come true.

The arrogant industrialist overhears her spiel, grabs the

paw away from her, and jokingly wishes for "another million dollars." The fortune-teller rebukes the man and tells him that since he used the magic of the monkey's paw with so little understanding and respect, she can tell him right then and there that his third and final wish will be for death.

Angered by the old woman's rebuke and her apparent effort to "spoil the party," the man throws her out without paying her. His wife is very upset and tells him to be more kind and more careful in his dealings with things he does not understand. He laughingly dismisses his wife as a "superstitious fool."

The next day, while the servants are cleaning up after the party, the man's lawyer comes to the house, very sad and apprehensive, and gives him a check for a million dollars. The man is surprised, both by the check and by the lawyer's nervousness, and asks the reason for both. Haltingly, the lawyer replies that the check is full payment from his son's life insurance policy. The industrialist's only son has been caught in a mine cave-in and killed; and since the son had made his father the sole beneficiary, the lawyer is simply fulfilling his legal obligation by delivering the million dollar check.

The industrialist is overcome with grief and regret. His wife overhears the lawyer and is convinced that it is the magic of the monkey's paw and her husband's ill-considered wish for another million dollars that has created this horror, so she grabs the paw and wishes fervently for their son not to be dead, but to be home again with them.

That evening the industrialist and his wife are both alerted by the sound of the dogs barking and baying. They go to the door to see what is upsetting the dogs, but before they open it, they hear the awful squelching, groaning, scraping sounds of someone or something dragging itself up the steps of the mansion. The husband and wife both realize at the same moment that it is their son. He has not been killed in the mine collapse; he has been crushed and maimed, and now he has clawed his way out of the rubble of the collapsed mine and crawled home to them in pain. They are both suddenly aware that they have brought this horror on their son and on themselves. At the same instant, they both reach for the monkey's paw and wish for death.

The "Disappearance" of the Trickster Figure

One of the things that makes this such a good example of the archetypal trickster motif in its modern guise is that there is no trickster figure per se in the story. Jung is right in noting that the *figure* of the Trickster has "vanished" (been repressed) from the "sacred narratives" of Western industrial society, but the archetypal energy of the trickster drama has only been enhanced and intensified by the repression.

The "shriveled mummified monkey's paw" itself is a very apt image for the repression of the Trickster in technological society. All that is visibly left of the figure of the traditional Trickster is this shriveled "preserved" remnant. But as the story makes metaphorically clear, the *power* of the drama has in no way been diminished by the exit of the specific figure of the Trickster from the stage. The trickster drama continues with undiminished energy, even though the figure of Coyote/Uzume has been reduced to a "mummified fragment."

In modern times, the archetypal trickster drama has evolved and lost the archaic, but essentially healthy, sense of a "riddle" to be solved, and has acquired instead the moribund quality of "tragic inevitability." In the Western technological world, the energy of the archetypal Trickster has taken on a veneer of false sophistication and become "the tragic view of life," along with the world-weary sense of inevitable disaster and misery that characterizes so much of modern European and American religious and philosophical thought. The repression of the *figure* of the Trickster has resulted in the diffusion of the archetypal *energy* of the Trickster throughout the psychosocial background of modern and postmodern Western culture.

The "primitive mentality" has an advantage in perceiving an actual trickster figure with whom communication, relationship, and negotiation is possible. For the contemporary Westerner, the drama of the archetypal Trickster has become the play of "inevitable irony" of "Murphy's Law"—the way in which things "always seem to work out" for the worst.

The Trickster's revenge on self-deceptive pride and hubris always demonstrates the Law of Irony: "Where consciousness is partial, irony is inevitable." (And since, no matter how developed and refined human consciousness becomes, it is *always* partial and incomplete, we are well-advised to cultivate a taste for it.)

Trickster's Archetypal Lesson

Since Trickster is the archetype of consciousness itself, we should embrace its presence and learn its lesson of basic humility and openness to new possibilities before the irony of trying to avoid and deny them destroys us. In this sense, humility is not some shining (and ultimately perfectionistic and unattainable) spiritual ideal; it is simply the realization that our waking sense of self and reality is always provisional, and thus it is always open to being altered by new experience, if we can only remain awake and aware and open to it.

The ironic, humbling, dark-shadow-side of the Trickster is only a part of the story. The Trickster is also simultaneously the messenger from the Source, the transpersonal center—what Jung called the capital-*S* Self—whence all creativity, new possibility, and evolving self-awareness arises. In the course of administering comeuppance to hubris, the Trickster also always delivers the creative energies and new perspectives that are necessary for transforming inevitable misery into expansive joy—but only if the attitude of hubris is abandoned and the consciousness is genuinely opened to the impact of the new experience.

This tale from the late medieval period in Europe may serve as an example of this obverse, irrepressibly creative aspect of the archetypal trickster drama:

The Story of the Rabbi of Seville

They say that in 1415 a little Christian boy disappeared from the Christian community of Seville, Spain. Upon learning of his disappearance, the leaders of the Christian community became convinced that the Jews had abducted and murdered the child in order to use his blood in the preparation of the Passover matzos. (Here is the perennial "blood-libel" in its late medieval form, a very real and historically attested accusation in the period in which the story is set.)

When the community leaders bring their suspicions to the Grand Inquisitor of Seville, he too becomes convinced; so he sends the Inquisition guards into the Seville ghetto to arrest the Head Rabbi and bring him back to stand trial for this heinous religious crime.

The Head Rabbi is arrested and dragged before the Inquisition court, but to everyone's amazement, he demonstrates an exquisite grasp and understanding of Christian canon law and defends himself very gamely. He defends himself so well that the trial drags on inconclusively for weeks, which threaten to stretch on into months.

Finally, in frustration, the Grand Inquisitor goes into "executive session." He says to the other inquisitors, "Look here, it's obvious to me that merely human means are insufficient to discover the truth in this matter. I propose that we call upon God himself to give us a sign." He goes on to suggest that God be provided with the opportunity to give this sign by putting two pieces of paper into a little leather bag—one blank, and one with the word *Guilty* written on it—and that the Rabbi be forced to pick one without looking. In this fashion, the Almighty himself can provide the true verdict.

The other inquisitors, who are "company men," picked for their unswerving loyalty and ability as "team players," are also frustrated with how long the trial was taking; so one by one, they all nod and agree.

"Yes."

"Indeed."

"Good plan."

The Grand Inquisitor then retires to his inner chamber to prepare the bag and to examine his conscience (in the fashion of grand inquisitors even today). Upon reflection, he decides that he is absolutely convinced of the Rabbi's guilt, and since he does not want God's justice to be contravened by mere chance, he writes "Guilty" on *both* pieces of paper before he puts them into the bag.

When the bag is brought into the inquisition chamber, the Rabbi is instructed to reach into it and pick a piece of paper without looking. He does so, and still without looking, he immediately pops the slip of paper he has chosen into his mouth and swallows it. There is much consternation in the courtroom, and the Rabbi speaks up loudly, proclaiming that he has acted on an inspiration from God to "cleave to his innocence." He goes on to say that if there is the slightest doubt in anyone's mind about which piece of paper he picked, all they have to do is open the bag and see what is left (Fig. 17).

Figure 17. (Medieval Europe) The Rabbi proclaims his innocence before the Inquisition (in the style of 15th-century Spanish manuscripts).

Trickster and the Evolution of Consciousness

In this tale, the Rabbi plays the Trickster. He delivers comeuppance to the Grand Inquisitor (and his hubris), undermining and destroying the Inquisitor's unquestioned assumption of power and impunity. The basic shape of the trickster drama emerges again, even more clearly: Human consciousness is unfinished, incomplete; and whenever this basic truth is forgotten, in the self-deceptive pride and satisfaction at the incredible creative accomplishments of consciousness, the archetypal energy pattern aptly called Trickster comes to the fore and reveals the thing that was left out, the thing that was there all the time, but that lay hidden, not yet brought to consciousness.

Jung himself (despite his blunder of seeing the Trickster only as representing a "vanishing level of consciousness") still understands the basic inevitability of the Law of Irony. Elsewhere he says, on several occasions, "What you do not make conscious, comes at you from outside, as if by fate." The only amendment I would offer (from the improved perspective of historical hindsight) would be to drop the "as if..."

In many ways, the predicament of the Rabbi is a symbolic analogue of the predicament of contemporary consciousness itself. We are presented with a bag of depressing rigged options—war, cultural decadence, economic collapse, ecological disaster, industrial planning failure—and told solemnly to "choose." If the unquestioned assumption of hubris is accepted—that is, that "the experts know best," that everything important is already known (or at least "on the verge of being discovered by science"), and that there is "nothing left but refinements in administration" (about which we may still argue passionately)—then we pick docilely (despite the theater of passionate debate about "administration") and the game ends, "not with a bang, but a whimper."

If, however, we run the risk of appearing momentarily foolish (like the Rabbi when he eats the piece of paper without looking at it) and open ourselves to "divine inspiration," freeing our imaginations to play with *previously unimagined possibilities,* then even the most seemingly inevitable disaster can, in fact, be transformed.

Another mythic narrative, this time from Africa, may serve to illustrate this point more fully. This story comes from the Tiv people of Nigeria.

Hare and The King of the World

They say that one day the King of the World looked out over the beautiful, hot, dry, sparsely vegetated land between the two rivers and felt a great sadness. The land was beautiful; but in his heart, the King had a vision of an even more beautiful land, a land that was green and wet and full of thriving, orderly vegetation, like a garden.

So he sent out a command to all the beings in the cosmos to bring their seeds and the essences and come to a Great Planting Festival. The invitations were carried by the King's messengers to everyone—to the sky and the clouds; to the mountains and the winds; to the rivers and streams; and to the dew, the morning, the heat of the day, and the cool of the evening; and to all the trees and the plants and the grasses; to all the birds, the insects, and the animals; and to all the peoples of the earth—and they all came.

On the day the King had appointed for the Great Planting Festival to Turn the World into a Garden, all the guests arrayed themselves with their essences and their seed bags; and the King looked out over the immense throng and felt a deep satisfaction that now the world would be As It Should Be, a beautiful garden for all. He nodded to all his subjects as they passed before him and bowed and offered their essences and their seeds to him for his Great Planting Festival, and he felt that it was good.

Then he noticed—someone was missing. But who could it be? Who would dare ignore the invitation of the King of the World? He surveyed the vast throng of all the living energies in the world and squinted and frowned. And then he realized—it was Hare—Hare was not present! The King of the World called angrily for the messenger whose job it had been to take the invitation to Hare.

The messenger hurried up and prostrated himself before the King.

"Where is Hare? Did you not give him my message?" asked the King.

"Oh, Your Majesty," replied the messenger breathlessly, "I did give your invitation to Hare, but he would not come out of his hole to talk to me. He just called out to me that he was busy right then, that he had better things to do, and that besides, he never comes out of his hole in the middle of the day."

"Oh," said the King of the World, controlling his mounting

rage. "Go and bring me Hare so that he may tell me these things himself!"

So the messenger gathered several other messengers to help him and went back to Hare's hole. He shouted down into the hole and told Hare that the King of the World was angry and that Hare had better come with them if he knew what was good for him. But Hare called out to them that he couldn't be bothered with such silliness in the middle of the day, and so the messengers were forced to dig him out of his hole and drag him by his long ears to face the King.

Hare was distinctly discommoded and out of sorts by the time the messengers tossed him down on his skinny knees before the King of the World.

"Just who do you think you are to ignore the invitation of the King of the World?" asked the King in a quiet, smooth, polite voice that always frightened people who knew him even more than his shouts of anger.

"I am Hare," Hare replied, standing up and brushing the dust out of his fur. "And I have better things to do than waste my time at your silly Planting Festival. Why, it's ridiculous! I could put on a better festival than this without half trying!" (Fig. 18).

"Oh? Is that so?!" thundered the King of the World, abandoning his fake-quiet voice. "Well, you have my permission to try. But if you fail, I will have you skinned alive just for my amusement, although your mangy, flea-bitten hide is hardly worth the trouble!"

Hare scurried away from his meeting with the King, glad that his long-eared head was still on his scrawny shoulders. The more he thought about the situation, the more distressed and depressed he became.

"Oh, woe," he moaned to himself, "I've let my alligator mouth run away with my hummingbird asshole again, and this time, the King is going to *kill* me. Oh, woe is me! What can I do? Maybe I can crawl back and throw myself on his mercy. But the way he was shouting and carrying on, I don't believe he would offer me any mercy at all! Oh, what am I to do?"

And so, with his little round eyes filled with tears of self-pity, his shoulders hunched, his head low, and his long ears hanging

Figure 18. (Central Africa) Hare argues brazenly with the King of the World (after a carving from Nok, Northern Nigeria, tentatively dated 1000 B.C.E.).

down so they dragged unnoticed in the dust, Hare wandered off into the bush in misery.

A little while later, Hare returned, carrying a big sack over his shoulder with something big in it. With difficulty, he climbed a great old tree growing right at the edge of the Great Planting Festival, hauling the awkward sack up into the branches with him. Then he opened the sack and took out—the First Drum.

Hare looked out over the Great Planting Festival stretching to the horizon and beyond and started to beat out a slow, solemn rhythm on his New Drum: thump-de-bump, thump-de-bump, thump-de-bump.

The mountains and the clouds and the trees and the plants and the animals and the birds and the insects and the people and the gentle breezes all started fall into the rhythm of Hare's solemn drumming and to bow and plant in time to the Drum's slow thump-de-bump, thump-de-bump.

When Hare was sure that all the beings were moving in unison, stooping and planting their seeds and essences in time to his slow, solemn drumbeat, he started to pick up the pace: thumpity-bump, thumpity-bump, thumpity-bump.

As he had hoped, the Planting Festival participants started to plant faster, keeping up with the quickening rhythm of the Drum. When Hare was sure that they were all keeping up with the beat, he started to accentuate the alternate beats and syncopate the rhythm: thumpity-bump, thumpity-bumpity, thumpity-bumpity-thumpity-bump, bump-bump-thumpity-bump, thumpity-bumpity-thumpity-bump.

And soon, all the participants were completely caught up in Hare's joyful, infectious, complex rhythms. Leaping and shuffling and clapping and singing wordlessly, they trampled their now-forgotten seed bags beneath their dancing feet.

At just that point, Hare leaned down out of his tree and called to the King of the World, who was dancing and swaying and clapping along with everybody else.

"Hey, King! See? I *told* you! *Everybody* came to my Dancing Festival, but *nobody* came to your stupid old Planting Festival!"

Trickster and the Archetypal Creative Impulse

The archetypal parallels between this story and the story of Hermes' invention of the first lyre, as well as Uzume's salvation of the world, are clear. In all three instances, the characters representing the established, "inevitable" order (Ama-terra-tsu, Apollo, and the King of the World) exhibit hubris in their total assumption of power and authority. They are subsequently brought up short and overthrown by acts of spontaneous creativity on the part of the lowliest and most despised trickster characters. In all three narratives, the archetypal, creative inspiration takes the symbolic form of the invention of musical forms. The tricksters achieve their ends without violence, coercion, or even threats; they employ only the gentle influence of "music that has never been heard before."

Homeric Greece, prehistoric Japan, and postcolonial Tiv land are widely separated in time and space, but the archetypal structure of the panhuman psyche reveals its fundamental oneness in the repeating symbolic structures of the one archetypal trickster story.

Uzume, Hermes, and Hare all exhibit their own hubris in defying the ultimate authority of their respective societies; and when they are cast into life-threatening circumstances in punishment for their transgressions, they respond by calling on the archetypal creative impulse, spurred on by their desperation. Each version of the story has its own unmistakable indigenous accent, its own unique richness of character and cultural detail, while at the same time, repeating the same essential psychospiritual story of human consciousness evolving in the midst of trouble and oppression and strife to claim new ground for human activity and awareness and creativity in the landscape of primal creation.

As the Trickster demonstrates over and over again, the greatest and most effective tool of oppression is always the disparagement of native imagination. In actual practical fact, if you persuade a person or a group of people that the spontaneous and playful products of their native imaginations are substandard or worthless, then they are enslaved, no matter how much money they have, or where they live. If, for example, we are persuaded that the stories we read in the newspapers and see on television are some sort of approximation of "the important truth," and that (as a consequence) we can't even really grasp, let alone influence, the vast geopolitical forces that shape our destiny, then *we* are enslaved, no matter where we went to college or how much money we have in the bank.

Conversely, if you *fail* to persuade people that the spontaneous, playful products of their native imagination are substandard and worthless, then those imaginatively alive people are never truly enslaved, no matter how poor or oppressed or underprivileged they are, because they are always in a state of creative ferment, thinking up new things to do and new ways to think and feel and express themselves that haven't been outlawed yet, because no one in authority ever thought of any of them before.

This is a universal drama, repeated in the evolving consciousness of every human being and every society and culture. In the midst of this archetypal drama, every remembered dream is a "Trickster's gift," designed exquisitely to reveal the as-yet-unimagined creative possibilities of the individual dreamer's life and the life of the species as a whole. If we have the courage and flexibility of mind and heart to hold it and see further into the depths of the dream, it always has previously unimagined and seemingly unimaginable gifts for us, symbolically analogous to the First Lyre and the First Drum—gifts that can change *every-thing,* without violence and coercion.

The Trickster does not triumph by brute strength or social prestige; the Trickster transforms everything with the gift of creativity, even in the face of "inevitable," "invincible" power and coercion. Every remembered dream reveals the current state of the archetypal trickster's drama in the specific details and location of the dreamer's own life, inviting each of us to see beyond our previously unquestioned assumptions and the limits of our imaginations.

To the extent that we do not understand our dreams, they always come to tell us that everything we need to know is *not yet conscious* and to invite and entice us into looking further. In the moment of being remembered, the dream tells us that we have an increasingly conscious and morally responsible role to play in the creative unfolding of our deepest life dramas and in the collective dramas of our community, culture, and global society.

Even when the manifest content of a dream makes its meaning seem obvious, there is *always* more there, if we take the time and energy to look further and deeper. It is only hubris that suggests that the dreams are meaningless, or that they are simply "blind compensations" that the waking mind can see through with ease. It is precisely that hubris which imprisons us in the seemingly inevitable dramas of our individual and collective lives.

From the point of view of the arrogant, prematurely closed worldview—the perspective that believes it has discovered the ultimate (religious, scientific, philosophical, historical, you-name-it) truth—the energy of growth, development, and change represented by the Trickster is always perceived as "evil," as *Shadow.* And, as always, the great secret of the Shadow is that it always holds, as a hostage of the negative way in which it is viewed and perceived, the "great gift"—the very thing that is missing, the absence of which has been the source of all the trouble in the first place.

From the point of view of those who are oppressed by the dominant, prematurely closed worldview (as well as by those aspects of the psyche that are repressed and constrained by the unquestioned assumptions of waking consciousness), the Trickster is always synonymous with the Divine Child (of new possibility and liberation). The Trickster, as the archetypal constellation simultaneously embodying both the creative and the self-deceptive qualities of evolving human consciousness, always shows both the face of the Shadow (to the part of consciousness that is attached to the prematurely closed worldview, that wants the part not only to "stand for" the whole, but to *be* the whole) and the face of the Divine Child (to the suppressed parts of the psyche that long for acknowledgment and freer expression).

Trickster and Willing Sacrifice

This eternal drama of struggle among Shadow, Trickster, and Divine Child eventually calls forth the healing and transformative archetype of the Willing Sacrifice. It is the Willing Sacrifice that is ultimately capable of reconciling the naturally opposed tensions embodied in the paradoxical Trickster. The Willing Sacrifice is capable of resolving the paradox of the Trickster's dual nature and, indeed, the dual nature of *all* archetypal energies.

The Willing Sacrifice is perhaps the highest expression of the drama of evolving human consciousness that we have yet discovered/created/encountered. Once human consciousness has constellated into a condition of partial self-awareness, it is only by giving up and relinquishing that partial, provisional sense of "self" in the world that further growth and change can take place. Once consciousness has been established, it is only in willingly sacrificing itself, only in letting go of the previously cherished sense of identity and purpose, that any new, more complete and aware self can come into being. This is one of the primary reasons why the image of death in the dream world is so deeply and repeatedly connected to specific moments in the dreamer's growth and development.

The Willing Sacrifice is given shape in "the one that dies so that others may live," in the one who takes the risk of self-destruction in the effort to win the prize, in the one who lets go of deeply cherished notions in the face of the growing awareness that there is more than the prematurely closed ideas of "religious truth," or "political necessity," or "economic development" that previously seemed to express the whole truth, the previously accepted limit of imagination and possibility.

The Willing Sacrifice may take on the grandest and most noble shapes, like Jesus on the cross, or Buddha in steadfast meditation achieving enlightenment under the Bo tree. Or it may be as simple and mundane as pausing to wonder, "Is this right? Is this what I *really* want to do? I always *thought* it was right. I always thought it was what I wanted—always, since I was a little kid—but is it really?"

Each time a dream is remembered and the dreamer pauses before dismissing it, wondering what deeper meanings it might hold, the archetype of Willing Sacrifice (of previously held, unquestioned assumption) begins to be acted out in specific human detail, and the possibility of actual psychospiritual growth and change becomes concrete and real.

Organized religion in general, and Christian religion in particular, has done us all a great disservice by promoting the notion that Willing Sacrifice is present only in the largest and most dramatic acts of painful self-sacrifice and martyrdom. These great moments do indeed give dramatic shape to the Willing Sacrifice; but for most people, those moments are to be worshipped from afar and avoided at all cost. For this reason, the mundane tasks of living are all too often, by definition, "not spiritual."

In reality, the Willing Sacrifice takes shape in mundane details of our daily lives on a regular basis. The smallest and the simplest acts—like getting up and plunging into the morning commute traffic to get to the less-than-satisfying job, so that the less-than-satisfying family can go on eating and clothing themselves; the decision to give my friend, or my kid, the benefit of the doubt and listen seriously to his or her latest craziness (despite the long history of failed possibilities); the willingness to laugh and accept, rather than judge and be angry—are all concrete exemplars of archetypal Willing Sacrifice.

All these acts, from the most spectacular example of reli-

giously motivated martyrdom and offering up one's best energies for the benefit of others, down to the most mundane gam-
ble—risking a new behavior in the hopes of winning a little more
time, a little more love, a little more insight—all embody and
exemplify the archetype of Willing Sacrifice. For that reason,
they all provide real, concrete occasions for old consciousness
and self-awareness to "die" and be renewed, deepened, and
expanded, and for broader and deeper realms of consciousness
and self-awareness to be "born."

Dreams are the best and most reliable guides we have in this
archetypal drama of personal and collective evolution and
unfolding. Every dream is a Trickster's gift, and every new "aha"
of insight gained from pondering and exploring a dream is an
embodiment of Willing Sacrifice (of the old, provisional personality), clearing the way for a more whole, provisional sense of
waking self to constellate.

There is a perennial folk narrative from Latin America that
gives symbolic shape to this deep truth.

A Dream of the Angel Gabriel

A poor Indian has a dream involving the Patron of the
hacienda and an angel. The Patron hears rumors about it and
commands the Indian to come and tell the dream. The Indian
tries to refuse, but the Patron's messengers threaten him (in
some versions, threaten *her,* emphasizing the doubly oppressed
circumstances of women) if he fails to appear.

The Indian comes to the Patron's mansion and the Patron
orders him to kneel and tell the dream.

"Patron, I dreamed that the Archangel Gabriel came to me
and told me that I must come to you and receive punishment for
my sins" (Fig. 19).

"And so you shall. Speak on."

"In my dream, the Archangel Gabriel commanded the people standing around to smear shit all over me and cover me up in
all manner of offal and dirt and garbage; and at the same time,
he ordered your servants to bathe you and anoint you with honey
and spices and sweet-smelling oils."

Figure 19. (Latin America) The Peasant tells the Patron the Trickster dream of the Archangel Gabriel.

"And so he should! Speak on."

"Oh, Patron, I dare not."

"It is a dream from God! You must tell it! Speak on!"

"When we were all anointed and covered as he had ordered, he turned to us and said, 'And now, to pay for your sins, you must lick each other clean.'"

The Trick of Willingness

In this fashion, even the arrogant, hubris-filled "Patron" (of waking ego consciousness and social convention) is tricked into playing the role of Willing Sacrifice. As the Zen Buddhists are fond of saying: "Enlightenment doesn't care how you get there." Trickster arrives and ironically "saves" the prematurely closed waking sense of self from itself. Trickster presides over the creative expansion of consciousness and self-awareness and tricks the arrogant part of the psyche into opening to change "voluntarily" (that is, "willingly"—even though it is a trick). In this way, Trickster "redeems" the original invention of language and deception by enlisting it in the service of evolving health and wholeness.

Human consciousness is still evolving. The Trickster is the facilitator of the evolution. Each time we solve some problem, each time we invent some new marvel or create some compelling new work of art, we are tempted to strut and preen and look down on those who have not achieved the successes and triumphs we have; and as we do so, the Trickster is awakened in our psyche. Each time we look at our desperate circumstances and grimly contemplate the seemingly inevitable "choice of evils" our lives have brought us to, the Trickster yawns and scratches and begins to move around.

Each time we pause to contemplate our lives and wonder in amazement at the patterns that are emerging, stunned at how unconscious we are and how much we do not know; each time we allow ourselves to feel our emotions to their fullest, to think our thoughts all the way through to their fullest clarity; each time we take the risk of expressing ourselves honestly and deeply, the Trickster breathes deeply and smiles and transforms into the Willing Sacrifice.

Each time we remember a dream and pause to contemplate its enigmas, each time we share our tentative conclusions about the meaning of our lives, we open ourselves to great mystery—what Laurens Van der Post called "the mystery that heals." Each time we overcome our fearful prejudices and look at another and realize, "I am that too...," we become more truly ourselves and more consciously aware of our shared connection with the divine. It is in this fashion that we actually grow and change and evolve into the shining beings we are becoming.

And all the while, awake and asleep, we tell ourselves stories—great compelling stories, little amusing stories, strange spooky stories—stories that stretch our awareness and pull us further and further into the great unknown possibilities of ourselves.

SUMMARY

Like the organs of a living body, all archetypal forms are fundamentally related to and intertwined with one another. Particularly intimate and ironic relationships exist among the archetypes of Shadow, Trickster, Divine Child, and Willing Sacrifice. Trickster narratives from Japan, Africa, and the United States are offered to illuminate the basic function and role of the archetypal Trickster in the evolution of consciousness. Trickster figures in the other myths discussed in earlier chapters are also discussed in greater detail.

Jung's assertion that the Trickster is a representative of "a vanishing level of consciousness" is challenged, and examples from contemporary collective "trickster dramas" are offered in support of the argument that the Trickster is a primary archetypal metaphor of evolving human consciousness itself and that it thus remains as relevant today as it was in the earliest developments of language and culture.

Since human self-awareness is partially conscious, in order to develop further, individuals and groups must consciously relinquish their cherished self-images in order to grow and change. The archetypal pattern of this conscious acceptance of growth and development is Willing Sacrifice. It is an important part of the archetypal role of Trickster to facilitate and bring about that change.

The separate figure of the Trickster has all but disappeared from modern mythic narrative, but it has dissolved into the overall background of Western culture and now manifests itself as a fake-sophisticated "tragic view of life." The archetypal Trickster is still alive and well in the psyche, so the appearance of hubris in all its forms has the effect of energizing and activating the trickster energy of previously ignored and denied possibility.

In this way, Trickster presides over the evolution of consciousness and brings the arrogant waking ego/worldview to willingly participate in its own transformation. The Divine Child of new transformative possibility is, in this sense, the child of the Trickster. To the extent that all these evolutionary energies challenge and eventually overturn the comfortable, prematurely closed notions and habits of the waking mind, they appear initially as distressing Shadow energies. By "tricking" the repressive waking ego/dominant society into participating voluntarily in its own "overthrow," the Trickster redeems the original invention of language and deception by bringing it into the service of health and wholeness.

Chapter 9
TEN BASIC HINTS FOR DREAM WORK

(1) The single most important thing to understand about dreams is that *all dreams come in the service of health and wholeness.* Even the nasty, scary, seemingly negative dreams we call nightmares take the emotionally gripping form they do simply to insure that the content of the dream will be recalled, at least for a little while, upon awakening. Dreams assume nightmarish form because the information they have to convey is of particular use and potential value to the dreamer.

For more than four million years, paying immediate and focused attention to nasty, threatening stuff has been a basic survival strategy. The animals who were able to pull off this trick of consciousness tended to survive, and the ones who couldn't quite get it together didn't. As a result of this evolutionary history, we human beings are inherently predisposed to pay close attention to threatening stimuli more readily than to soothing, supportive stimuli. For this reason, among others, the unconscious source from which the dreams spring is inclined to dress important information up in the form of a nightmare when it is especially relevant or important.

What is true of nightmares is also true of all remembered dreams—they come to serve the dreamer's evolving health and psychospiritual wholeness. The more seemingly nasty or "stupid" or mundane a dream appears to be, the more important it is to ask the question how it might possibly serve the dreamer in a way that a more benign dream might not be able to do.

Another consequence of the fact that all dreams come in the service of health and wholeness is that all dreams, even the most dismal and repetitive, come to offer aid, solace, creative energy, and ideas contributing to the solution of the dreamer's problems. No dream ever came to anyone to say, "Nyeah, nyeah—you have

262

these problems and you can't do anything about them!" If a person dreams about a seemingly insolvable problem in his or her life, the simple fact that a dream about this problem has been remembered means that there *are* possibilities for growth and change and creative/transformative responses to this problem that have been overlooked. In the service of health and wholeness, the dream is calling the dreamer's attention back to the problem because there is something that can be done about it.

Carl Jung says the most important question to be asked about any dream is "Why this dream now?" Another way of phrasing the basic question is "How does the arrival of this particular dream experience in this precise moment in the dreamer's life serve his/her health and wholeness?"

(2) The second most important thing to remember in this process of exploring dreams to discover more of their multiple meanings is that *only the dreamer can say with any certainty what his or her dream means.* This certainty usually comes in the form of a wordless "aha" of recognition. Whenever someone says something true and to the point about the possible meaning or significance of a dream, the dreamer usually feels a flash or a tingle of confirmation. This recognition reaction *of the dreamer* is the only reliable touchstone of dream work.

This "aha" is a function of memory. The old Anglo-Saxon term for "unconscious" is *not-yet-speech-ripe*. Those things that our dreams are inviting us to see are not yet sufficiently conscious to be put into words. When someone else puts some of these potential insights into words, the dreamer consciously remembers, for the first time, what he or she already knew *unconsciously* (preverbally) about the meanings of the dream when it first occurred.

The only one who can remember with any accuracy what meanings lie woven in the dream is the original dreamer. However, since the language of the dream is in fact universal, the ideas that other people come up with about the possible meanings of a dream are very likely to evoke aha's of recognition in the dreamer as well.

(3) *All dreams speak a universal language of symbol and metaphor and address all human beings in essentially the same way,* regardless of the dreamer's unique circumstances—regardless of

race, sex, age, beliefs, and convictions—regardless even of the dreamer's relative state of mental and emotional health. In fact, the only substantial difference between truly crazy people and ordinary garden-variety neurotics is that the truly crazy people wake up and their dreams do not end. The only thing that separates sanity from profound mental and emotional disturbance is the ability to distinguish between the dream (what Freud called "primary process," the stuff of dreams) and the consensual reality of waking life.

Another consequence of this universal quality of the experience and imagery of dreams is that the health and wholeness that the dreams serve cannot be limited just to the individual dreamer. Dreams and myth together speak a universal language that serves the health and wholeness of the entire species, and by implication, of the cosmos as a whole. Dreams come to help effectuate "the reconciliation of each with all."

(4) In addition, *all dreams have multiple layers of meaning and significance* woven into them. Even the tiniest fragment will reveal multiple meanings when it is examined with curiosity and care. These multiple meanings turn out to be related to one another, but they are always different enough to warrant separate articulation and appreciation.

(5) One practical consequence of this fact about dreams is that the work of understanding and "interpreting" a dream or series of dreams can never be truly complete. There is always more there to be unpacked. For this reason, *all endings in dream work are strictly arbitrary.* One can never say that the work is complete, and even when there is a satisfying sense of closure, it is illusory. Most of the time, the work with a dream has to be ended while the sense of unexplored possibility is still very strong.

This means that "closure" must be achieved arbitrarily. I ask myself two questions to decide when to bring a piece of group dream work to a close: (a) Have I and everyone else (including the dreamer, but no more than anyone else) had any "aha's" about this dream while we have been exploring it? (If I haven't, and no one else has either, it probably means we should try a little longer.) (b) Are we spending more time on working this dream than we usually do? Are the basic laws of fairness being observed? (Barring unusual circumstances, each dreamer in the group should have roughly the same amount of the group's time and attention.)

One of the reasons why exploring dreams in a group with the help of other people's projections and speculations is so productive and valuable is that the chances of touching on something like the full range of possible meanings that a dream may hold is much greater if several different people are involved in the process.

(6) It is also true that *no dream ever comes to tell the dreamer just what he or she already knows.* Often there will be several aha's of recognition from a dream, but they will simply reinforce what the dreamer already thought and felt before the dream appeared. Although these elements of previous thought and feeling are clearly present in the dream, the larger purpose of the dream is always to take the dreamer beyond these already known elements into new areas of self-revelation and insight.

Individual human consciousness rests on a foundation of selective perception. Although the dreamer is the only one who can "remember" what his or her dream means, the dreamer is not at all likely to get to these radical layers of new information alone, because the dreamer is uniquely blind to precisely these layers of meaning. (As Carl Jung was fond of saying, "The problem with the unconscious is that it really *is* unconscious!") Here again, the speculations and projections of others about what the dreamer's dream may signify are absolutely invaluable. The hardest thing to do is to see one's own dreams with fresh eyes. Conversely, the easiest thing to do is to see someone else's dreams with fresh eyes. Members of a dream group always bring one another the invaluable gift of the fresh eyes and ears with which they apprehend the dreamer's dream.

The only apparent exception to this general principle is that occasionally a dream will come to "tell the dreamer what he or she already knows" because the quality of that purely intellectual self-knowledge has been too isolated and circumscribed to lead to authentic behavior change. In such instances, the dreams will often offer the dreamer grotesquely exaggerated metaphors of what he or she already thinks and feels to make the point that these thoughts and feelings are really important and ought to lead to some sort of concrete expression or course of action in the dreamer's waking life.

(7) *Anyone who is interested in his or her dreams should keep a regular dream journal.* Even the most seemingly compelling dreams will slip away from memory if they are not recorded.

If you wake up in the middle of the night and remember a dream, make brief notes on the dream. (My wife and I both use little penlight flashlights with ballpoint pen refills taped securely to the barrel. This means that if either one of us wakes up with a dream, we can make notes without having to turn on a light and disturb the other.)

Some people like to use tape recorders to record their dreams. This is a very practical and easy way to catch the experience, but it requires the extra step of transcribing the tape recorded narratives into written form. Being a skilled typist helps in this process immensely. (In fact, I wouldn't recommend using a tape recorder to catch your dreams unless you have above-average typing skills.)

Remember to draw pictures of your dreams as you record them. In keeping a dream record, a picture (even the crudest little stick figure sketch or floor-plan diagram) is worth a great deal more than a thousand words. Remember, the point is not the finished, artistic quality of the drawing, but the fact that the act of drawing brings the visual associative system into more conscious play and makes for a whole different level of aha's about the many meanings of a dream.

(8) *Record the dream(s) in the present tense, rather than the habitual past tense with which we refer to waking events* the moment they have passed. It will make the dream records more vivid and compelling for the dreamer and will draw dream group members into their own imagined versions of the dreams more fully and immediately when the dream is shared and worked on. Recording the dream experiences in the present tense is also a way of acknowledging the truth that a dream remains an active, "alive" experience long after it initially appears. The vividness with

which a dream is recalled, no matter how long ago it initially appeared, is a very reliable indicator of the value of exploring the dream now.

(9) When working on a dream or series of dreams with other people, it is always important to *preface any interpretive comment or remark about possible meanings with some version of the idea: "If it were my dream..."* There are many reasons for doing this. Let me mention three of the most significant:

(a) It is the only intellectually honest thing a person can say when talking about the possible meanings of another person's dream. The only way to generate interpretative comments is to imagine one's own version of the dreamer's dream; therefore, all ideas about possible meaning and significance must of necessity be projections, born out of the interpreter's own imagined experience of the dream.

(b) The first person form of address is always "confessional," whereas the use of the second person is always "accusatory." Even when the content of a "you" statement is positive, it is still an accusation. Human beings are inherently predisposed to respond to accusations with hurt feelings and arguments (particularly when the accusations are true!). There are few things in this world that are more pointless or silly than arguing with people about the meanings of their dreams. The best way to avoid this pointless interaction is to remove from the process the primary invitation to argument, which is the use of the second person form of address.

(c) The most important reason for using some version of the "if it were my dream..." form is that each time someone takes the trouble to do this, he or she is saying to the dreamer in effect: "There is nothing in you or your dream—no matter how odd or distressing or downright repugnant the (symbolic) surface appearance may be—that I am not perfectly prepared to find in myself as well in this moment" The repetition of this affirmation of the deep, shared (archetypal), common humanity revealed by the dream can turn what might otherwise be a merely emotional or intellectual exercise in symbolic analysis into an authentic spiritual discipline—that is, an activity the result of which is the increasing conscious awareness of the energies of the divine in our individual and shared collective lives. The "if it were my dream..." form points to the importance of the deep shared humanity out of which the dream springs and directs our attention back to the felt sense of depth that is our primary communion with one another and with the divine.

(10) As mentioned in the "Note on Anonymity and Confidentiality" that opens this book, *all group dream work should consciously reiterate the agreement to keep the individual dreamers anonymous in any subsequent discussion of the work, and further emphasize that each dreamer has both the right and the responsibility to speak up and ask for strict confidentiality at any point where he or she feels the slightest need for it.* In the absence of a specific request for confidentiality, the agreement to anonymity allows discussion of dreams and insights gained from working with dreams as long as no individual dreamer is identifiable in the details of anything that is said. As soon as anyone asks for confidentiality, everyone in the group agrees to move immediately, without hesitation or question, into that more restrictive mode.

There are many more things that can be said about the ethics and dynamics of "if it were my dream..." group dream work, but my experience over the past thirty years is that this set of ten basic principles is sufficient for anyone to begin to undertake this work productively.

Appendix I
BACKGROUND RESOURCES FOR THE EXPLORATION OF MYTHS AND DREAMS

If you enjoyed this book, you would probably also like to look at my two earlier books: *Dream Work: Techniques for Discovering the Creative Power in Dreams* (Mahwah, NJ: Paulist Press, 1983) and *Where People Fly and Water Runs Uphill: Using Dreams to Tap the Wisdom of the Unconscious* (New York: Warner Books, 1992). The focus of these two books is on practical strategies for discovering and exploring the multiple layers of meaning in dreams. (For a brief presentation of the fundamental theoretical issues and practical strategies for participatory group dream work, see chapter 9.)

These two books also examine the nature of the unconscious itself, with particular emphasis on the role of the unconscious in spiritual experience and the development of character and personality. The emphasis in both books is on the advantages of exploring dreams with friends in participatory dream groups. Each of these books also contains practical suggestions for working with your own dreams in solitude, and each includes an extensive, annotated bibliography and resource guide.

General Background Material on Jungian Psychology

The best general introduction to the fascinating and important work of Carl Jung is his *Man and His Symbols* (Garden City, NY: Doubleday, 1964). Don't be too put off by the sexism of the title—it really does address the psychology and authentic experience of women as well as men. The book was inspired by a dramatic dream late in Jung's life in which he found himself addressing a huge audience in a gigantic hall and feeling both pleasure and amazement that they appeared to be grasping and appreciating what he had to say. This dream suggested to the aging Jung that he had not yet fulfilled his desire and his responsibility to make his rather complex and abstruse ideas more easily available to a general audience.

Inspired by his dream, Jung called on his most trusted and qualified students and associates to write introductory essays, each focused on one of the most important aspects of his work. Jung himself wrote a draft of a general introductory essay; but, alas, he died before he could complete the task of reviewing and editing the manuscripts. This has placed *Man and His Symbols* in an odd, "stepchild" position in relation to the rest of Jung's work; but I believe that his ideas are presented in easily accessible language, more clearly and compellingly in this book than anywhere else. The book is also profusely illustrated and makes a conscious effort to touch the feelings and intuitions of its readers through the relationship of pictures and text. For this reason, I would recommend reading the large, hardbound edition in which the pictures have their full color and impact, rather than the Dell paperback where, unfortunately, the impression of the illustrations is reduced to something like an auction catalogue of postage stamps in black and white.

When I teach formal classes in "Jung and Myth," I usually suggest to my students that they also obtain a copy of Anthony Storr's selection of excerpts from Jung's collected works, *The Essential Jung* (Princeton University Press, 1983) and pursue the areas of Jung's work that they are particularly interested in through the index (looking up all the references to "dreams" or "mythology" or "synchronicity," for example) to get a clearer, more direct sense of the breadth and depth and subtlety of Jung's own prose.

There are two other single-volume anthologies of the most important selections from Jung's collected works: *The Portable Jung*, edited by Joseph Campbell (New York: Viking, 1971), and *The Basic Writings of C. G. Jung*, edited by Violet de Lazlo (New York: Modern Library, 1959), both of which offer slightly different editorial views and emphases.

Valuable Resources for Approaching
World Myth and Sacred Narrative

An overall familiarity with at least a few of the various traditions of world myth and sacred narrative is a vitally important element in gaining a more conscious understanding of the
universality of the archetypes and how they manifest themselves
and function in our individual and collective lives in general and
in our dreams in particular. The best introduction I have yet discovered to world myth as a whole is *The Universal Myths: Heroes,*
Gods, Tricksters, and Others by Alexander Eliot (Harrisburg: Merid-
ian/New American Library, 1990). This book includes two brilliant general essays: "Myth and Mythical Thought" by Mircea
Eliade and "Myths from West to East" by Joseph Campbell, which
together provide an excellent overview of the history and basic
ideas associated with the serious study of myth. In the main body
of the book, Eliot takes crucial, evocative, emotionally charged,
archetypally significant moments and scenes from a wide diversity of myths from around the world and groups them together by
theme. The scenes and episodes are very well written. The problem is that the reader only gets enticing snatches from much
longer and more profound and complex narratives and is in danger of not really grasping how these brilliantly luminous vignettes
fit into the larger structures of the myths they are drawn from.

To solve this problem, I recommend three other books that
also have a diverse representation of mythic tales and sacred narratives from different world cultures, but that offer fewer stories,
told in more complete versions. The best written of the three is
Myths of the World (originally titled *Orpheus* when it was first published by Macmillan in 1930) by Padraic Colum (New York: Gros-
set & Dunlap/Universal Library, 1974). The other two are *World*
Mythology: An Anthology of Myths and Epics by Donna Rosenberg
(Lincolnwood: National Text Book/Passport Books, 1986) and
The World of Myth: An Anthology by David A. Leeming (Oxford
University Press, 1990). *Parallel Myths* by J. F. Bierlein (New York:
Ballantine, 1994) is another good resource, particularly interesting because of its numerous quotes from leading Western schol-
ars, from Ananda Coomaraswamy to Paul Tillich, illuminating
their diverse attitudes toward and understanding of mythology.

In 1994, Larousse Kingfisher Chambers of New York published an American edition of a charming and comprehensive British book, *Goddesses, Heroes, and Shamans: The Young People's Guide to World Mythology* by various editors and contributors. Like many other such publications aimed at young people, it provides a wonderfully clear, succinct, and beautifully illustrated introduction to the subject that is quite stimulating and accessible to adults as well.

This book that you are holding in your hand is also an effort to fill the growing need for an accessible and in-depth, multicultural introduction to the diversity of world myth and sacred narrative on the one hand, and to its fundamental archetypal unity on the other.

Appendix II
REFERENCES, POINTS OF CLARIFICATION, AND SUGGESTIONS FOR FURTHER READING

In an effort to promote ease of reading and avoid cluttering the pages with distracting technical scholarly paraphernalia, I have gathered all the specific publication and page references for the works quoted directly, along with bibliographic information about other works consulted, in this appendix. I have also included, with this reference information, the evaluations, extended discussions, and digressions that in a more formal, academic presentation would go into substantive footnotes and an annotated bibliography.

An Introductory Aside

If we were not still laboring under the historical and psychological weight of Roman imperialism, we would probably not use quite so many words with Latin roots in our technical vocabulary. "Unconscious" is one of these time-honored, Latinate technical words; and on the face of it, it is simply a contradiction in terms. If we were not still dazzled by the fact that the word is cobbled together from Latin roots, we would probably have abandoned it long ago in favor of the more evocative, accurate, and communicative expression from the Anglo-Saxon word hoard, *not-yet-speech-ripe*.

In many ways, the Anglo-Saxon phrase is far superior as a technical term because it describes the actual condition we experience. The "unconscious" energies and dramas are there within us, growing and pressing insistently against our interior awareness, but not sufficiently evolved to be rendered clearly into conscious thoughts formulated in words. Throughout this book, I use the word *unconscious* because it is the most generally accepted term, but it should be remembered that despite the implications of intellectual abstraction and emotional distance that the word has acquired over the years, *unconscious* refers to something very real, something we each experience in our own lives as pressingly present and alive within us that is simply "not-yet-speech-ripe."

Crick and Mitchison's article, "The Function of Dream Sleep," appeared in the British journal *Nature* (vol. 304, July 1983). The lines quoted attacking the practice of dream work appear on page 114. Stan Krippner's comments about the fundamental failings of Crick and Mitchison's work appear in *Dreamtime and Dreamwork* (Los Angeles: Tarcher, 1990, pp. 37–38). *Dreamtime* is a particularly good anthology and offers an exemplary range of different styles and ideas about working with dreams. Another excellent anthology is *Dreams Are Wiser Than Men,* edited by Richard Russo (Berkeley: North Atlantic Books, 1987).

For a fascinating examination of dreams as they reflect the dreamer's social and cultural reality, see "The Dream as a Tool for Historical Research: Reexamining Life in Eighteenth Century Virginia Through the Dreams of a Gentleman: William Byrd II, 1674–1744" by Susan Sleeper-Smith, in the professional journal of the Association for the Study of Dreams, *Dreaming* (vol. 3, no. 1, Spring 1993, p. 49).

The question of what these statistical patterns of recurrent imagery in the dream content of children, women, and men *mean* is even more interesting than the indisputable but under-appreciated fact that these repeating similarities in manifest content exist. At least one of the important reasons why children dream of animals more than adults do is that children are less socialized than adults and tend to be more immediately aware of their instincts and spontaneous urges than are most adults. The animals in dreams and myths often symbolize the life and vitality of the instincts.

The patterns of difference between adult men and women with regard to experiencing and remembering color in dreams appear to be a reflection of the archetypal association between color and emotion. To the extent that women in our patriarchal society are generally trained and socialized to be more aware of feeling and emotion than men, the higher incidence of remembered color in the dreams of women makes sense. The recurring difference in the amount of talking with other dream figures versus fighting and manipulating machines can also be seen as reflections of the collective, statistically observable effects of sexism and the psychological and emotional consequences of sex role stereotyping. In individuals, and in a society struggling to free itself from the limiting effects of sexism, changes in these statistical patterns of content in men's and women's dreams might well be monitored as relatively objective criteria for evaluating the actual individual and collective success of those efforts toward liberation.

Dr. Milton Kramer made his succinct remarks to me in the hall of the Sheraton New York at the Twelfth Annual Conference of the Association for the Study of Dreams in July of 1995. He was taking me to task for what he perceived to be "an antiscientific bias" in my presidential address, which he felt was uncalled for since, as he said, science had come to the same conclusion I was promoting: that dreams are demonstrably and inherently meaningful.

Chapter 1

Often our modern triumphs of intellect, will, collective organization, and technological manipulation of the physical environment are so dramatic that they seem to separate us radically and completely from our more "primitive" and "superstitious" ancestors. Sometimes we are even tempted to imagine that we have moved so far beyond our "unenlightened" predecessors that our sophisticated and profound individual and collective dilemmas are completely new and unprecedented. However, when viewed at this level of deeply shared, collective psychology, our modern political, ecological, and spiritual problems are exactly the same as they have always been. It is simply that the immediate observable and undeniable consequences of our ancient fear, greed, and stupidity have grown to gigantic, global proportions as a result of our sorcerer's apprenticeship in science and technology. Apart from this inflation of the dire consequences of the failure to individuate and know ourselves below the surface of mere appearance, the mythic, archetypal symbol dramas themselves are virtually unchanged.

Our dreams and modern myths regularly reveal us to be exactly the same sort of people as the ones who first stood upright, began to use articulate language, and started to use their opposable thumbs, perhaps four and a half million years ago. We have developed and changed as a species in many ways, but the deep unconscious foundations of our common humanity remain fundamentally the same.

All people dream. The laboratory evidence is in; there is no such thing as a person who does not dream. Anyone who says "I never dream" is simply confessing that he or she habitually forgets this vital aspect of the universal human experience of being alive and self-aware.

Not only do all human beings dream, but all complex, warm-blooded, viviparous animals dream. Dreaming is a universal phenomenon among all relatively highly evolved species. This is particularly significant, given the dangers of dreaming to individual organisms. While we are asleep and dreaming, neural inhibitors paralyze all voluntary nervous impulses, rendering the individual dreamer completely helpless and vulnerable. There is even reason to suppose that this neural inhibition associated with dreaming may be the cause of sudden infant death syndrome (SIDS) and its increased incidence in premature babies.

However, despite these dangers, and in the face of the tremendously wide range of adaptations different mammalian species have made to maximize their survival in various ecosystems, no mammalian species has found it advantageous to abandon the behavior of dreaming. In the face of this evidence, we are left with no choice but to assume that there are survival benefits, both individual and collective, to this seemingly anomalous behavior that far outweigh its obvious dangers and apparent disadvantages.

There is even substantial inferential evidence to suggest that humanity evolved into the condition we recognize as "human" today because our distant, prehuman, hominid ancestors *dreamed* about articulate speech, laying down the first neurological pathways and connections necessary for articulate speech while paralyzed in the dream state.

The electroencephalographic evidence is clear—the brain responds to the "illusory" experience of the dream *as though it were really taking place.* The neural inhibitors that isolate and neutralize the brain impulses directed through the voluntary nervous system in response to the dream are what keep us from *physically acting out* every dream we have, while we're having it. It has been argued that in premature infants, the distinction between "voluntary impulses" and "involuntary impulses," which is the last thing to develop in the fetus, has not had an opportunity to develop to its necessary full extent. When the child falls asleep and starts dreaming, the natural neurological inhibitors that operate during dreaming sleep are "too effective," blocking the involuntary nervous impulses that stimulate the heart and the diaphragm, and thus the infant smothers to death. Since the neurological inhibitors that operate naturally during dreaming sleep leave no discernible trace, it is impossible to demonstrate that they are responsible for SIDS; but they are, at present, the most likely candidate.

The Thai version of the enchanted frog story on which I draw primarily is *Sang Thong–A Dance Drama from Thailand,* written by King Rama II and the poets of his court, and translated by Fern Ingersoll (Rutland and Tokyo: Charles Tuttle, 1973). Her comments about the disturbances caused by the appearance of the ethnic Negrito actor/dancer Kenang in the role of the enchanted prince appear on pages 30–45.

A charming Tlingit example of this archetypal motif, "The Woman Who Married a Frog," a version of the story that emphasizes the collective implications of the encounter with the enchanted frog for society as a whole, may be found in *Native American Animal Stories,* told by Joseph Bruchac (Golden, Colo.: Fulcrum Publishing, 1992, pp. 53–56).

Chapter 2

I found the inspiring quote from Sir James Jeans that opens this chapter in a charming book of quotes, *Dimensions of Man's Spirit,* edited by Virginia Bass (Los Angeles: Science of Mind Publications, 1975, p. 225).

The Shakespeare quotes equating sleep and death with the afterlife and dreaming come from *The Tempest* and *Hamlet* respectively. The Tibetan Buddhist line is my own rendition of lines from the *Bardo Thodol*, the so-called *Tibetan Book of the Dead*, compiled and edited by W. Y. Evans-Wentz (Oxford University Press, 1960). I also made use of *Teachings of Tibetan Yoga*, translated and annotated by Garma C. C. Chang (Hyde Park: University Books, 1963).

The anthropologist Lucien Levy-Bruhl sums up the evidence of the deep archetypal association between dreaming and the experience of the discarnate soul after death by saying, "Through the agency of dream the living man [*sic*] communicates in the simplest and easiest way with the dead, and with mystic powers in general" (*Primitive Mentality* [Boston: Beacon Press, 1966], p. 160). This passage is also the source for the meaning of the West African word *drokuku*.

Kuo Hsiang's wise words about the subjective relativity of all perceptions of difference and similarity can be found in John Ferguson's *Encyclopedia of Mysticism and Mystery Religions* (New York: Crossroad, 1982, p. 101).

Toward the end of his alcoholic life (when his own huge body was starting to show its age and response to wear and tear) the great American poet Charles Olson even went so far as to explore the possibility of particular myths, dreams, and archetypal symbolic forms being directly associated with particular organs of the body and to talk about the "dreams of the pancreas" and the "myths of the liver and the intestines."

Jung's words about the "irresistible bait" for projection come from paragraph 253 of his essay *The Spirit Mercurius*, which can be found in volume 13 of his *Collected Works* (Princeton University Press, 1979).

John E. Mack's book, *Abduction: Human Encounters with Aliens* (New York: Scribner's/Macmillan, 1994), documents his fascinating and humane work with people who have compelling and very similar stories to tell about their experiences of being abducted and experimented with by aliens. The quote about these experiences producing a greater sense of connection and meaning comes from page 418 of that book. Dr. Mack does not discuss the possibility that there is an *archetypal* pattern being developed in their experiences, but it seems to me that the data calls out for such an analysis, *whether their stories are true or not,* and I am quite willing to entertain the possibility that they are. John Mack is also notable for his earlier book (published prior to his public interest in UFO's), *Nightmares and Human Conflict* (Boston: Houghton Mifflin, 1970), which remains a major contribution to the study of nightmares and dreams in general.

Jung's *Flying Saucers: A Modern Myth of Things Seen in the Sky,* originally published in German in 1958, was published in English in 1969 by New American Library in New York. The dream quoted is only one of several he cites and discusses in depth in the chapter "UFO's in Dreams" (pp. 35–84).

The famous "butterfly dream" of Chuang Tzu can be found in many slightly different versions in several different places. I have combined several translations to give the exact phraseology presented here, relying primarily on Burton Watson's *Complete Works of Chuang Tzu* (Oxford University Press, 1968). For a most illuminating discussion of Descartes' famous dream, see Marie Louise von Franz's essay, "The Dream of Descartes" included in her book *Dreams* (Shambala, 1991, pp. 107–191).

Most folklorists, mythographers, ethnographers, and anthropologists have generally preferred to focus on only one version of a myth or folk practice as "primary." They have expended great energy in searching for the "oldest" and therefore supposedly most "pure and authentic" text or enactment, and in placing all other versions in graded positions as "derivative" or "degenerate." This intellectual strategy has tended to miss and obscure the basic point that it is only in the examination of the multiple versions in their wondrous diversity throughout the world in different periods of history that the full impact and significance of the archetypal symbols and themes can be most clearly seen, felt, and appreciated. This attitude has also tended to dismiss and ignore any and all new, contemporary versions of the great archetypal stories and themes. In fact, it is often in the more modern versions of the ancient archetypal stories that their compelling relevance to present circumstances can be most clearly recognized.

The basic tool for research into recurring motifs in world

myth and folk tale remains *The Types of the Folktale: A Classification and Bibliography,* second revision, 1961, by *Antti Aarne and Stith Thompson* (Helsinki, Folk Lore Fellows Communication #184). It is cumbersome and of use only as a jumping off place for searching through primary sources. However, a charming and carefully annotated anthology, which includes a wide range of well-told representative stories from around the world as well as scholarly classifications and cross-referencing of multiple versions of the tales from different cultures, has recently been re-published in paperback: *World Folktales: A Treasury of Over Sixty of the World's Best-Loved Folktales,* edited by Atelia Clarkson and Gilbert B. Cross (New York: Scribner's, 1980).

In fact, it is the persistence of the same archetypal elements in these multiple versions, extending into contemporary times, that constitutes one of the most important pieces of evidence that there are shared universal qualities of the human psyche and the human condition. Myths and dreams grow out of, and appeal to, this universal layer of human experience, regardless of the particular circumstances of any given individual life or society.

Jane Goodall's work documenting chimpanzees breaking off twigs to fish termites out of termite mounds and then trimming the twigs to maximum effective length by trial and error put an end to the idea that tool use and tool fabrication are exclusively human abilities. The ongoing research with primates and cetaceans, such as Francine Patterson's work teaching Koko the gorilla to communicate in standard sign, also makes it clear that language "is in the eye of the beholder," and is also not an exclusively human ability or activity.

Matthew Fox's works are all exceptionally wise and transformative. His remarks about the deep relationship between all forms of addiction and failed spiritual search are most accessible in his book *Creation Spirituality* (San Francisco: Harper & Row, 1991).

Chapter 3

There are many versions of the Izanagi and Izanami story cycle available in English. I have made particular use of *The Kojiki:*

Records of Ancient Matters, translated by Basil H. Chamberlain, and *Nihongi: Chronicles of Japan from the Earliest Times to A.D. 697,* translated by W. G. Aston, both published by Charles Tuttle, 1981 and 1972 respectively. When he gets to the sexually explicit passages of the *Kojiki,* Chamberlain resorts to the quaint Victorian stratagem of translating the ancient Japanese text into Latin instead of English. The most engaging and accessible general introduction to the Japanese tradition of myth and sacred narrative that I have discovered is *Japanese Mythology,* by Juliet Piggott (London and New York: Paul Hamlyn, 1969).

Another cross-cultural example of the archetypal animus/anima anxieties depicted in the Izanagi/Izanami myth is the Arctic Eskimo tale of the benevolent giant, Inugpasugssuk, who proposes a "wife exchange" with a human friend. The humans agree, but when the giant makes love to the human woman, she is "split wide open" by his huge erection. And when the human man tries to make love with giant woman, he falls into her vagina. The man dissolves inside her, and his bones are expelled in her urine. Inugpasugssuk is devastated by the unfortunate outcome of the exchange of spouses and adopts a human boy and raises him in an effort to expiate his guilt (see *Dictionary of Native American Mythology* by Sam Gill and Irene Sullivan [Santa Barbara, Denver, and Oxford: ABC-CLIO, 1992]). Although the possibility of "cultural diffusion" from Japan to the Arctic is certainly possible, it in no way undercuts the quality of universal interest that this particular gender fantasy evokes in all the cultures where it appears. It is that quality of "fascination" that marks archetypal symbolic material when it rises in conscious awareness.

I would recommend the whole series of large format, beautifully illustrated introductory mythology books published by Hamlyn.

With regard to the idea that the penis was once regarded as a female organ only given to men on loan, a recent comment by the actor Dustin Hoffman during a televised interview is amusing and instructive. While discussing the archetypically masculine habit of giving the penis a separate "pet name" (a practice which in itself points to the anxiety-producing experience of the penis as "other"), he leaned forward and made even stronger eye contact with the interviewer and said, "You know, it's like living with a *madman!*"

Aldous Huxley is quite devastatingly articulate in his criticism of "fuzzy" Jungian/archetypal thinking and analytical methods:

> Jungian literature is like a vast quaking bog. At every painful step the reader sinks to the hip in jargon and generalizations, with never a path of firm intellectual ground to rest on, and only rarely, in that endless expanse of jelly, the blessed relief of a hard concrete fact. (Quoted by Peter Bishop in his essay "Jung, Eastern Religion, and the Language of the Imagination," in *Self and Liberation,* ed. Meckel and Moore [Paulist Press, 1992, p. 175].)

Unfortunately, the quality of subjectivity and intellectual uncertainty that so annoys Huxley is inherent in the analysis of symbolic form itself, regardless of the particular school of thought. Understanding of symbols is *always* reliant on the detection and interpretation of patterns lying below and beyond the surface of appearance created by "hard concrete facts." Either the interpretations are interesting, compelling, and convincing, or they are not, and the assertion that one school of symbolic thought is "scientific" while another is not is simply not supportable.

The intellectually distressing tendency of archetypal images to dissolve into one another and to defy firm, mutually exclusive definition is a problem dictated by the nature of human consciousness and symbolic form itself, and the schools of thought that attempt to avoid or deny this problem (like virtually all forms of Marxism, Objectivism, and Logical Positivism) unfortunately end up in actual practice supporting the most destructive kinds of denial and self-deception.

As Jung himself said to Georges Duplain in 1959:

> There are so many possible forms of truth. We must find simple words for the great truths; we must try to approach the living truth behind things—it's [hu]mankind's greatest effort. In our time, it's the intellect that is making darkness because we let it take too great a place. Consciousness discriminates, judges, analyses, emphasizes the contradictions.

It's necessary work up to a point, but analysis kills and syn-
thesis brings life. We must find out how to get everything
back into connection with everything else. We must resist
the voice of intellectualism and get it to understand that we
cannot only understand. (Quoted in *C. G. Jung Speaking:
Interviews and Encounters*, ed. McGuire and Hull [Princeton
University Press, 1977], p. 420.)

And again:

The ground principles, the *archai*, of the unconscious are
indescribable because of their wealth of reference, although
in themselves recognizable. The discriminating intellect naturally keeps on trying to establish their singleness of meaning and thus misses the essential point; for what we can
above all establish as the one thing consistent with their
nature is their *manifold meaning*, their almost limitless
wealth of reference, which makes any unilateral formulation
impossible. (*Collected Works of C. G. Jung* [Princeton University Press, 1968], vol. 9, p. i.)

Demaris Wehr, in her excellent book, *Jung and Feminism:
Liberating Archetypes* (Boston: Beacon Press, 1987), and Robert
Hopke, in his groundbreaking book, *Men's Dreams, Men's Healing*
(Boston and London: Shambala, 1990), both argue, quite convincingly it seems to me, that Jung's formulation of the Shadow,
animus, and anima are oppressive and do not correspond either
to the spontaneous dream experiences of contemporary people
or to the mythic narratives of the ancients. They both argue that
for these reasons, the classic Jungian formulations of these particular archetypes must be reshaped, because the basic concept
of "archetypes" is far too useful and descriptive of the actual situation in the collective psyche to be scrapped or abandoned.

The story of the Bogadjimbri appears in several sources. I
have made particular use of Pamela Allardice's *Myths, Gods, and
Fantasy* (Bridgeport: Prism Press, 1991, p. 40); *The World's
Mythology in Colour* by Veronica Ions (London: Hamlyn, 1974, p.
299); and *Encyclopedia of World Mythology* (New York: Galahad
Books, 1975, p. 34) all of which offer different versions and
selections (as well as spellings) of the myths of Bogadjimbri.

The story of the tortoises and the humans badgering God

to allow them to have children is found in several versions. I have relied primarily on the version told by Ulli Beir in his wonderful little book, *The Origin of Life and Death: African Creation Myths* (London: Heinemann Educational Books, 1966, pp. 58–59).

The story of Earthmaker and Coyote arguing over the creation of the world comes from *The Maidu Indian Myths and Stories of Hanc'ibyjim,* edited and translated by William Shipley (Berkeley: Heyday Books, 1991, pp. 49–52).

In waking life I have a relatively difficult time imagining and discerning the symbolic and metaphoric significance of numbers. I have tried for a long time to see the deeper archetypal patterns of number theory and specific numbers because I *know* that numbers have the same overdetermined and resonant symbolism as words and images, but even armed with that certainty, I still find it much more difficult to see and understand them. The discussion of the symbolic implications of the "twos" and the "twinning" in the sex/death creation stories in the main text is distilled down from a very wide range of research.

For me, the most succinct and best introductory essays on the archetypal symbolism of numbers are the essays on "Numbers" included in J. E. Cirlot's *A Dictionary of Symbols* (New York: Philosophical Library, 1962, and often reprinted) and J. C. Cooper's *An Illustrated Encyclopedia of Traditional Symbols* (London: Thames & Hudson, 1978, recently re-issued in paperback). These two books together make a very good beginning nucleus for building a library of resources to help in exploring dream symbols with particular reference to their archetypal resonances (the strategy of dream work that Jung called "amplification").

The basic trick of using a dream and symbol dictionary to explore the meanings in dreams is to use more than one. Dreams and symbols in dreams are overdetermined and always have multiple layers of meaning and significance. The "aha" of recognition of the dreamer is the only reliable touchstone in the search for the authentic meanings in dreams. I am personally convinced that the same holds true for the explication and analysis of the symbols in myth, sacred narrative, and art as well. Bearing this in mind, even the most aggressively authoritarian and trivial dream/symbol dictionary can sometimes yield very satisfactory "aha's," particularly for dreamers who for whatever reason are unable to work their dreams with other people and are forced to pursue their interior investigations in solitude. The more dream symbol books you have at your disposal, and the more diverse the traditions they reflect, the more like hearing the multiple ideas and projections of a dream group it will be.

The Chinese rain-making ceremony of the two teams of naked men and women hitting one another is referred to briefly in Wolfram Eberhard's *Dictionary of Chinese Symbols* (London and New York: Routledge, 1986, p. 203). A slightly different translation of the line from the *I Ching* will be found on page 262 of that same volume.

The practice of giving dreams titles when you record them, as the woman did when she called her dream "In the Front Row with Gorilla-Man," is an excellent idea. The moment of picking the title is always an invitation to insight and often generates spontaneous "aha's" about the dream's larger meanings and implications. Even more importantly, if you get into the habit of giving your remembered dreams short, evocative titles, then you will be able at any point to go back and look over everything you have recorded at once. This means that you have a much better chance of seeing the shape of the whole forest instead of just the shape of the individual trees. It is a primary way of making the transition from beginning dream work to intermediate and advanced work with dreams. Instead of asking, What does this dream mean and portend? the dreamer can begin to ask, What is the overall direction and thrust of my dreams over the months and years? How are the repeating themes and motifs of my dreams evolving over time and increased experience?

The main task a good dream title should fulfill is to recall the basic *experience* of the dream to memory. A good title should recall the experience of the dream to mind months or even years later. Dreams have gifts of insight and creative energy to give that often can not be adequately appreciated until time has passed. Thus, "In the Front Row with Gorilla-Man" is a much better title than "Accepting My Animus," even though that may be a primary significance of the dream. In general, such "insight synopses" serve best as subtitles.

Erich Neumann's *Amor and Psyche–the Psychic Development of the Feminine: A Commentary on the Tale by Apuleius* (Bollingen Foundation Series LIV, Princeton University Press, 1956, reprinted in paperback in 1971) is one of the best renditions of the narrative *The Golden Ass.* Diane Wolkstein's and Samuel Noah Kramer's *Innana* (New York: Harper & Row, 1983) is a very good version of the older Mesopotamian myth, one of the few extant narratives in written form from the prehistoric matriarchal tradition.

Chapter 4

The Great Goddess's Celtic/Welsh name is usually rendered as "Ceridwen" and her son's as "Afagaddu." He is also sometimes called "Moorna." Little Gooyion is usually rendered as "Gwion Bach"; *bach* is an adjective suggesting "young" or "small in stature." Gooyithno is usually rendered "Gwyddno."

I have chosen here and throughout to use the older names and to render them phonetically to make them easier to pronounce more or less correctly, and to avoid the complicated scholarly game of transliterating the Welsh alphabet. These stories are far too lively and universally important to be left exclusively to the domain of the small minority of academicians with primary interest in ancient Welsh orthography and epigraphy.

Erich Neumann's *The Great Mother* (Princeton University Press, 1955) remains the most exhaustive scholarly examination of the both the archeology and the psychology of this archetype. Many books have been published more recently exploring this archetypal form from a more consciously feminist point of view. I am particularly fond of *The Myth of the Goddess: Evolution of an Image* by Anne Baring and Jules Cashford (Penguin Books/Viking Arcana, 1991). This book also contains an exhaustive bibliography. The works of Marija Gimbutas, *The Goddesses and Gods of Old Europe, Myths and Cult Images* (University of California, 1982) and *The Language of the Goddess* (Harper & Row, 1989), are particularly clear and comprehensive with regard to the prehistoric worship of the Great Mother in Europe. Geoffrey Bibby's brilliant book, *Four Thousand Years Ago: A World Panorama of Life in the Second Millennium B.C.* (Alfred Knopf, 1961), remains the best overview of the (archetypal) religious and cultural developments in the ancient world during the transition from prehistoric to historic times.

The description of the Mesoamerican goddess Tonantzin is quoted in John Bierhorst's *The Hungry Woman: Myths and Legends of the Aztecs* (New York: William Morrow, 1984, pp.10 and 23). He, in turn, is quoting from a translation of an even earlier French work transcribing firsthand accounts of Aztec beliefs recorded by the Spanish clerics who "converted" the Mesoamerican peoples to Christianity soon after the destruction of the Aztec empire by Cortez.

The quote about male ignorance of paternity comes from Malinowski's *The Father in Primitive Society* (W.W. Norton, 1927, pp. 14 and 95).

The Bible renderings so clearly suggestive of reincarnation are assembled from Matthew 16:14, Mark 8:28, and Luke 9:19, respectively. It is worth noting that this exchange immediately precedes the account of Jesus turning to Peter and pressing his questions in a seemingly unexpected direction: "And who do *you* say that I am?" Peter becomes the first one to say it out loud: "I believe that you are He—the Christ—the Anointed One—the Messiah...!" It appears to be on the strength of these reports from his spies, together with Peter's willingness to say what no one has had the nerve to say before, that Jesus is moved to say, "OK, enough of this lurking in the suburbs. Go get me an ass to ride. We're going into the city at last."

A succinct account of the Yuletide tradition of the "Mari Lwyd" can be found in John and Caitlin Mathews' *The Aquarian Guide to British and Irish Mythology* (Wellingborough: Aquarian Press, 1988, p. 114).

Chapter 5

The chilling reply of the papal legate is reported in a number of sources. I first came across it in Stephen Howarth's interesting and distinctly sober book, *The Knights Templar* (New York: Barnes & Noble, 1993, p. 191). The papal legate is named in *The Unknown*

South of France by Henry and Margaret Reuss (Boston: Harvard Common Press, 1991, p. 108).

There are many versions of the "Raven Steals the Sun for the People" available in English. I have made use of several of them in creating the version here, including *Raven Tales: Traditional Stories of Native Peoples*, selected and edited by Peter Goodchild (Chicago: Review Press, 1991); *Once Upon a Totem* by Christie Harris (New York: Atheneum, 1968); *The Raven Steals the Light* by Bill Reid and Robert Bringhurst (Seattle: University of Washington Press, and Toronto: Douglas & McIntyre, 1984); *Portrait Masks from the Northwest Coast of America* by J. C. H. King (London: Thames & Hudson [Blacker Calman Cooper Ltd.], 1979); *9 Tales of Raven* by Fran Martin (New York: Harper & Brothers, 1951); *Indian Legends of the Pacific Northwest* by Ella E. Clark (Berkeley: University of California, 1953); and *The Trickster: A Study in American Indian Mythology* by Paul Radin (New York: Bell Publishing, 1956). This last volume is particularly interesting because it includes two very important essays: "The Trickster in Relation to Greek Mythology" by Karl Kerenyi and "On the Psychology of the Trickster Figure" by Carl Jung, as well as Radin's succinct renditions and elaborate analyses of several key Native American Trickster myths, along with associated rituals and ceremonies. It is worth noting that in other Native American cultures, farther south and east, where water is less plentiful than it is in the Pacific Northwest, it is often the First Water (of Life) that Raven steals from the Old Chief for the people.

From our very limited perspective, the human species appears to be the primary cosmic laboratory experiment in the development of consciousness at present. We have begun the clumsy search for other "signs of life" in the universe; and not too surprisingly, we have not yet found any totally convincing indications of extraterrestrial life. However, I believe it is the height of hubris and self-deception to imagine that we are the only such experiment—or worse yet, the only possible one—in this seemingly infinite cosmos where the archetypal principles and patterns that shape our possibilities and experiences seem so interested in preserving and protecting and *expanding* this conscious self-awareness that we are in the process of evolving.

The "Book of Revelations" is not closed, and to assert that it is, is only to invite the archetypal Trickster (of consciousness itself) to prove us wrong.

I am particularly fond of the details of the "Flight into Egypt" provided by the beautifully melodic traditional British folk song "The Cherry Tree Carol." In the song, Mary's energy flags as they flee; and as she rests by the side of the road, she asks Joseph to pick her some cherries to revive her:

> And Joseph spoke in anger,
> In anger spoke he.
> "Let the father of the baby
> Gather cherries for thee!"
>
> Then up spake baby Jesus,
> From in Mary's womb
> "Bow down, you tallest cherry tree,
> Let my Mother have some!"
>
> And so the tallest cherry tree
> Bowed down to the ground,
> And Mary gathered cherries
> While Joseph stood around...

Here is another tiny, exquisite Divine Child story. In these few lines, Joseph's lingering doubts and resentments are resolved and dispelled, and his world is forever altered. The Divine Child exhibits his miraculous powers, and the whole of nature responds, renewing the world.

I called my earlier book *Where People Fly and Water Runs Uphill: Using Dreams to Tap the Wisdom of the Unconscious* (Warner Books, 1992) because of my deep interest in creativity and the ways in which the metaphor of flying and "defying gravity" tends to reflect and comment on the creative energies and the possibilities of genuinely new and innovative solutions to the individual and collective problems we face.

I am particularly taken with what Lao Tzu has to say about "conventionality" in the inner chapters of the *Tao Te Ching*. After reading many different translations, I would render it in this way:

Conventionality arises when loyalty and honor are starting to decay. Conventionality is the doorway to chaos.

Chapter 6

Although it is generally agreed that the story of Oedipus is Greek, the largest statue of the Sphinx is in Egypt, where there is also a "Kingdom of Thebes" and a documented tradition of royal incest. Immanuel Velikovsky, the rebel scholar who accurately predicted the surface temperature of Venus long before it was measured by the Mariner space probe (arguing that both Venus and the moon are late arrivals in the solar system, one a comet and the other an asteroid, captured by the gravitational fields of the Sun and the Earth), wrote a most interesting book suggesting that the Oedipus "myth" is actually a slightly fictionalized account of the life and difficulties of Akhenaten, the rebel monotheist pharaoh (*Oedipus and Akhnaton: Myth and History* [New York: Doubleday, 1960]).

The subsequent tragedies of the children of Oedipus and Jocasta are chronicled in the various versions of *Seven Against Thebes* and *Antigone.*

In Sophocles and elsewhere, the crossroads where Oedipus fights and kills his father is "a place where three roads come together." Freud argues forcefully that this description is a symbolic diagram of the female genitalia, the true venue of the struggle between son and father.

The remarkable quote from Freud acknowledging the reality and importance of the collective unconscious comes from his *Outline of Psychoanalysis* (p. 28). I was absolutely stunned when I first came across it (quoted in Ann Mankowitz's *Change of Life: A Psychological Study of Dream and the Menopause* [Toronto: Inner City Books, 1984], p. 31), particularly when one remembers the ferocious attacks Freud mounts on Jung and the notion of the collective unconscious as "unscientific." Clearly, there is no useful distinction to be drawn between the level of unconscious life Freud calls "phylogenic" and "archaic" and defines as *prior to individual experience* (even relating it directly to mythology and "the earliest human legends") and Jung's notion of the "collective unconscious" or "objective psyche."

Geza Roheim's global applications of Freudian theory can be found throughout his work. I would particularly recommend *Fire in the Dragon and Other Psychoanalytic Essays on Folklore,* edited and introduced by Alan Dundes (Princeton University Press, 1992).

By saying that it is "an aesthetic question" which archetypal energy one chooses to make paramount and use as the center point to orient and organize the rest of the pantheon into a coherent pattern, I do not wish to suggest that it is a trivial or unimportant question. In my view, the *aesthetic* question—what one is prepared to find and relate to as beautiful, and what one is prepared to view as ugly and thus reject and avoid—is a philosophical, moral, and psychospiritual question of the utmost importance. "Beauty" and "meaning" are different sides of the same coin, different aspects of the ultimately important aesthetic question.

The most meaningful formulation is by definition also the most beautiful. True beauty is defined and conferred by the depth and all-encompassing quality of meaning. Only the seemingly meaningless is truly ugly. (And on closer examination, nothing is meaningless.)

The primary problem with Freud's assertion that the Oedipal drama is the benchmark against which all other psychospiritual experience must be measured is that it ignores and denigrates the experience of women on the one hand, while on the other hand, it reduces all questions of meaning and psychospiritual significance to variations of self-deception—mere "masks" worn by more basic, instinctive, "animal" biological urges. In Freud's view, the evolution of those "primal urges" into increasingly conscious and profound expressions of deepening self-awareness becomes a mere "sublimation" of the more authentic and true (and bestial) instincts. In Jung's eyes, they become the expressions of a meaningful cosmos evolving to become more aware of itself, simultaneously using and enabling human beings to achieve that end.

Obviously, such basic, primal/sexual urges are present at

all times and must be taken into account in any honest effort to assess the depth of meaning and significance of human experience, but the mere fact that they are present does not make them the prime determinants of human activity and behavior. Growing out of "mere unconscious (animal) existence" is the uniquely human and the uniquely conscious and self-aware possibility of meaning, significance, and conscious relationship to (archetypal) patterns of harmony and collective reconciliation that extend far beyond the urge to reproduce and survive as individual organisms.

Prior to World War II, the Indo-Europeans were called "Aryans" or "Indo-Aryans." The first comprehensive study of their origins and archaeology was done in 1925 by the archaeologist and anthropologist V. Gordon Childe. His book, *The Aryans: A Study in Indo-European Origins,* is still in print (New York: Dorset Press, 1987).

When the Nazis centered on the term *Aryan* as their preferred name for their "glorious racially superior ancestors," the progenitors of the "Master Race," it became distinctly unfashionable in the non-German academic world to use the term, and *Indo-European* came much more into fashion. More recently, there have been (in my view) two notable additions to the evolving study of our "Caucasian" ancestors and the archetypal patterns of their religion and society: *Archeology and Language: The Puzzle of Indo-European Origins* by Colin Renfrew (Cambridge University Press, 1990) and *Myth, Cosmos, and Society: Indo-European Themes of Creation and Destruction* by Bruce Lincoln (Harvard University Press, 1987).

An interesting précis of the archaeological finds at Mohenjo-Daro can be found in Jacquetta Hawkes' *Atlas of Ancient Archeology* (New York: McGraw Hill, 1974). This is a very valuable reference volume for following the archaeological evidence for religious and social lives of ancient peoples around the world.

The biblical David and Goliath story offers an interesting glimpse of possibilities of social organization that are literally unimaginable to the patriarchal mind. The Philistines were a matriarchal people, and it is they who propose that the battle between them and the nomadic, pastoralist Israelites be settled by single combat between designated champions. Goliath is defeated and they retreat, even though they outnumber their foe and are better equipped. The biblical narrator(s) suggest that it is their "terror" at the demonstrated superiority of the Israelite God that causes them to quit the field, but there is substantial evidence from other sources that it is an agreement, that the Philistines are adhering to a divine social contract and are simply behaving in their own version of "civilized behavior" when they quit the field after the defeat of their champion.

In the Irish epic of *The Cattle Raid of Cooley*, the Ulster hero Cuhoolan (usually transliterated "Cu Chulainn") fights a series of single combats with chosen champions of the invading army of Queen Maeve; and at no point, despite her rage and frustration at Cuhoolan's repeated victories over her champions, does Maeve even consider attacking him with her whole army, which stands idly by, day by day, watching the combats. This "unthinkable" behavior offers further inferential evidence of the social contract that appears to have contained and ritualized warfare across the ancient matrifocal world, from the Near East to Ireland, in prehistoric times.

What would contemporary sports commentators say if, after a team was defeated, their supporters in the stands came down on the field to beat up the winning team in an attempt to reverse the defeat? It would be deemed "uncivilized," no matter how big and attractive the prize for winning might be. This may be an appropriate analogy to the social contract that appears to have governed intercommunal conflict among matriarchal societies.

An interesting piece of inferential evidence for the Indo-Europeans using the "excuse" of following the migrating herds as a justification for conquest can be found in the twelfth-century Irish *Book of the Dun Cow,* where several much more ancient tales are told of kingdoms that rise and fall and go to war with one another over the possession of cattle, and where the practice is described of warriors releasing a cow and following her into battle wherever she wanders. All of these tales have strong claim to be part of a very ancient Indo-European tradition of "following the herd" in whatever direction it travels, as an indication of "God's will." The concept of the "sacred cow" and the persistence of cattle worship in contemporary Hindu India are also clear examples of this Indo-European psychospiritual heritage.

For a more complete rendition of the myth of the birth of Hermes and its relationship to the transformation of ancient Indo-European society, see chapter 15, "The Gifts of Hermes and the Transformation of Culture," in my earlier book *Dream Work: Techniques for Discovering the Creative Power in Dreams* (Paulist Press, 1983, pp. 184–195).

In the British Isles, the phrase "and pigs can fly" is one of the strongest derisive comments one can make. In the prehistoric matriarchal period in the British Isles, there was a persistent myth of the Goddess, in her guise as the Great Sow, flying over the land and dropping litters of piglets to the ground at sites that were particularly sacred to her. Archaeological evidence is very strong that raising pigs in sanctuaries dedicated to the Goddess was a common practice. The persistence of this derisive phrase, and the emotional vehemence with which it is usually uttered (in a culture not noted for its effusive emotional expression), suggest the kind of derision that the Indo-European patriarchs appear to have heaped on the literalistic interpretation of the sacred narratives of the matrifocal society it supplanted. Flying pigs and women giving birth to children without male assistance are/were equally worthy of disdain and ridicule.

Hamlet's Mill, published originally in hardcover by Gambit in Boston in 1969, has been reprinted twice in paperback. It is somewhat turgid, and both authors throw up their metaphoric hands in horror at the idea that they might be discussing something so subjective and "unscientific" as an archetype, but clearly, despite their protestations, the discovery and demonstration of repeating patterns of metaphor in sacred narrative—discernible in materials from widely separated cultures in ancient times—is, in itself, a functional definition of archetypal form.

The "precession of the equinoxes" refers to an observational phenomenon resulting from slow and inexorable gyrations in the earth's axis of rotation over thousands of years. The axis of rotation of the earth is not perpendicular to the plane of its path around the sun (known as "the plane of the ecliptic"). Because of this tilt (28 degrees from vertical), we on the surface of the planet experience the cycle of the changing seasons as the earth travels around the sun, alternately showing the Northern Hemisphere more directly to the rays of the sun, then the Southern Hemisphere, then the Northern again, in endless repeating sequence. It takes a year (365 1/4 days) for the spinning earth to make one complete cycle around the sun. When the tilt in the rotational axis exposes the Southern Hemisphere to the sun, we in the Northern Hemisphere experience fall and winter, while the denizens of the Southern Hemisphere experience spring and summer.

In winter, the sun is not visible above the horizon north of the Arctic Circle; in fact, the Arctic Circle is defined geographically by the winter shadow of the earth where the sun does not appear above the horizon for six months. At the same time, the South Pole experiences endless daylight, and the sun appears to spiral around in the sky without setting.

As the earth travels on its path around the sun, it reaches a point where the tilt in the axis of rotation faces exactly 90 degrees away from the plane of the ecliptic, and for that one day, the Northern and Southern Hemispheres receive equal amounts of sun. Viewed from both the poles, this day is characterized by the sun being split by the horizon as it makes a complete 360-degree circuit around the visible horizon before setting (or rising) fully. At the same time, observed from the equator, the sun appears to stand directly overhead at noon, instead of appearing to the north of the equator, as it does in spring and summer, and to the south, as it does in fall and winter. The Tropics of Capricorn and Cancer correspond to the farthest points, north and south of the equator, that the sun is observed to reach before "turning back" as the seasons change.

These moments of equal amounts of light falling on each hemisphere occur twice a year, once in the middle of autumn, and once in the middle of the spring. We experience those rotational moments as the times when all over the world, no matter at what latitude, the day and the night are of equal length—hence the name *equinoxes*. The next day after an equinox, one hemisphere receives more light than the other and has a longer day than the other, and the cyclic imbalance of exposure to the rays of the sun that causes the changing seasons marches onward.

A quarter of the way further along on the earth's path around the sun, we experience the longest and shortest days and nights of the year, the *solstices*. These are also midseasonal moments.

The Romans insisted on twisting their (and hence our) calendar a quarter turn "out of true" by declaring that the solstice and equinox points mark the *beginning* of the seasons, but this is clearly out of sync with our experience. Shakespeare has it right—the shortest night of the year is *Mid*-summer's Night, not the first night of summer. It is typical of the Romans, and of the masculinist Indo-European heritage we share with them, that they prefer the linear clarity of having seasons begin and end at clearly observable moments, rather than giving recognition to the way the seasons *feel* to us as we live through them. The arguments over the calendar that characterize dynastic rule in the Northern Hemisphere during the period of recorded history clearly reflect the ongoing struggle to reconcile the religious and spiritual ideology of patriarchy with the older, instinctual, experiential relationship to the physical world and the cycle of the seasons celebrated in the Goddess tradition.

When looking at the background of "fixed" (i.e., vastly distant) stars that form the observational background of sunrise and sunset on these equinox days, they always appear to be the same from year to year. But in fact, each year there is a tiny, incremental difference in this observed background of stars, because the tilt of the axis is itself rotating or "gyring," only this movement is so slow as to be virtually imperceptible over the course of a lifetime, or even several lifetimes, of even the most careful observation of the sky with the unaided eye.

The analogy that is used most often to describe this gyring motion is the decelerating of a child's spinning top. As you may remember from playing with spinning tops yourself, as they slow down, they start to fall over; but because of the centrifugal force of their rotation, they start to gyre, so that the axis of the top's spin starts to wobble and describe larger and larger circles, only at a much slower rate than the rate of the top's spin. The tilted axis of the earth's rotation is undergoing a similar gyre, but it takes something in the neighborhood of 26,000 years for this gyre to complete one full rotation. In other words, it takes about 1,300 human generations to observe one full cycle. That's very slow by human standards. (No wonder the nomadic hunter-gatherers and the matriarchal farmers appear to have missed it.)

For purposes of clarity and measurement of time, we earth-surface dwellers have divided up the sky into twelve sections, roughly corresponding to the division of the yearly calendar into twelve months. These divisions appear observationally as the twelve constellations of fixed stars that lie along the plane of the ecliptic, the band of space in the sky where the moon and the planets are observed to travel around in their own respective passages around the sun (defined by the path of the earth's orbit around the sun). The word *planet* itself drives from the Greek word for "wanderer," because the planets appear to "wander" in seemingly erratic (but ultimately predictable) fashion along the plane of the ecliptic.

Obviously, these constellations are relatively arbitrary constructions of human consciousness, but once their boundaries have been established by general agreement, their appearance is easily observable by anyone. Since the background of stars on the morning of the Vernal (spring) Equinox appears "fixed," it has become the traditional "set point" for the calendar, in large measure because the time of spring planting is a matter of such tremendous practical as well as cultural and religious significance in societies dependent on agriculture. (If you get the timing of this one wrong, you don't eat.)

The matriarchies that invented agriculture set their calendars to the Vernal Equinox to solve the problem of when to plant. The invading, conquering patriarchs (among which we must still include Western industrial society) became equally dependent on agriculture, and therefore on the agricultural calendar, despite the fact that all agricultural concerns are relatively late additions to nomadic patriarchal culture.

Because of this excruciatingly slow (at least from the perspective of individual human life spans) shift in the background of stars on the day of the Vernal Equinox, the constellations are

not fixed, and every 2,000 years or so, it will be observable and
obvious to anyone that the background of stars is "off" by one-
twelfth in comparison to the background 2,000 years earlier.
Instead of the sun appearing against the background of the constellation that tradition has always said it will, the sun appears
against the background of the next constellation over.

It is this phenomenon that is known as the "precession of
the equinoxes." When people talk about the "dawning of the
Age of Aquarius," it is precisely this observational phenomenon
to which they are referring. For the past 2,000 years or so, the
sun has been observed to rise against the background of the constellation Pisces on the morning of the Vernal Equinox. Thus the
present era, since about the time of Christ, is often referred to as
"the Piscean Age." At some point (impossible to determine by
official Roman calendar standards, because the boundaries of
the constellations as we see them in the night sky are arbitrary
and not subject to exact visual measurement), anyone looking at
sun rising on the day of the Vernal Equinox will see that the
background constellation is not Pisces, as it has been for more or
less the entire Christian era, but rather Aquarius. At that point,
when even the most casual observer will have no doubt that the
background of stars on the morning of the Vernal Equinox is
indeed Aquarius, the "Age of Aquarius" may be said to have
"dawned" (Fig. 20).

This roughly 2,000-year period has also been called a "Pla-
tonic Year" because Plato suggested that it marked a cycle of
time when the dominant spiritual/philosophical perspective
that held sway for the previous 2,000-year period was destined to
be superseded by some new worldview.

Because Aquarius is a constellation associated with an earlier part of the solar year than Pisces, this slow but inevitable
"slippage" of the background of "fixed" stars is going "backward" (in relation to the "forward" movement of time through
the seasons), and thus the phenomenon is known as *pre*cession,
rather than *pro*cession.

Jung, in conversation with Laurens van der Post about the
possibilities of life after death and the emotional and psychological

problems of grieving survivors, is reported to have said, "Trust the meaning. Trust the thing that gives most meaning..."

The fascinating epic, *The Secret History of the Mongols–The Origin of Chingis Khan (Based Primarily on the English Translation by Francis Woodman Cleaves)* by Paul Kahn (San Francisco: North Point Press, 1984), is perhaps the first manuscript ever to be written in the Mongol language. Originally composed by a now unidentifiable member of the royal family immediately after the death of Chingis Khan in 1227 C.E., it contains much folk and mythological material, including accounts of how the "younger gods" battle with one another to succeed the older patriarch when he is no longer able to "master the herds." *The Secret History* offers ample evidence for the archetypal patterns of Mongol social life and religion. In many places it reads like a Celtic cattle raid epic, with the same kinds of heroic struggles of personal friendship and family loyalty conflicting with larger dynastic and divine loyalties, and espousing the same ultimately tragic/heroic view of life as demanding supreme effort and sacrifice, even though it is doomed to ultimate failure.

A similar demonstration of the same basic archetypal, patriarchal pastoralist patterns of religious practice and tragic/heroic worldview can be found in *The Heart of the Ngoni: Heroes of the African Kingdom of Segu,* by Harold Courlander with Ousmane Sako (New York: Crown Publishers, 1982).

Chapter 7

It may seem ironic, if not downright odd, that such a dramatic feminist reframing of the Oedipus story should come in channeled form to a man rather than a woman. My own suspicion is that it is just one more indication that a satisfactory resolution of the contemporary gender wars requires a raising of conscious awareness of the interior emotional and intuitive life of "the other," whoever he or she may be. We are all an amalgam of gendered desires and attitudes, and unless we fully and consciously acknowledge the whole range of our own interior experiences, we will inevitably deny the humanity of those who appear different.

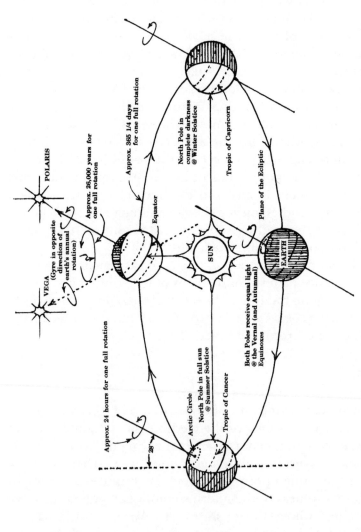

Figure 20. (Worldwide) Diagram of the Earth's rotational dynamics as viewed against the background of the most distant, "fixed" stars that create the phenomenon known as "the precession of the equinoxes."

Some of my women ritualist and liturgist friends have adopted *Queen Jocasta* into the "canon" of sacred stories they use in their work. They have reported to me that there is usually a certain amount of disbelief expressed when it comes out that the piece was channeled by a man. (As I said, I was pretty surprised myself.) I have become convinced that we are capable, individually and as a species, of understanding each other at great depth and of reflecting that knowledge back to the world in the form of healing expressive art. I hope that *Queen Jocasta* may serve that purpose.

I am very grateful to all the people who carry this story further into the world and bring it to new audiences. Please feel free to make whatever creative use of the text you may be drawn to. (If you use it to make money, charging admission to hear and see it, you owe me 10% of the gross as "royalties." In such a circumstance, you may send the money to me in care of my publisher, Paulist Press, at 997 Macarthur Boulevard, Mahwah, New Jersey 07430.)

Chapter 8

Paul Radin's words at the beginning of this chapter can be found on page xxiii of his wonderful book, *The Trickster: A Study in American Indian Mythology* (New York: Schocken Books, 1979). The quotes from Jung on the nature of the archetype of Trickster can be found in that book as well, in his essay, "On the Psychology of the Trickster Figure," which is reprinted there in full (pp.195–211).

Once again, there are many versions of the adventures of Ama-terra-tsu, Susan-o-wo, and Uzume. As in chapter 3, I have made extensive use of *The Kojiki: Records of Ancient Matters,* translated by Basil H. Chamberlain, and *Nihongi: Chronicles of Japan from the Earliest Times to A.D. 697,* translated by W. G. Aston, both published by Charles Tuttle, 1981 and 1972 respectively.

There is a very interesting and informative discussion of the academic controversies surrounding the idea of the Trickster in the *Dictionary of Native American Mythology,* by Sam D. Gill and Irene F. Sullivan (Santa Barbara, Denver, and Oxford: ABC-CLIO, 1992, pp. 308–311). Of particular interest is Ann Doueihi's article in *Soundings: An Interdisciplinary Journal* (vol.

67, no. 3, 1984) in which she argues, quite convincingly, that the academic debates that surround Trickster are as much a part of a larger "discourse of power... which distorts and abuses the Indian so that he [*sic*] fits into an idealized image serving Western man's nostalgia and yearning as...(older) approaches that relegate the Indian to the status of primitive savage or decadent heathen." Although she limits her point to the debates surrounding Trickster as an organizing principle in the study of Native American sacred narrative, Jung's assertion that Trickster, wherever it is encountered, is a character indicating "primitive stages of development" plays the same sad, counterproductive role.

Ganesha, the elephant-headed God of India, is said to have been "born" from the scrapings of the Goddess Parvati's skin, without male involvement. This marks him clearly as a figure with ties to the pre-Vedic religions of the Great Mother. Like his European counterpart, Hermes, he is a god of flocks and herds, a "Lord of the Animals." When he seeks to give a gift to his Divine Mother, he faces the same dilemma as Susan-o-wo. He too plunges his hands into his chest and tears it open in the search for something unique and new to give back to her in return. Only in his case, all the stars of the night sky come spurting out like blood. Many Hindus believe that the Milky Way is the remnant of the first spurt of stars that burst forth from Ganesha's willingly opened and "sacrificed" heart (Fig. 21).

The story of the clever rabbi and the inquisitors can be found in Ausable's *Legends of the Jews*. If it seems to you that "grand inquisitors even today" is an overstatement, let me direct your attention to reports of the CIA and National Security Council deliberations regarding the revelations of their respective roles in supporting the torture and murder of American citizens (let alone foreign nationals), particularly in Latin America and Africa during the last twenty years.

I am particularly grateful to Dr. Charles Keil, the eminent ethnomusicologist, currently at the State University of New York at Buffalo (my *alma mater*), for sharing the story of "Hare and the First Drum" with me, directly from his field notes taken during his ethnographic researches among the Tiv, the Hausa, and the Falani in Nigeria (I think in the late 1950's).

Figure 21. (India) Ganesha opens his heart and looks within, seeking for a gift for his Mother, the Great Goddess, and discovers all the stars of the night sky, while his animal "vehicle," the Rat, Subramunion, looks on in awe and wonder. (Swastikas have been associated with Ganesha for thousands of years—long before they were adopted by the National Socialist Party in Germany in the 20th century; they symbolize creativity at all levels, from making fire with the "firedrill" to making love, to all forms of creative expression in the arts and sciences.)

One of the more ironic contemporary trickster stories that I am aware of involves the CIA and their research into the mind-altering effects of LSD, and its potential for influencing individuals and large populations. The CIA decided, in their grand inquisitorial fashion, to run some "blind" experiments to see what the effects of LSD might be on various personality types. As part of these experiments, they secretly introduced LSD into the water coolers in the staff stations in the psych ward at the Stanford University Medical Center and watched the staff who drank from them.

At the time, a struggling graduate student of English and Creative Writing at Stanford named Ken Kesey was trying to complete his graduate degree by working the night shift at the psych ward and going to school in the daytime. He unwittingly imbibed undetermined quantities of LSD—it was a hot summer— and began struggling with obsessive thoughts and volcanic feelings, the "paranoid" sense that "people were spying on him"(!) and the inescapable thought that he was losing his mind.

In an effort to "save his soul," he threw himself into his writing and attempted to alchemically transform the emotions and visions that were threatening to overwhelm him into written prose. The result is the now justly famous novel, *One Flew Over The Cuckoo's Nest*. One might argue that all his subsequent work also bears the stamp of that heroic effort to contain and shape the raw energies of the unconscious that were called up in him, in large measure by the immoral experiment in "mind control" that the CIA carried out on him without his knowledge.

So, ironically, in the midst of their arrogant and callous search for even more effective chemical means of manipulating and controlling individuals and large populations, the CIA unleashed one of the most talented spokespersons for anarchy and individual self-determination that the English-speaking world has yet produced. It is irony of this order that always accompanies the activation of the Trickster and the subsequent acting out of the archetypal drama of the "Trickster's Revenge."

Were there other unwitting subjects of the callous CIA drug experiment who did not make it through the artificially induced "dark night of the soul" with the same creative success as Ken Kesey? There may well have been. Unfortunately, their stories have not come to the attention of the press in the same way, although there continue to be persistent rumors of "out of court settlements" made to families of people who were apparently permanently injured and debilitated by these "experiments."

Index

Page references in italics refer to illustrations.